POLITICAL INSTITUTIONS
IN THE UNITED STATES

POLITICAL INSTITUTIONS IN THE UNITED STATES

Richard S. Katz

OXFORD
UNIVERSITY PRESS

OXFORD

UNIVERSITY PRESS

Great Clarendon Street, Oxford OX2 6DP

Oxford University Press is a department of the University of Oxford.
It furthers the University's objective of excellence in research, scholarship,
and education by publishing worldwide in

Oxford New York

Auckland Cape Town Dar es Salaam Hong Kong Karachi
Kuala Lumpur Madrid Melbourne Mexico City Nairobi
New Delhi Shanghai Taipei Toronto

With offices in

Argentina Austria Brazil Chile Czech Republic France Greece
Guatemala Hungary Italy Japan Poland Portugal Singapore
South Korea Switzerland Thailand Turkey Ukraine Vietnam

Oxford is a registered trademark of Oxford University Press
in the UK and in certain other countries

Published in the United States
by Oxford University Press Inc., New York

British Library Cataloguing in Publication Data

Data available

Library of Congress Cataloging in Publication Data

Data available

ISBN 978–0–19–928383–5

10 9 8 7 6 5 4 3 2

Typeset by Laserwords Private Limited, Chennai, India

Printed in Great Britain
on acid-free paper by
Ashford Colour Press Ltd, Gosport, Hampshire

CONTENTS

LIST OF TABLES

LIST OF FIGURES

PREFACE

Europeans often find American politics bewildering in ways that far exceed the puzzlement, for example, of the British regarding the machinations of the Italians or the Italians regarding the immobilism of the Swiss. Questions range from the apparent marginality of world-shaping issues of foreign policy in the electoral politics of the world's only remaining super-power, to the inability of the national government to block executions by the states, to the central political importance of the courts. Much of the government of the United States appears irrational, if one approaches the subject with expectations and understandings rooted in modern European experience—if one assumes that the American Republicans are fundamentally like the British Conservatives (or German Christian Democrats); if one assumes that national elections are supposed to choose a national government and to resolve national issues; if one assumes that courts should be outside the political process; if one assumes that criminal justice is a responsibility of the national state. Although it would be an exaggeration to say that each of these assumptions is totally false (or that the corresponding assumptions would be totally true about every European state), to assume that they are true renders much of what happens in the United States bizarre or unintelligible.

This book is intended as an introduction to the government of the United States primarily for non-American undergraduates. It differs from the majority of introductory American government texts in three respects. First, and most obviously, it is shorter than most. I have not written it to be *the* text for a semester-long course, but rather to be one of several country books in a comparative politics course, or the basic overview in an American politics course that will then explore specific topics in greater depth on the basis of more specialized readings. Second, this book focuses more on the enduring institutions of government than on the topical, but transient, questions of contemporary politics. Of course, this distinction can easily be overdrawn. One of the most significant factors contributing to the longevity of democracy in America has been the adaptability of its institutions—indeed, the proper functioning and roles of 'the enduring institutions of government' are among the major 'questions of contemporary politics'. For the most part, examples are drawn from recent events, but those events are not themselves the primary focus. Third, even if it was not written exclusively for non-Americans, it was written with a non-American audience very much in mind. George Bernard Shaw (as well as Winston Churchill, Noah Webster, and perhaps others) is reputed to have said that 'England and the United States are two countries divided by a common language'. Although perhaps not as different as the meaning of 'jumper' (to Americans, a sleeveless one-piece dress; to the English, a long-sleeved knitted sweater—that might be worn under an American jumper) or the word for green summer squash (to Americans, zucchini, from the Italian; to the English, courgette, from the French), the vocabulary of political institutions (both the choice of words and their meanings) varies from one system to another, but particularly between presidential systems (like the United States) and parliamentary systems (like many other democracies). Rather than assuming that readers are coming to the text with the cultural understandings and experiences typical of Americans, I have tried to remember what European colleagues have found surprising or counter-intuitive about American politics—and to assume that those of their students who read this book will find them so as well.

The primary focus of this book is on the institutions of American government, in particular the electoral and party systems; the separation of powers among executive, legislative, and judicial branches of government, as well as the internal organization of each branch; federalism, and the division of powers between the federal government and the states. Although they will be raised in passing, questions of political behaviour and the content of policy (as opposed to the process by which it is made) are not major topics. Instead, by giving students a solid understanding of the 'rules' of the American political game, the 'pitch' on which the game is played, and the basic characteristics and orientations of the 'teams' that are playing the game, this book aims to equip them to study these topics more easily and with greater understanding later. While it is inevitable in a textbook that the need to present a range of material will dilute any central argument, one underlying theme that runs throughout the book is that the way in which power is divided between the levels of government, among the branches of government, and among individuals within a single branch of government undercuts responsibility, both in the sense of a careful weighing of options and consequences before a decision is made and in the sense of a clearly identifiable institution, or party, or person who is to be blamed when things go wrong or praised when they go well.

Writing an academic book about the politics of one's own country presents a distinctive challenge. Professional norms dictate a level of detachment—of standing above, or at least outside, the partisan debate—being unbiased. But, to quote comedian Ron Corddry (faux news reporter on American cable television), 'How does one report the facts when the facts themselves are biased?' Increasingly in the United States, 'unbiased' has been taken to be synonymous with 'balanced', and 'balance' to have been achieved when one says something nice (or something nasty) about both sides, or alternatively to mean saying nothing with any evaluative implications at all.[1] While I have tried to be objective, I have worried rather less about being balanced. To those who think that makes this book biased, I can only say that bias means intentionally tipping the scales, not objectively reporting that the scales are out of balance.

Most books about American politics are written by Americanists. Although I am an American, I am not an Americanist, but I have profited enormously from the advice of friends and colleagues who are. Erin Ackerman gave me the benefit of her experience teaching American government to German undergraduates as part of the exchange agreement between Johns Hopkins and the University of Mannheim, while Shlomit Barnea, as a non-American student of comparative politics, added the viewpoint of someone near to my intended audience. Three colleagues at Johns Hopkins—Joseph Cooper, Joel Grossman, and Adam Sheingate—collectively read most of the manuscript (I refrained from inflicting all of it on any one of them), and made many helpful suggestions, including correcting detail that I got wrong and warning me when lack of imposed balance veered into actual bias. Robin Kolodny at Temple University also read many chapters, as well as pointing me in the right direction when I wanted some obscure facts. If I failed to heed all of the advice they offered, that is not their fault.

Although this is hardly my first book, it is the first book I have written explicitly as a textbook. The editorial staff at the Oxford University Press have been extremely helpful in guiding me along this somewhat unfamiliar path. As with virtually everything I write, my wife Judy did her best to assure that all my sentences have both subjects and verbs, and that the words are spelled (spelt for those who prefer English English) consistently. I am grateful to them and to her.

Unless there are corrections that I make on the proofs that OUP fail to get into the final book (an unlikely occurrence, if experience is any guide), any remaining errors of fact, interpretation, grammar, or spelling are mine.

....

NOTE

1 A contemporary example might be the news coverage of the Jack Abramoff scandal (described in greater detail in a note in Chapter 9). When originally reported in the *Washington Post*, the story was phrased to suggest that Abramoff had made or directed substantial contributions to members of both parties, making it a 'bipartisan scandal'. It quickly turned out that what really had occurred was that some of Abramoff's clients had made contributions to Democrats as well as to Republicans, but that after hiring him their contributions to Democrats had been cut while their contributions to Republicans had been greatly increased.

1

The Foundations of American Government

Overview

This chapter reviews the evolution of the American political system from the Articles of Confederation through to the 1970s, showing that not just the growth, but particularly the dominance, of the federal government are quite recent developments. These sections introduce the two central institutional features of American government: separation of powers (the parcelling out, and sharing, of powers among the legislative, executive, and judicial branches of government); and the division of powers (the allocation of powers and responsibilities between the federal and state levels). It also introduces three elements of American political culture: individualism; suspicion of government; and suspicion of political parties. The chapter then puts the United States in context by comparing data from the United States, the European Union, and Canada both regarding aggregate demographic, government finance, and social welfare characteristics and regarding attitudes concerning both personal religious beliefs and the proper role of religion in politics.

In the mid-1980s, it became customary, and essentially accurate, for the Democratic leaders of Congress to describe the budgets submitted by Republican President Ronald Reagan as 'dead on arrival' (DOA). Indeed, in 1987, even Republican Senate leader Robert Dole described the President's budget as merely 'a starting point for work on a final document'.[1] In the mid-1990s, with the Republicans in control of Congress, the same language was often used to describe the fate of Democratic President Bill Clinton's budgets. Even more tellingly, the 'DOA' phrase was used to describe the Senate reception of President George W. Bush's 2003 tax proposals, even though the Republicans controlled the White House and both houses of Congress.

In most European countries, if the head of government were to be unable to get his (or her) major policy proposals, and especially the budget, adopted by the parliament, it would signal a major crisis of government. In the United States, it is business as usual. In Europe, the overwhelmingly dominant 'legitimizing myth' of contemporary government is 'party government': politicians are organized into cohesive national teams (parties) that compete for popular support on the basis of coherent programmes; voters think in terms of parties and their leaders rather than local candidates; the party or coalition that wins the most seats in parliament (which in most cases means that they won the most votes) forms the cabinet and takes both control of, and responsibility for, the government until the next election. Of course, like all myths, this is both a simplification and a distortion of reality, but it encapsulates the predominant way in which Europeans think democracies should work.[2]

The point here, however, is that although this 'responsible parties' idea of democracy has had its supporters in the United States, the American political system is predicated on a very different understanding of how government should be structured. Rather than being coherent teams, American parties are better understood as loose alliances of local politicians and their supporters, none of whom feel bound to support the national platform—including indeed the presidential nominee whose supporters wrote it. Rather than voting for a candidate as the standard bearer of his party, Americans tend to value voting 'for the man, not the party' at every level of government—from the presidency to the inspector of hides and animals (elected in some counties of Texas) or commissioners of cemetery maintenance districts (an elective office in Utah). Rather than the winner of a general election assuming control of the government, and indeed rather than there being a singular winner of a general election in the first place, control is divided between state and national governments, and at each level control is divided among the independent executive, legislative, and judicial branches of government. And beyond this, control is divided within the legislatures between two independently elected houses,[3] while in many states the executive branch includes many independently elected officials in addition to the governor. The result is that no one, either an individual or a party, is likely to be unequivocally responsible for anything.

While this lack of clear accountability sounds like a design flaw, it is merely a pejorative way of expressing the central design objective of American political institutions. Unequivocal responsibility requires undivided power, and the founders of the American republic were primarily concerned with the dangers that undivided governmental power posed for the independent farmers and merchants that they were and represented. As James Madison wrote in *The Federalist*, 'the accumulation of all powers, legislative, executive, and judiciary, in the same hands, whether of one, a few, or many, may justly be pronounced the very definition of tyranny'.[4] The resulting imperative that authority be divided and shared is reflected in both the separation of powers (the phrase used to describe the allocation of power and responsibility among legislative, executive, and judicial branches) at both national and state levels of government, and the division of powers between national and state levels. The balance of powers among branches of government and between levels of government has evolved over the more than two centuries since the Constitution was ratified, and it remains a recurring point of both principled and opportunistic debate in American politics. Along with its consequence of blurred and confusing lines of accountability, it is also the central theme of this book.

American political development

The colonial heritage

The thirteen colonies that on 4 July 1776 declared themselves to be 'absolved from all Allegiance to the British Crown' had been founded for a variety of reasons, ranging from providing a haven from persecution for religious dissenters of various denominations (some of whom then proceeded to persecute each other) to commercial profit for their backers, and with a variety of particular forms of government. They all shared a number of characteristics that played into the development of the institutions established by the Constitutional Convention that met in Philadelphia in 1787.

First, all of the colonies had legislatures with at least one house elected by the colonists. As in England, the electorate was limited to men of substance, generally defined by the ownership of land, although in some colonies voters also could be qualified on the basis of personal property or the payment of substantial taxes.[5] The meaning of these restrictions, however, was quite different. Even what are now regarded as dramatic underestimates of the extent of the colonial franchise suggest that roughly 25 per cent of adult males could vote (Rossiter 1953: 20), with a more realistic figure probably closer to 50 per cent (Dinkin 1977: 41). In contrast, Junz (1960) estimates that prior to 1832 only 5 per cent of adults (translating into roughly 10 per cent of adult men) in Britain could vote.

Second, the colonies in general had strong class systems, but these too were significantly different from Britain. At the upper end, there was essentially no nobility; at the bottom, there were substantial numbers of unfree persons, including both chattel slaves and indentured servants. But there was also a very real possibility (although not a terribly high probability) of substantial class mobility within the lifetime of a single person; one could arrive in America as an indentured servant and die as a wealthy landowner. While the elite were well aware that their interests often conflicted with those of the *hoi polloi*, they did not regard 'the lower orders' (except, of course, for the slaves) as a separate race.

Third, all of the colonies were far from London. Although only Connecticut and Rhode Island had governors chosen in the colony and the ability to legislate free of royal veto, all of the colonies had substantial self-rule within the framework of the English common law, if only because it could take months for legislation to reach London and a veto to return to America. Beginning however with the Seven Years' War (1756–63, known in the United States as the French and Indian War), the British government attempted to increase the revenue generated by the colonies with a variety of taxes imposed from London. It also tried to limit westward expansion into territory inhabited by native peoples. Whether these policies were justified or not, they were resented by the colonists, and broke the political alliance among the beneficiaries of royal patronage, southern planters, and New England merchants, leading the latter two groups to realign with the small farmers, artisans, and labourers. The conflict between the colonists and London escalated, ultimately leading to open rebellion justified in the American view by the long list of grievances against arbitrary power catalogued in the *Declaration of Independence*.

Fourth, by the historical standards of Europe, the colonies were all new. When the American Revolution broke out in 1775, Englishmen had lived in the colonies for less than 170 years. Unlike the 'constitutions' of seventeenth- and eighteenth-century Europe, which were basically the accretion over centuries of tradition, custom, and practice, each of the governments of the colonies was established by a single written document, which even in the oldest case was hardly hallowed by time. Moreover, while in 1700 there were roughly 250,000 colonists, in 1750 there were about 1 million, and in 1775 there were about 2.5 million. The colonial economies both expanded and diversified. These changes required adaptation in the government, furthering the idea that political institutions can be made and remade on the basis of rational deliberation.

Even before the first shots were fired at Lexington and Concord, many of the cornerstones of American political culture were already firmly in place: strong representative institutions chosen by a broad, although far from universal, suffrage; social divisions moderated both by belief in the possibility of social mobility through individual effort and by alliances that cut across lines of social cleavage; experience of self-government and suspicion of centralized power; belief in the capacity of rationality to resolve social and political problems.

The Revolution and the Articles of Confederation

With armed hostilities a reality, coordination among the colonies was an obvious imperative. As Benjamin Franklin is reputed to have said to his fellow signers of the Declaration of Independence, 'We must all hang together, or most assuredly we shall all hang separately'. But what form would that coordination take during the war, and what would be the form of government once the war was successfully concluded?

Although we now read the Declaration of Independence as the founding document of the UNITED STATES OF AMERICA as a single entity, it could also plausibly be read as a common declaration of 13 states of their independence not only from Great Britain but from each other as well. Indeed, the constitution initially adopted, 'The Articles of Confederation and Perpetual Union', described its creation as 'a firm league of friendship' rather than a government.

Congress and its committees were the only organs of government established; there were to be neither national courts nor a national executive. Congress itself consisted of delegates appointed, paid, and at any time replaced by the state legislatures. Each state had one vote and most important decisions, including any involving the appropriation of money, required the approval of nine states—which was sometimes more than the number of state delegations actually present.

'The United States in Congress assembled' was given the power to conduct foreign relations, to appoint senior army officers and to build and equip a navy. The Articles established the framework for a national economy—giving Congress the authority to regulate the value of money and to establish uniform weights and measures; providing for free movement of inhabitants to another state with equal 'privileges of trade and commerce' as the inhabitants of that state; requiring each state to give 'full faith and credit' to the legal actions of other states—but stopped far short of allowing Congress truly to regulate commerce, either among the states or with other countries. Congress could assess the states for money (in proportion to the value of land) or troops (in proportion to the white population), but had no direct authority to enforce either kind of assessment. These powers could be expanded, and indeed all provisions of the Articles could be altered, only by the unanimous agreement of the states—the eighteenth-century American equivalent of the national veto in the twentieth-century European Union, and with even stronger paralysing effect.

The Constitution

The Articles of Confederation reflected the fear of central power that animated many of the radicals who had made the American Revolution. The Congress of the Confederation successfully negotiated the Treaty of Paris, which ended the Revolution; enacted the Northwest Ordinance, which set the precedent for the governance of territories and their eventual admission to the United States as fully the equals of the original states; and passed a bill of rights, which was a prototype for the Bill of Rights in the Constitution of 1787. Overall, however, the Articles quickly proved inadequate for the tasks confronting the United States after the war was over. The central government proved incapable of enforcing treaties into which it had entered, or of preventing the individual states from negotiating with foreign powers. The central government also was incapable of preventing the erection of tariff barriers and other trade restrictions between the states, and indeed of preventing armed conflict between the states. Finally, the central government proved incapable of acting decisively when confronted by Shays' Rebellion, a rising of small farmers facing foreclosure which, while put down by the state militia in Massachusetts, raised the fear of 'mob rule' among the upper classes.

In May 1787, delegates of all of the states except Rhode Island met in Philadelphia 'for the sole and express purpose of revising the Articles of Confederation.' Disregarding this limited mandate, over the next four months the delegates instead drafted an entirely new constitution, which was then submitted to the states for ratification with the provision that it would go into effect when ratified by nine states, rather than the unanimous agreement of all 13 states required to amend the Articles of Confederation. This quorum of nine was achieved in June 1788, and the First Congress convened on 4 March 1789, although the thirteenth state, Rhode Island, did not ratify the Constitution until the end of May 1790.

In gross terms, and in reaction to the obvious inadequacies of the Articles of Confederation, the Constitution embodied the triumph of the supporters of order and central authority over the 'democrats' who favoured less government and a weaker centre. The two questions implicit in this conflict—How much should government do? And at what level of government should it be done?—have continued to be contentious subjects, although in comparison to the eighteenth century, the range of answers offered has shifted dramatically in favour of bigger government in general and a more dominating role for the federal government in particular.

Within the broad agreement in Philadelphia that a stronger central government was necessary, a number of compromises were required to arrive at a draft that was acceptable to enough delegates to allow the project to go forward. (The draft ultimately was signed by 39 of the 55 delegates, some having left during the convention and others refusing to sign in protest.)

The first compromise was between the large and small states and decided the structure of Congress. The so-called Virginia Plan called for a bicameral legislature, with the upper house chosen by the lower, and the lower house elected by the people; representation in both houses would be proportional to population. The New Jersey Plan, reflecting the fear of the small states that they would always be outvoted, called for a single chamber in which the states would each have one vote, as under the Articles of Confederation. The Great (or Connecticut) Compromise essentially gave both sides half of what they wanted. Congress would consist of two chambers, a House of Representatives, directly elected by the people and with representation apportioned among the states according to population, and a Senate in which the states would be represented equally (by two senators rather than having a single vote).

The second compromise was between the north and the south, and responded to the radically different economies of the two regions. The northern elite were primarily engaged in commerce and were poised to develop a manufacturing economy; they wanted protection from foreign competition. The southern elite were primarily engaged in plantation agriculture; they were interested in freedom to export their crops to Europe. In addition, the southern elite depended on slave labour, whereas slavery was a dying institution in the north. The compromise reached had several parts. With regard to trade, Congress was barred from levying taxes on exports, and approval of two-thirds of the Senate was required to ratify treaties (thus affording the south protection against commercial treaties that might threaten its interests). With regard to the relative weight of the states, representation in the House of Representatives would be based on resident population, with slaves—whom the south wanted included as inhabitants notwithstanding that for all other purposes they were considered property—counted at a discounted rate, the 'Three-Fifths Compromise'. Finally, with regard to the institution of slavery itself, the 'compromise' was simply to put off the evil day on which the problem would have to be faced; Congress could not prohibit the importation of slaves until 1808, and in the interim could not impose an import duty of more than $10 per person.

The third compromise was over the nature and method of choice of the executive. Both the Virginia and the New Jersey Plans called for the executive to be elected by Congress, and would have allowed (Virginia) or specified (New Jersey) a plural executive. Those who favoured a stronger executive argued for a single president and feared that election by Congress would make the president subordinate to Congress, perpetuating one of the agreed weaknesses of the Articles of Confederation. The ultimate decision was for a single president to be chosen by an electoral college, in which each state would have as many electors as the sum of its members of the House and Senate (thus reiterating both the Connecticut and the Three-Fifths compromises). In the event that no person had a majority of the electoral votes, which given the absence of national political parties or a common meeting of the electors from the various states was expected to be the usual situation, the president would be chosen by the House of Representatives from among the five (reduced to three by the Twelfth Amendment to the Constitution) candidates with the most electoral votes, with each state casting a single vote. The method by which the electors would be chosen was left to the state legislatures—a decision that allowed the indirect choice of the president effectively to be converted to direct popular election (albeit with a potentially distorting electoral system) without any change to the Constitution itself.

Taken together, all of these can be understood as part of two grand compromises, but also of two grand temporizes, over the division of powers between the states and the federal government and over the degree to which the new government would be democratic. In comparison to the Articles of Confederation, the powers of the central government were dramatically increased. Among other powers, it (literally, Congress) was given the authority to lay and collect taxes, to regulate both interstate and foreign commerce, and in the so-called elastic clause to 'make all Laws which shall be necessary and proper' for the execution of any powers vested in the United States. The central government was given its own courts, and the Constitution and laws of the United States were made superior not only to state laws, but to the very constitutions of the states as well. Unlike the Articles of Confederation, the Constitution was not made by the states, but rather by 'We the People'. The new government was also more democratic than the Confederation in that the members of the House of Representatives were to be chosen by the people rather than by their state legislatures, but the House was the only directly elected organ of the federal government: the president was to be chosen by an electoral college which originally was itself chosen by the legislatures in a majority of the states; senators were to be chosen by the state legislatures as well; judges were to be appointed by the indirectly chosen president subject to the 'advice and consent' of the indirectly chosen Senate.

In comparison to other national constitutions, one of the American Constitution's most remarkable features is its brevity. In one edition (Peaslee 1965–70), the original Constitution of the United States runs to 11 printed pages; in the same edition, the Austrian constitution is 47 pages, the Belgian constitution 17, the Danish 15, the Finnish 37, the French 19, the German 38, and so forth. This brevity left plenty of room for ambiguity, interpretation, and evolution. As already said, the future of slavery was explicitly deferred for twenty years and the presidential electoral system was left sufficiently vague that it could be democratized without formal amendment. Similarly, the extent of the suffrage was left to the states—the federal suffrage was coterminous with that for the most numerous branch of the state legislature, and therefore could (and still does) vary among the states. Although the presumption at the time was that Congress would be the dominant branch, the relative standing of the three branches of government (most immediately, the power of the courts to declare the actions of the other branches void as violative of the Constitution and whether the presidential veto was to be used only if the president believed the proposed law to be unconstitutional or also if he felt it merely to be unwise) was left unclear. The extent of congressional power to regulate commerce, and the 'elasticity' of the elastic clause continue to be redefined by practice.

The Constitution in theory: *The Federalist*

Once the draft Constitution was completed, it required ratification by special conventions in at least nine states. Having been drafted in secret and without benefit either of a legal mandate or popular feedback, it was by no means clear that such ratification would be forthcoming. What ultimately was published under the title *The Federalist Papers* was a series of 85 articles addressed 'To the People of the State of New York' by Alexander Hamilton, John Jay, and James Madison (the first and last of whom had been part of the Constitutional Convention) arguing in favour of ratification. The opponents of ratification, collectively known as the antifederalists, produced arguments on the other side, and although they lost the overall argument, they were successful in exacting a promise that a federal Bill of Rights would be proposed by the First Congress. Both *The Federalist* and the writings of the antifederalists continue to be cited, for example by the Supreme Court, as authorities on the correct interpretation of the Constitution (*American Insurance Association v. Garamendi* 538 US 959; *Blakeley v. Washington* 542 US 961), but as the document of the winning side, *The Federalist* clearly is the most significant.

The Federalist had two objectives. The first was to demonstrate that a strong union was necessary: to protect the United States from foreign domination; to resolve disputes among the states; to protect each state from the dangers of an insurrection that it would be incapable of putting down;

to assure a large and secure base for commerce. So much was learned from the failures of the Confederation.

But could a strong federal government be trusted not to repeat the perceived sins of the British government that had led to the revolution? The second objective of *The Federalist* was to show that the Constitution allowed this question to be answered in the affirmative. In addressing this task, Hamilton, Jay, and especially Madison laid out the basic philosophy of the American republic.

In general terms, *The Federalist* perceived two dangers posed by the new (or any) government. The first was tyranny by the governors in their capacity as governors. Having rejected the idea that 'a mere demarcation on parchment' would be adequate to prevent this,[6] they argued that separation of legislative, executive, and judicial powers was essential, but if 'separation' is taken in its simple meaning of 'legislative powers given to Congress, executive powers given to the president, judicial powers given to the courts', it would be inadequate. Rather, 'ambition must be made to counteract ambition',[7] through an overlapping of powers that would give each branch of government the ability to defend itself against encroachments by the others. The most obvious examples would be giving the 'power of the purse' to Congress, thus allowing it *in extremis* to starve the executive, balanced by the presidential veto, giving the president the power to require an extraordinary (two-thirds) majority of both houses of Congress to enact a bill of which the president disapproves. Thus, conflict among the branches of government, and even potential gridlock, far from being pathologies, would be evidence that the potential for tyranny was being thwarted.

The other danger was tyranny arising from the governed—that some interest or combination of interests would take control of the government and use it to tyrannize over the others. The term used for such a combination 'of citizens, whether amounting to a majority or a minority of the whole, who are united and actuated by some common impulse of passion, or of interest, adverse to the rights of other citizens, or to the permanent and aggregate interests of the community' was faction, and thus the problem was one of 'curing the mischiefs of faction'.[8]

Having dismissed the possibility of curing the causes of faction as being 'worse than the disease', *The Federalist* addressed the problem of limiting the effects of faction. In the Madisonian view, 'relief [from minority factions] is supplied by the republican principle, which enables the majority to defeat its sinister views by regular vote'. The real problem, therefore, would be a majority faction. Two main defences were suggested. First, by having a large and diverse republic, one would increase the number of interests, and therefore decrease the likelihood of a majority forming with a common interest in invading the rights of others. If such a majority were to exist anyway, a large and diverse republic would make their self-recognition and coordination more difficult. In this, Madison took direct issue with the antifederalists, who claimed that small and homogeneous societies provide more fertile ground for liberty. Second, by having representative government, which would filter popular passions through a group of (presumably) wiser and more temperate citizens, and even more by limiting direct election to the House of Representatives (and by having the other organs of government chosen through varying means and with varying terms of office), both the size and the durability that any majority faction would have to attain in order to defeat the separation of powers would be dramatically increased.

With the benefit of hindsight, it is clear that *The Federalist* underestimated the capacity of national political parties to surmount the obstacles to majority rule implicit both in the separation of powers and in the supposed virtues of a large and diverse republic. Indeed, in the responsible parties model of democracy, that is precisely what they are supposed to do. To a certain extent, *The Federalist* recognized this and is, in consequence, profoundly anti-party (which *The Federalist* equated with being anti-faction), notwithstanding that the Federalists themselves in coordinating their campaign for ratification might now be recognized as a national political party, and that within a few years of the Constitution's going into operation, they formed what was clearly the first national political party in the United States. On the other hand, although the organization of national parties has made the electoral college into a vestigial organ of government,[9] and both houses of Congress are structured around national parties, the tacit claims that the diversity of the country and the incentives imposed by separation of powers would prove impediments to the formation of *strong national* parties have proven quite prescient.

Reading *The Federalist* highlights a number of enduring tensions in American political culture. One, evident in the *Declaration of Independence* as well, is the belief that the United States is not just another country, but is instead a kind of noble experiment, a beacon and exemplar for the rest of the world. In that respect, principle is extremely important. As with most idealistic creeds, there is the recurring danger that the quest for righteousness will, at least from the perspective of one's opponents, degenerate into self-righteousness in a way that overt pursuit of self- (or national-) interest does not. At the same time, however, there is a deep belief in pragmatism, and in the necessity, if not necessarily the virtue, of compromise and tolerance of difference.

A second tension is a love–hate relationship with government, particularly at the federal level. Although increasingly expecting government to solve a variety of social and economic problems, Americans tend still to see government as it was portrayed in *The Federalist*: as a necessary evil, and moreover as an evil that has to be kept in check because of the naturally self-aggrandizing tendencies of all human institutions. One clear reflection of this is that in contrast to the 'inalienable rights ... [of] life, liberty, and the pursuit of happiness' of the *Declaration of Independence*, the rights of the Bill of Rights are all negative: freedom from rather than freedom to.

A third tension is between the democratic ideal of a sovereign *demos* using government to pursue its single common interest and the liberal ideal of autonomous individuals who need government to provide the stability that will allow them to pursue their individual interests. But while the dominant inclination at this abstract level, and in the construction and justification of the Constitution, is towards the liberal ideal, the 'policy of supplying, by opposite and rival interests, the defect of better motives'[10] conflicts with a sense that alliance with or pursuit of 'special interests' is morally blameworthy. (Of course, 'special interests' are always on the other side of any conflict.) This then feeds the suspicion of political parties, and especially of national parties.

These tensions might be summarized (and radically oversimplified) by saying that although Americans love democracy (by which they basically mean liberal republicanism), they distrust politics.

From Jacksonian democracy to the Civil War

The constitutional system worked in practice more or less as the framers had expected until 1861. The country grew enormously, to include (either as states or territories) all of the current United States except Alaska and

Hawaii, but the basic governmental structure remained unchanged. After the Bill of Rights, the Constitution was only amended twice until 1865: once to bar individuals from suing a state in federal court and once to have members of the electoral college vote separately for president and vice-president.[11] The federal government's budget was small, and almost entirely spent on the post office, the army, navy, veterans' pensions, and debt service; with the exception of brief spikes occasioned by wars, the federal administrative budget was generally well below 2 per cent of realized national income, and therefore an even smaller percentage of gross domestic product (GDP).[12] Roughly 70 per cent of the civilian employees of the federal government worked in the post office.[13]

Given the personal standing of the first three presidents—Washington, Adams, and Jefferson—combined with the initial lack of structure or experience of governing in the first Congresses, the president and cabinet (especially the first Secretary of the Treasury, Alexander Hamilton) dominated politics for roughly the first fifteen years of the new republic. After that, however, Congress developed more effective committees and leadership structures, and assumed a dominant position that was occasionally challenged, but never really broken. The presidential establishment consisted of no more than a few clerks. Although Washington and Adams delivered what would later be known as the State of the Union Message to Congress in person, presidents from Jefferson to Taft (1909–13) merely sent written reports with suggestions for legislation. The period between 1837 and 1861 was characterized by one-term presidencies. There was only one executive department (Interior,[14] created in 1849) represented in James Buchanan's cabinet (1857–61) that had not been in John Adams' cabinet (1797–1801); in fact, the eighth cabinet department, Agriculture, would not be established until 1862, and not raised to cabinet rank until 1889.

Within the basic structure, however, there was substantial democratization. The election of 1812 was the last in which as many as half of the state legislatures chose the presidential electors; by 1832, only South Carolina chose its electors in this way. Property requirements for voting were replaced by taxpaying requirements, or abolished altogether. In 1828, more than half of the age, race, and gender eligible population voted in a presidential election for the first time; participation averaged over 75 per cent in the presidential elections between 1840 and 1860. The presidential nominating process also changed; beginning in 1832, presidential candidates were chosen by national nominating conventions rather than by the congressional caucuses. This led to additional national party development and gave the president somewhat more independence from Congress, but not from the state party leaders who ultimately controlled the conventions. Although patronage was important to parties everywhere, in some states it formed the basis for strong party organizations, while in others the parties were weaker (McCormick 1973). The focus of politics overall remained at the state and local level, and the focus of national politics remained in Congress.

While the general structure of politics remained relatively stable within the context of democratization, the grand temporizes of the Constitutional Convention about the power of the federal government and especially about slavery came home to roost. Differences of economic interests among the commercial north, the plantation south, and the developing agrarian west were significant factors in congressional politics and presidential elections, and often were cast as questions over the authority of the federal government *vis-à-vis* the states. A focal point for this debate was tariff policy, with the nadir reached in 1832 when South Carolina declared the federal government's tariff to be null and void within the state. The threat of secession was overcome by a compromise tariff passed the following year.

The twin foci of the slavery issue were the extension (or barring) of slavery in the territories and the admission of new states into the union, both of which threatened to upset the balance between north and south. Two major compromises (the Missouri Compromise in 1820 and the Compromise of 1850) put off the inevitable, but following the election of Abraham Lincoln as the candidate of the avowedly abolitionist Republican Party, 11 of the 15 states in which slavery was legal left the union, provoking the American Civil War.[15]

The Civil War to the First World War

Whether the Civil War was simply about slavery was a subject of controversy at the time, and continues to be uncertain. What is certain is that while the war resolved the question of slavery, it did not solve the problem of race. Lincoln's Emancipation Proclamation freed the slaves in those states that were in rebellion when it was issued in 1863, and slavery was forbidden nationally with the ratification of the Thirteenth Amendment in 1865. Three years later, the Fourteenth Amendment clarified that all persons born in the

United States (including the former slaves) were citizens both of the United States and of the state in which they resided, and two years after that, the Fifteenth Amendment prohibited denial of the right to vote on the basis of 'race, color, or previous condition of servitude'. From 1867 through 1876, the states of the confederacy were subject to military reconstruction, which enforced the rights of the freed slaves, but as part of the deal to resolve the disputed presidential election of 1876, reconstruction was ended, and the southern states, through a variety of legal devices and tolerance of physical intimidation, effectively disenfranchised their non-white populations and established pervasive regimes of legally enforced racial segregation which lasted into the 1960s.

By the end of the Civil War, it was resolved that presidents could veto bills on policy as well as constitutional grounds, but vetoes were quite rare (on average, less than one per year). Between 1865 and 1913, the average was almost 20 per year—and although this average is highly skewed by Grant and Cleveland, who were responsible for 94 and 584 vetoes, respectively, only the presidencies of Hayes (13) and Garfield/Arthur (12) had fewer than 29 vetoes per four-year term. On the other hand, it was not until well into the last quarter of the nineteenth century that the president's unilateral power to remove executive department officials whose appointments had required congressional approval was firmly established.

Notwithstanding the more extensive use of the veto power, Congress continued to be the dominant branch of government. This dominance was based on strong state and local parties that controlled nomination for office, including selection of delegates to the presidential nominating conventions, the mobilization of campaign workers and voters, and most of the patronage (given the practice of 'senatorial courtesy', including much of federal patronage) and money that was 'the mother's milk of politics'. Control over money, much of which came in the form of 'contributions' from the holders of patronage jobs, became a particularly important basis of party control over the president as the cost of campaigns skyrocketed, even as presidential candidates began to take control over their own, more vigorous, campaigns; between 1872 and 1876, the total estimated cost of the two major parties' presidential campaigns increased from $300,000 to $1,850,000. Congressional dominance was also furthered by the evolution of rules, particularly in the House of Representatives, that concentrated power in the hands of the congressional leadership, by a dramatic increase in the size of the congressional establishment (between 1861 and 1881 the number of employees of Congress increased by a factor of more than six), and by the development of congressional campaign committees—which did not just strengthen the partisan character of politics, but did so with particular roots in Congress. This was an era of party government, but the voice of the party was in Congress rather than in the White House—although party government was still limited by the fact that for more than one-third of the fifty years between 1863 and 1913 one of the House of Representatives, the Senate, and the White House was controlled by the party that did not control the other two and by the presidential veto, which was frequently used even when the president and both houses of Congress were of the same party.

The Civil War marked a significant increase in the size of the federal government. From a norm of about 1.5–1.8 per cent of realized national income, the budget grew to a norm of 2.2–3 per cent, an increase of roughly 50 per cent, but still extremely small. In 1881, the number of civilian employees of the federal government was 2.7 times what it had been in 1861; in 1901, the figure was 2.3 times what it had been in 1881, and in 1915 it was about four times what it had been in 1881. More significantly, beginning in the 1880s, both the scope of the federal government and the organization of the executive began to change. With the Interstate Commerce Act of 1887 and the Sherman Anti-Trust Act of 1890, the federal government began to regulate private business for the public good. In 1903, the Department of Commerce and Labor was added to the president's cabinet, and in 1913 it was divided into separate cabinet-level departments of Labor and of Commerce. In 1914, both the Federal Reserve system and the Federal Trade Commission began operation.

After a few very limited programmes of grants to states and localities to promote activities deemed worthy by Congress in the nineteenth century, in the second decade of the twentieth century fire protection, agriculture, highway construction, and vocational education all become subjects for federal grants conditioned on federal approval of state plans, matching funds from the state, and federal oversight. Ultimately this changed dramatically the relationship between the states and the federal government, as the former became more dependent on federal funds, and thus more subject to the conditions attached.

The last quarter of the nineteenth century also saw the introduction of civil service reform, spurred in part by the assassination of President

Garfield by a disappointed office-seeker. When introduced in 1884, appointments based on competitive examination covered only about 10 per cent of federal civilian employees, but by 1913 the figure exceeded 70 per cent. The twin effects were to give the executive branch a more capable and loyal (to their departments, if not necessarily to the president) workforce, and to reduce the volume of patronage available to maintain the congressionally and locally based party machines.

Other reforms at the same time also began to undermine the political machines. The introduction of the state-printed 'Australian ballot', government-organized systems of voter registration, and the direct primary all involved extensive state regulation of what had previously been internal party affairs, and in some ways over time converted American parties into instruments of election administration. The direct election of senators weakened another support for machine dominance of national politics. These forces also combined to undermine the centralized power of the Speaker of the House of Representatives, so that by the time the United States entered the First World War, the 'Czar' rule of the Speaker was on its way to being replaced by a more fragmented leadership structure in which seniority rather than loyalty would play the decisive role.

From the First World War to Nixon

Immediately after the disruption of the First World War, which saw, *inter alia*, the federal budget in 1919 grow to over 22 per cent of gross national product (GNP), there was a call for a 'return to normalcy'. With the war over, the budget fell, but not to pre-war levels. Between 1910 and 1916, the federal budget was never as much as 2 per cent of GNP (2.5 per cent of realized national income); after 1920, it was never as low as 3 per cent. The explosion of the federal budget did, however, have one permanent effect. Prior to 1920, the budget was constructed in Congress from departmental estimates mechanistically compiled and delivered by the Secretary of the Treasury. In 1921, the Bureau of the Budget was created—initially in the Treasury Department, but after 1939 in the newly organized Executive Office of the President—and given responsibility for submitting a presidential budget.

'Normalcy' came to an end with the Great Depression and the administration of Franklin Roosevelt. Between 1933 and 1940, the number of federal civilian employees grew by over 72 per cent; federal spending more than doubled. With a host of new programmes and regulatory agencies, the federal government began to take an active role in assuring the welfare of its citizens, in place of the previous view that the government was responsible only for assuring the conditions under which individuals could look after themselves. The Social Security Act established a (far from universal) system of public old-age pensions and unemployment insurance.[16] Supervision of the financial sector, labour relations and working conditions, of agricultural production and pricing, and of public utilities became permanent responsibilities of the federal government, which also established massive but temporary programmes of public employment.

Even with this growth, the federal government was far smaller than it became after 1945. At its pre-war maximum, the federal government spent 11.2 per cent of GNP; from 1952 to 1970, the figure was generally just under 20 per cent. The number of civilian employees of the federal government more than doubled from 1940 to 1952. The 19 years between 1952 and 1970 saw the creation of three new cabinet departments (Health, Education and Welfare; Housing and Urban Development; Transportation), consolidating the substantial growth in the range of federal responsibilities.

This expansion in the activities of the federal government also altered the nature of the relationship between the federal government and the states. One reflection of this is the growing importance of the federal grants, and of the conditions attached to them, to the operations of state and local governments. In 1932, just under 3 per cent of all state and local revenue came in the form of transfers from the federal government; in 1952 the figure was 8.3 per cent; in 1968 it was over 14.5 per cent. Thus, for example, when the federal government wanted to impose a national highway speed limit or the minimum age for the sale of alcohol (both clearly within the jurisdiction of the states), it needed only condition federal highway grants on state compliance with these standards—in effect, the federal government bought out state sovereignty.

Until the 1940s, the United States was essentially a supernumerary on the world stage. The Monroe Doctrine, which was more a statement of isolationism with regard to Europe than of interventionism with regard to Central and South America, was enforced primarily by the British navy. With the Spanish American War (1898), the United States acquired a small, but far-flung, colonial empire (although it was not identified as such), and began to pursue interventionist policies with regard to the Caribbean basin. In the First World War, the United States played a decisive role, but primarily as a source of supply and as balance tipper at the end of the war. With the Second World War, however, the United States both became and came to see itself as a major power.

The impact on the United States of the transformation from peripheral to world power can be seen both militarily and economically. Before the Spanish American War, the American military was about 0.05 per cent of the population; from the Spanish American War until just before the Second World War, it gradually grew to about 0.25 per cent of population; after 1950 it generally ranged between 1.4 and 1.7 per cent. From 1900 until the Second World War, defence spending was generally less than 10 per cent of the federal budget; after the Second World War, it ranged from roughly 30 per cent to more than 50 per cent of the federal budget. The military–industrial complex about which President Eisenhower warned in 1961 became a major force in American politics.

Taking a sample of 56 countries that together in 1992 produced 93 per cent of world output as the base, in 1820 the United States accounted for about 2 per cent of the world economy. By 1870 the figure had risen to 9 per cent and by 1900 it was almost 17 per cent; in the late 1940s, with the economic devastation of Europe, the figure reached a peak of almost 30 per cent of total output, before declining to roughly 22 per cent (all calculated from Maddison 1995). While the growth in the American economy meant that the United States accounted for a growing proportion of international trade,[17] the proportionate importance of foreign trade in the American economy dropped; overall trade was roughly 11–14 per cent of GNP from the 1890s to the First World War, roughly 10 per cent during the inter-war years, and then around 7–8 per cent until 1970. With the exception of strong dependence on imported petroleum (which only developed in the 1950s, and was not generally recognized as significant until the oil embargo of 1973), the American economy was largely self-sufficient. As a result, the United States could afford the policy of isolationism in the economic as well as the military sphere, reflected for example in tariffs that into the 1930s were more than twice those of France, Germany, Italy, or the UK. It was only in the post-Second World War period that the United States assumed the role of world economic leader, and that was driven far more by the politics of anti-communism than by the economic 'fundamentals'.

The emergence of the United States as a world power in both military and economic terms was, of course, important for the rest of the world; the United States became the proverbial 800 pound gorilla in the room: powerful and somewhat prone to clumsiness. It also had a profound effect on the balance of power within American government, giving the president, as commander-in-chief and as the negotiator of international agreements, a pre-eminence that was unprecedented.

Along with the president, in the post-Second World War period the Supreme Court also became a far more significant political actor. The Court had made a number of important decisions since it first asserted its power to declare Acts of Congress unconstitutional and therefore void in 1803 (*Marbury v. Madison* 1 Cr 137). Some argue that the pro-slavery decision in *Dred Scott v. Sandford* (19 How. 393) made the Civil War inevitable. From the end of the nineteenth century, the Court invalidated or emasculated numerous attempts by both the federal government and the states to regulate business, ultimately leading to the so-called court packing crisis of 1937.[18] During the same period, the court approved racial segregation under the 'separate but equal' doctrine (*Plessey v. Ferguson* 163 US 537, 1896), but also gradually extended many of the protections of the Bill of Rights to apply against actions of the states as well as those of the federal government.

With the appointment of Earl Warren as Chief Justice in 1954, however, the Court assumed an even more prominent role in defining American politics. Three decisions in particular deserve mention. In *Brown v. Board of Education* (347 US 483), the Court overruled its earlier decision in *Plessey*, and began the process of legally enforced desegregation. In *Baker v. Carr* (369 US 186), the Court entered 'the political thicket' of legislative apportionment, ultimately leading not only to an insistence on equal population districts—and seemingly endless litigation—but also to the restructuring of some local governments altogether. In *Roe v. Wade* (410 US 113), the Court overturned state laws banning abortion, but in reaction energized first conservative religious groups but then liberal groups (for example, exponents of homosexual rights) both to federalize a range of moral issues that previously had been regarded as purely the province of the states and to judicialize issues that previously had been regarded as purely the province of the 'political' branches of government. In addition, the growing volume and complexity of legislation, along with the growing tendency of Congress to delegate rule-making authority to executive agencies, meant that the courts, in resolving the contradictions and ambiguities of legislation and rules, increasingly were making policy themselves.

Aside from the obvious direct consequences of these and related developments, they also revived the question of the proper role of the judicial branch in American politics. Conservatives, including conservatives in the White House, began to rail against 'activist judges'. But where Andrew Jackson is reputed to have said in response to a Supreme Court decision that he proposed to flaunt, '[Chief Justice] John Marshall has made his decision; now let him enforce it', presidents no longer feel able to ignore edicts of the Supreme Court. With the courts deciding an increasing range of politically charged issues, the appointment of federal judges, but especially of members of the Supreme Court, became a significant issue in presidential politics.

Post-Nixon American government

The Nixon presidency was marked by two national traumas: the increasingly sharp protests against the Vietnam War coupled with a sense of national betrayal felt by the war's supporters when the United States left South Vietnam; and the Watergate scandal, impeachment, and resignation of Richard Nixon. While both these events had a long-lasting impact on American politics—for example, in leading to a far more aggressive press—neither fundamentally altered either the institutional or the partisan balance of the country. Nonetheless, the period beginning in the mid-1960s saw a number of significant changes in both.

With regard to electoral politics, the period saw the collapse of the New Deal Democratic coalition. Beginning with the civil rights agendas of the Kennedy, and especially of the Johnson, administrations, the urban riots of the 1960s, and the white backlash to forced integration, the south shifted from being solidly conservative Democrat to being predominantly conservative Republican. While this shift, which was initially motivated by race, brought many southern evangelical Protestants to the Republican fold, the social issues epitomized by abortion moved many Catholics, whose partisanship previously had been determined by their ethnicity, to the Republican Party as well. On the other side, African Americans, many of whom either had been disenfranchised or were supporters of the 'party of Lincoln', became the most solidly Democratic group in the electorate. Accompanying these realignments, there was also a substantial dealignment, with marked declines both in levels of partisan attachment and in rates of voter turnout, and increased rates of 'split-ticket' voting (Green 2002: 318).[19] The Watergate scandal stimulated a series of campaign reforms, ostensibly designed to limit the influence of money in politics, but in fact simply altering the ways in which the ever-growing power of money was manifested. The result of all of this was to increase the ideological coherence of the parties, but not their organizational strength.

The balance between the federal government and the states continued to shift towards the national level. In part this was furthered by the growing willingness of majorities in Washington to use federal grants-in-aid to leverage control over policy areas traditionally within the purview of the states, or to enact regulations that pre-empted rather than supplemented state action. In part it was furthered by the increased willingness of the federal courts to federalize questions which they had previously regarded as non-justiciable or on which they had deferred to the states. And in part it was furthered by growing predominance of television, with its focus on national personalities, as both news source and agenda setter. Notwithstanding this shift, however, the states remained both tremendously important in the American system and substantially independent of federal control.

Within Congress, the balance between centralization and decentralization of leadership shifted twice, first towards decentralization with a series of Democratic reforms to limit the power of conservative southerners who owed their positions to seniority, and then strongly back to concentration in the hands of the majority party leadership as the Republicans attempted to consolidate their control after 1994. Within the executive branch, there has been both great growth of, and a growing concentration of power in, the Executive Office of the President, and a corresponding decrease in the policy significance of the cabinet departments and their secretaries. Within the judiciary, the explosion of federal regulatory activity has dramatically increased the significance of the Court of Appeals for the District of Columbia (where appeals concerning the rule-making of many regulatory agencies are heard)—to the extent that it is sometimes called the 'little Supreme Court'. Corresponding to this increase in judicial intervention in the policy process, appointments to all of the Courts of Appeals, and even to the federal district bench, have become increasing objects of partisan rancour.

The United States in context

In some respects, the United States is simply one more advanced industrial democracy, perhaps with unique political institutions, but still fundamentally like the other, predominantly European, industrial democracies. In other respects, however, the United States seems to be *sui generis*. While the resolution of the 'American exceptionalism' debate is largely a matter of interpretation, it is important for both Americans and non-Americans to recognize that the United States may be less (or more) like other countries than they think. To that end, Table 1.1 compares the United States, the pre-2004 (15 member) European Union (EU), and Canada on a variety of geographic, economic, social, and attitudinal dimensions.

TABLE 1.1	Demographics, economics, government finance, and social welfare in the United States, the European Union, and Canada		
	United States	EU–15	Canada
Demographics			
Population (2001, millions)	278.1	378.5	30.8
Area (thousands km^2)	9,167	3,240	9,894
Population density (2000, per km^2)	29.4	119.4	3.1
Urban proportion (2001)	77.4	73.5	78.9
Economics			
GDP (2002, billion PPS)	9,289	8,811	856
GDP per capita (2002, in PPS)	32,159	23,110	27,300
Inflation (CPI, 2001–02)	1.6	2.1	2.2
Trade dependence (EU average weighted by GDP, 2002)	12	34.1	41.5
World trade share (import+export)/2	15.1	19.2	
Inequality of income (2001, top 20% divided by bottom 20%)	8.4	5.6	5.8
Unemployment (2002)	5.8	7.8	7.6
GDP Growth (% change 2001 to 2002)	2.2	1	3.2

continues

Table 1.1 continued

		United States	EU−15	Canada
Government finance				
Total government expenditure as proportion of GDP (2000)		39	51.4	47.9
Central government proportion of total government expenditure (2000)		49.8	72.7	41.3
Military spending as proportion of GDP (1990)		5.3	2.8	2
Social welfare				
Medical spending as proportion of GDP		13.2	8.7	9.2
Proportion of population with total medical coverage[1]		24.7	95.5	100
Life expectancy at birth (2000)	M	74.2	75.5	76.0
	F	79.9	81.4	83.0
Infant mortality (per 1,000 live births 2000)		6.9	4.7	5.3
Incarceration rate (per 100,000 of population)		686	101	102
Students in third-level education per 1,000 population (2000)		55	34	60
Intentional homicides per 100,000 (2000)		5.51	3.93	4.25
Intentional homicides per 100,000 (1990)		9.4	1.7[2]	4.3
Serious assaults per 100,000 (2000)		323.6	149.4	145.9

PPS (purchasing power standard) is an artificial currency unit that allows cross-national comparisons adjusted for differing price levels; CPI is consumer price index

[1] Luxembourg Income Study, excluding Greece, Italy, Luxembourg, Portugal, Spain. Even if one made the ridiculous assumption that no one in these countries had total medical coverage, the European average would still be over 65 per cent.

[2] Data are missing from Belgium, Luxembourg, the Netherlands, Portugal, and the United Kingdom

Sources: Eurostat (http://europa.eu.int/comm/eurostat/newcronos/queen/display.do?screen=welcome&open=/&product=YES&depth=2&language=en (7/15/04): Statistics Canada; British Home Office; Statistical Abstract of the United States

In comparison to the countries of Europe, the United States is big and relatively empty: while the EU as a whole has more people, the most populous European country (Germany) has less than 30 per cent of the population of the United States; even the EU of 27 members envisioned for 2007 will have less than half the area of the United States while the geographically largest (France) is less than 6 per cent of the size of the United States. The population density of the EU, and of all but three of the individual countries, are many times that of the United States. Canada is a bit larger geographically, but has a much smaller population. This combination of large size and low population density arguably has had two complementary effects on the culture of the United States. On the one hand, it has fostered the idea that interpersonal problems can be solved by putting space between people, whether it be antagonistic social groups or anti-social neighbours. On the other hand, it has meant that a variety of problems that have confronted much of Europe for centuries—waste disposal, deforestation, exhaustion of agricultural land or mineral resources—could be 'solved' simply by moving on. What would today be described as social responsibility simply has been less necessary.

A second geographic feature that has played a role in shaping the American consciousness is that the United States is very far away. Protected by the Atlantic and Pacific Oceans, there has not been a significant attack by a foreign military power on the territory of the continental United States (and Hawaii was not a state when Pearl Harbor was attacked in 1941) since the War of 1812. For most of American history, foreign entanglements have been something to avoid; it is not just world leadership, but real engagement in the world system, that were new to the United States in the post-Second World War era. Moreover, it is the shattering of this ingrained sense of isolated safety that contributed to making the attacks of 11 September 2001 so deeply traumatic for Americans.

Economically, the United States is rich, both in aggregate (with a GDP slightly bigger than the countries of the EU–15 combined) and on a per capita basis (with only Luxembourg among these countries richer). The EU and the United States account for roughly equal shares of world trade, but Europe is much more heavily dependent on trade. Thus, the United States does not face the same imperative to be sensitive to the opinions of its trading partners.

The American economy has been less heavily regulated than the economies of most other industrial democracies, and the public sector is relatively smaller; where governments in the average European country spend (and therefore either tax or borrow) at a rate exceeding 50 per cent of GDP, the comparable figure for the United States is under 40 per cent. Conventional wisdom (which is not always accurate, but which shapes expectations whether it is accurate or not) suggests that this accounts for the higher rates of economic growth and lower rates of unemployment that the United States has enjoyed. Within the public sector, the United States spends far more on the military, and far less on social welfare, which contributes to America's markedly more unequal distribution of income.

One field in which the inequality of American society has become a salient political issue is health care. While in most European countries, virtually 100 per cent of the population has total medical coverage,[20] for the United States the figure is only 25 per cent. As a result, although the United States spends markedly more for medical care, the aggregate outcome as indicated by the standard measures of life expectancy and infant mortality are consistently worse. The problem is that although good American medical care is the best in the world, a large fraction of Americans do not have access to it.

This inequality of outcomes is supported by attitudes that are significantly more favourable to competition as a way to stimulate hard work and new ideas and to both the desirability and the reality of personal responsibility for outcomes. Americans are more likely than Europeans to believe in the efficiency and justice of the unfettered market.

The United States is generally perceived to be a violent society, and to a certain extent the crime figures bear this out: in 2000, the American intentional homicide rate was more than 40 per cent above the EU average, and the serious assault rate was more than twice the EU average. At the same time, however, in each case there was at least one European country for which the crime rate was higher than in the United States, and while the American figures have been falling, those for Europe have been rising. The American incarceration rate is more than six times the EU average, and indeed is so large that it too contributes to the apparently low American unemployment rate. Moreover, particularly because the numbers are not only large, but also heavily skewed by race and class, the high incarceration rate has great political and social significance beyond whatever it may say about criminality *per se.*

Relative to most European countries, the American population is quite diverse in terms of national origin and culture, religion, and language, although with increased migration both to and within Europe, the gap is closing. On the other hand, the self-conception of the United States is that of 'a nation of immigrants' where European self-conceptions have tended to be based on myths of homogeneity of culture or ancestry. Notwithstanding periodic waves of nativism and moves to restrict immigration into the United States, the integration of legal immigrants into the national mainstream has been less problematic than in Europe. Simply, it is easier to become 'an American' than it is to become 'German' or 'British' or 'French'.

When Alexis de Tocqueville visited the United States in 1831, he was struck by the American propensity to form unofficial groups to address social problems; what in Europe would be left to the authorities, in America was in the private sphere. This comparison remains true today. When shown a list of voluntary organizations and activities doing such things as providing social welfare services for the elderly, American respondents to the World Values Survey were, for each activity, significantly more likely to say that they were members or participants, often by a multiple of two or three times; analogously, American organizations providing these services tend to be far more heavily dependent on voluntary contributions—but also in aggregate more poorly funded.

Tocqueville also noticed the importance of religion in American life, but he also 'showed . . . how the American clergy stand aloof from secular affairs' (Tocqueville 1956 [1834]: 154). Americans remain an astonishingly religious people in comparison to Europeans, whether measured by church attendance, professed belief in God, or prayer outside formal settings. (See Table 1.2.)

On the other hand, the greater separation of church and politics that Tocqueville praised no longer distinguishes the United States from Europe. Indeed, quite the reverse is true. More than three times as many Americans agree that politicians who do not believe in God are unfit for public office; more than twice as many disagree that religious leaders 'should not influence how people vote in elections' and that they 'should not influence government decisions'. And the American clergy have become far more deeply

TABLE 1.2	World Values Study responses for the United States, the European Union, and Canada		
Question	United States	EU−15	Canada
Belong to voluntary organizations and activities: social welfare services for elderly, handicapped or deprived people (%)	17	7	13
Religious or church organizations	57	12	29
Education, arts, music or cultural activities	37	11	21
Local community action on issues like poverty, employment, housing, racial equality	13	3	8
Third world development or human rights	5	4	5
Conservation, environmental, animal rights groups	16	5	9
Youth work	26	4	11
Sports or recreation	36	18	27
Peace movement	4	1	2
Voluntary organizations concerned with health	17	4	11
Believe in God	96	75	89
Believe in life after death	81	52	72
Believe in hell	75	29	50
Frequency of attendance at religious services apart from weddings, funerals and christenings (% saying 'more than once a week' or 'once a week')	45	19	25
How important is God in your life? (% picking 10 'very important' on a 10-point scale)	58	16	37
How often do you pray to God outside religious services? (% saying 'every day' or 'more than once a week')	71	32	49

continues

Table 1.2 continued

Question	United States	EU–15	Canada
Politicians who do not believe in God are unfit for public office (% agree or agree strongly)	38	12	19
Religious leaders should not influence how people vote in elections (% disagree or disagree strongly)	22	12	14
Religious leaders should not influence government decisions (% disagree or disagree strongly)	29	14	19
Some people feel they have completely free choice and control over their lives, while other people feel that what they do has no real effect on what happens to them (% picking 10 'a great deal' on a 10-point scale)	24	11	19
Scale from 'Private ownership of business and industry should be increased' (1) to 'Government ownership of business and industry should be increased' (10) (% picking 1)	26	14	18
Scale from 'Government should take more responsibility to ensure that everyone is provided for' (1) to 'People should take more responsibility to provide for themselves' (10) (% picking 10)	19	14	10

Source: World Values Study

involved in politics, from leadership in the civil rights movement to organization of the 'moral majority'. Indeed, reminiscent of the European Catholic Church of 50 or 100 years ago, some American bishops have threatened to withhold the sacraments from politicians, or even the supporters of politicians, who take the pro-choice side of the abortion debate.

Conclusion

These brief reviews of American political development, of the economic, sociological, and geographic conditions of the United States, and of a few elements of American political culture and beliefs lead to several generalizations that are essential to understanding American politics and ultimately the policies of the United States government in the twenty-first century. They also form the background for the chapters that follow.

Because of size, wealth, and distance from Europe, for most of its history the United States has been able to pay scant attention to a range of issues that have confronted most other countries with far more immediacy. With regard to foreign policy, the United States could afford to be far more inward-looking in its politics than most other countries. It has been less constrained by reality, and more able to indulge urges towards symbolism and posturing; to assume that it could act in (which for most of its history meant withdraw from) the international arena without regard for the opinions of the rest of the world. In domestic politics as well, the combination of isolation and wealth has made limitations imposed by reality less intrusive, and allowed missteps to be absorbed without devastating consequences.

The political institutions of the United States were not designed to be efficient. Rather, if efficient governments are those that can take decisive action quickly, then the government of the United States was intentionally designed to be *inefficient*. The Framers of the American Constitution were concerned about the weaknesses of the central government under the Articles of Confederation, but they remained even more fearful of an over-powerful government. Their objective was to protect against a government that would trample on the fundamental rights of citizens, but like other liberals of the period (and since) they were unable to distinguish between current privileges that might be limited for the public good and fundamental rights, a problem exacerbated by their inclusion of property rights in the latter category. In making it easy for groups to defend their rights, they also made it easy for them to defend their privileges. The resulting equation in practice, if not in theory, of private interest and natural right has (with some exceptions, like the internment of American citizens of Japanese descent during the Second World War and some of the policies of the government in the so-called war on terror) been quite effective in protecting Americans from abuses by the government, but has left the government fettered in protecting citizen from abuses by each other. As with slavery and child labour in the past, government attempts to limit abusive labour practices, environmental degradation, libellous reporting, and so forth often are found to have fallen afoul of constitutional limitations intended to protect individual rights.

The separation and division of powers, coupled with the loose structure of American political parties that is in part their consequence, make it hard for individuals or parties to take, or reasonably to be assigned, clear responsibility either for policies or for outcomes. This leads to a style of politics in which what David Mayhew (1974, speaking specifically of Congress) described as 'position taking' and 'credit claiming' dominate over real responsibility. There are few incentives for politicians to take responsibility for policies that will be unpopular in the short run, no matter how desirable their effects are likely to be in the long run, or to impose costs even if the benefits will outweigh them. But as with the limitations on the powers of government, the richness of the country has allowed these inefficiencies to be tolerated.

Although the formal institutional structure of American government has hardly changed since the Constitution was ratified, the actual distribution of power and influence, among branches of government, between levels of government, and within the individual branches of government, all have changed substantially. In particular, the centrality of the federal government, the dominance of the executive branch, and the pre-eminence of the president within the executive branch all, in one way or another, are fairly recent developments. Nonetheless, in comparison to most other democracies, the American states have remarkable autonomy from the central government and the Congress is remarkably independent of the executive. As was the intention in 1787, American politics is rarely about the winners imposing their will on the losers. Rather, it is about compromise among groups, none of which definitively win, but correspondingly none of which completely lose. At the same time however, and in contrast to the rather rosy picture implied in the previous sentence, the highly inequitable distribution of resources, coupled with the tremendous importance of money in American politics (itself in part a consequence of the weakness of political parties), means that some interests win far more, and more often, than others regardless of the outcome of elections.

KEY TERMS

- Articles of Confederation
- Connecticut Compromise
- Constitution
- division of powers
- elastic clause

- party government
- responsible parties
- separation of powers
- Three-Fifths Compromise

NOTES

1 *New York Times*, 7 January 1987, p. D2.

2 That said, it should be admitted that this model fits the French 'semi-presidential' system rather poorly, and the Swiss system hardly at all.

3 With the exception of Nebraska, which has a unicameral legislature.

4 *The Federalist*, no. 47.

5 The property of married women was considered to be owned by their husbands, and consequently these women could not satisfy property requirements. The colonies differed in their treatment of unmarried female property holders, and there is some evidence that, as in England, at least some of the richest of these women did vote in colonial America (Darcy et al. 1987: 4–6).

6 *The Federalist*, no. 48.

7 *The Federalist*, no. 51.

8 *The Federalist*, no. 10.

9 The electoral college mechanism remains important in influencing the strategic imperatives faced by presidential candidates and in weighting the choices of the several states, but the role of electors has been turned into that of an automatic transmission belt for translating the

plurality choice of their states into blocks of electoral votes. See Chapter 3.

10 *The Federalist*, no. 51.

11 The latter (Twelfth) Amendment was inspired by the election of 1800, in which Thomas Jefferson and Aaron Burr, who were supposed to have been the presidential and vice-presidential candidates respectively of the Democratic–Republicans, received equal numbers of electoral votes, thus forcing the election into the House of Representatives.

12 Realized national income figures are from Robert F. Martin, *National Income in the United States 1799–1938* (New York: National Industrial Conference Board, 1939), pp. 6–7.

13 In contrast, from 1941 to 1970, the figure never exceeded 25 per cent.

14 Unlike Ministries of the Interior in many other countries, the American Department of the Interior is primarily responsible for the administration of federal lands, and has no authority over either law enforcement (police) or local governments.

15 The four slave states that remained in the Union were Delaware, Maryland, Kentucky, and Missouri. In addition, the western counties of Virginia seceded from that state and remained in the Union as the new state of West Virginia.

16 In the United States, the phrase 'Social Security' usually refers specifically to the Old Age, Survivors and Disability Insurance programme (and especially to the Old Age portion) of the Social Security Administration, rather than to social programmes more generically.

17 Taking the total trade of Australia, Canada, Denmark, France, Germany, Italy, Japan, Norway, Sweden, the UK and the US as the base, the US share of the total grew from 12.4 per cent in 1870 (even with Germany and Japan excluded from the denominator) to 13.2 per cent in 1890, 16.8 per cent in 1913, and 19 per cent in 1960—reaching 26.8 per cent in 1980.

18 Frustrated by the repeated invalidation of New Deal programmes by the 'nine old men' on the Court, Roosevelt proposed that the president be allowed to appoint an additional Justice for every Justice over the age of 70 who refused to retire.

19 Because of the American practice of simultaneously electing candidates to a wide range of offices using a single ballot (see Chapter 3), it is possible for a voter to support candidates of different parties for different offices at the same election. This is called 'split-ticket voting', and generally is measured in one of two ways. On one hand, respondents to surveys may be asked for whom they voted for two or more different offices, and these may be compared for evidence of split-ticket voting. On the other hand, the vote totals for the most and least popular candidates of a single party may be compared. Both methods almost necessarily understate the overall levels of split-ticket voting, and yet both indicate that more voters now split their ballots than vote only for candidates of a single party.

20 As defined in the Luxembourg Income Study. Within that study, the exceptions were the Netherlands (75 per cent) and Germany (90 per cent).

....

GUIDE TO FURTHER READING

AMAR, A. R. (2005), *America's Constitution: a Biography* (New York: Random House).

A legal scholar's analysis of the origins and evolution of the American Constitution.

HAMILTON, A., J. JAY, and J. MADISON (2003), *The Federalist*, ed. T. Ball (Cambridge: Cambridge University Press).

A series of essays explaining and defending the draft constitution in the context of the debate over ratification.

SKOWRONEK, S. (1982), *Building a New American State: the Expansion of National Administrative Capacities, 1877–1920* (Cambridge: Cambridge University Press).

A political and historical analysis of the development of national administration in the United States.

TOCQUEVILLE, Alexis de (1956 [1834]), *Democracy in America: Specially Edited and Abridged for the Modern Reader* (New York: Penguin).

A Frenchman's observations on travelling through the United States in the early 1830s.

2

Federalism American Style

Overview

Many of the powers of European central governments are, in the US, exercised by the states. This has been an evolving balance, with the federal government really growing in importance only since the 1930s. Even with the growth of federal power, the states play a pivotal role in the implementation of many federal programmes. One result is that the quality of government services received by citizens varies widely, both among the states and within a single state.

Although the Preamble to the Constitution of the United States begins 'We the People', the Constitution could equally be read as a compact among the states. Its authors had been sent to Philadelphia in an essentially ambassadorial capacity; in deciding on its provisions, their votes were recorded by states; when the finished document was to be ratified, ratification was by states—although by special conventions rather than by the state governments; the result of ratification was 'the Establishment of this Constitution between the States'.

The structure of the government created also gave a central position to the states. Most obviously, each state was given two senators, originally to be chosen by its state legislature, and only directly elected since the ratification of the Seventeenth Amendment in 1913. (On the other hand, since the introduction of direct election of senators, the state governments themselves have had no direct representation at the federal level—in contrast, for example, to the representation of the *Länder* governments in the German Bundesrat or of the national governments in the Council of the European Union.) In addition, however, although membership of the

House of Representatives was to be based on population, the first step in the apportionment process was (and still is) to allocate numbers of representatives to the states. Not only are the electors who choose the president allocated to the states, the actual constitutional language is that they are appointed by the states.

Federalism is manifested in American government along two distinct dimensions. The first concerns the division of powers and responsibilities between the federal government, on the one hand, and the state and local governments, on the other. In this regard, it is important to note that even when the states reproduce some of the structural characteristics of the federal system in their own constitutions, the states themselves are not federal; rather county, city, and other local governments all are creatures of their state government. The second dimension concerns the variability and relations among the several states.

The federal government *vis-à-vis* the states

In broad terms, the division of powers and responsibilities between federal and state levels has been defined by four major factors. The first is the text of the Constitution as adopted in 1787. As suggested in the last chapter, this dramatically strengthened the national government in comparison to its powers under the Articles of Confederation, but it still defined a system in which the vast majority of the governing would be within the purview of the states. This interpretation was re-emphasized by the Tenth Amendment, which declared that: 'The powers not delegated to the United States by the Constitution, nor prohibited by it to the States, are reserved to the States respectively, or to the people.' At the same time, however, in addition to the specifically enumerated powers of the federal government, Congress was given the implied power to 'make all Laws which shall be necessary and proper for carrying into Execution' the powers granted to the federal government, and by the supremacy clause 'Laws of the United States . . . made in Pursuance' of the Constitution were made 'the supreme Law of the Land . . . any Thing in the Constitution or Laws of any State to the Contrary notwithstanding'. Moreover, the courts have accepted that the federal government has some additional powers which are inherent in the fact that it is a national government. On the one hand, these provisions created a system of 'dual federalism', in which the federal government could work directly within the states, rather than, as under the Articles of Confederation, only working through them, but in which the states exercised exclusive power over most questions of domestic governance. On the other hand, they left considerable ambiguity concerning the boundary between federal and state powers, making claims about 'states' rights' the subject of active political and legal debate, even after the question of whether the Constitution was to be seen as a reversible compact among the states or as an irreversible decision of the people was resolved in favour of the latter position.

The second factor is the Fourteenth Amendment, which was one of the three post-Civil War amendments. (The Thirteenth Amendment abolished slavery in the United States, and the Fifteenth Amendment prohibited denial of the right to vote on the basis of race, colour, or previous condition of servitude.) In particular, section 1 says that: 'No state shall make or enforce any law which shall abridge the privileges or immunities of citizens of the United States; nor shall any State deprive any person of life, liberty, or property, without due process of law; nor deny to any person within its jurisdiction the equal protection of the laws.' Over time, the twin results of this section were to extend the protections against federal action afforded by the Bill of Rights to apply against state actions as well, and to involve the federal courts in a wide range of policy questions that could be framed by one side or the other as involving the substantive meaning of 'equal protection' or 'due process.'

The third factor is a dramatically expanded reading of the power of the federal government to 'regulate Commerce with foreign Nations, and among the several States...'. Originally understood to apply only to regulation of the physical shipment of goods across borders or the erection of interstate trade barriers, in the latter half of the nineteenth century it was also interpreted by the federal courts through an expansive reading of the 'dormant commerce clause'[1] to bar state regulations that could have a substantial although non-discriminatory impact on interstate commerce, which in the absence of congressional action was more a decision in favour of laissez-faire than in favour of federal power.[2] Although Congress began in the last decades of the nineteenth century to regulate business practices as well as the simple shipment of goods, through the mid-1930s federal power was still both limited in scope by the Supreme Court and sparingly used by Congress. Beginning in 1937, however, the Court vastly broadened its interpretation of the commerce clause, in the first place allowing wage and hour regulation not only for workers directly involved in transporting goods across state lines but for those manufacturing the goods to be shipped as well,[3] and ultimately expanding it to include a wide range of health and safety issues, environmental protection, as well as other policies with an indirect impact on interstate commerce.

The fourth factor was the expanded use of federal grants first to 'bribe' and then to coerce (through threatened loss of the bribes) the states to pursue federal policies or adopt federally determined standards in fields that would otherwise be matters for state control. Beginning as subsidies for a few activities deemed desirable by Congress, these grew in both scope and magnitude so that in 2002 over 30 per cent of total state revenue came from intergovernmental transfer, the vast majority of which was transfer from the federal government.

Contemporary federal–state relations

Although these four factors can be separated analytically, historically they worked in varying combinations to produce a sea-change from 'dual federalism' through varying shades of 'cooperative federalism' (with an emphasis on shared responsibility) to what has been described as 'regulatory federalism' (with the federal government effectively regulating state governments themselves in a number of areas, most notably including civil rights, education, and the environment). The result is that although the states retain great importance, the reach of federal government action—and particularly affirmative congressional and executive action, as opposed to 'boundary setting' by the federal judiciary—has expanded into numerous areas that until quite recently would have been regarded as exclusively the responsibility of the states.

Money only tells part of the story, which is further obscured by the fact that having revenue does not always imply having discretion about how it is to be spent. Figure 2.1 nonetheless is indicative of the changing balance between federal and state (plus local) levels of government over the period from 1929 to 2001, and expands on the story told in Chapter 1. Beginning in the 1930s, and then rapidly accelerated by war in the first half of the 1940s, there was a dramatic reversal in the relative financial resources of the federal and subfederal governments. In 1932, subfederal revenues were nearly four times those of the federal government; in 1944, federal revenues were more than four times those of state and local governments. After the war, there was some redress of the balance, but state and local revenues have never (since 1941) exceeded those of the federal government, and have settled at about two-thirds of federal revenue. Starting to grow significantly a few years later, and peaking in the late 1970s, before settling at about 20 per cent of the total, federal grants-in-aid have become an important share of state and local revenue. Since these transfers are included in the state and local revenue figures, they suggest that the 60–40 division of total revenues indicated in Figure 2.1 may somewhat understate the relative financial power of the federal government.

Highway construction, education, and social welfare all are fields that traditionally belonged to the states but in which the federal government has

FIGURE 2.1 **Federal and subfederal shares of government revenue, and federal grants-in-aid**

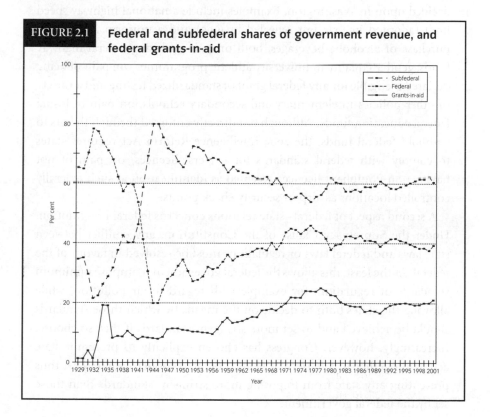

assumed a major role through the provision of 'grants-in-aid' (transfers of funds for specific programmes and subject to specific guidelines or controls). Often these require matching contributions from the states. Sometimes the formulas by which these grants are distributed are skewed in favour of the poorer states, thus reducing the differences among the states, but generally the states are free to supplement the base federal programme with funds of their own. In other cases, the federal formulas actually are skewed in favour of the richer states. All this means that the actual services provided to citizens under federal programmes may vary enormously from one state to another. For example, although Unemployment Insurance is a national programme, virtually every aspect of it—eligibility requirements, definitions of crucial terms like 'dependent', benefit levels—is defined by the states and differs among the states.

The strings attached to grants-in-aid have allowed Congress, or the agencies it creates, effectively to force the states to make policies actually decided upon in Washington. Examples include a national highway speed limit (adopted in 1974 but repealed in 1995) and a uniform age for the purchase of alcoholic beverages, both on pain of losing federal highway funds; gender equality in university athletic programmes (on pain of being declared ineligible for any federal grants); standardized testing and a variety of other policies in elementary and secondary schools, on pain of losing federal education funds. Although not directly enforced through threats to withhold federal funds, the 2004 Intelligence Reform Act requires states to comply with federal standards for drivers' licences, on pain of not having non-compliant licences accepted as identification at such federally controlled locations as airport security check points.

A second aspect of federal–state relations concerns federal pre-emption. Under the Supremacy Clause of the Constitution, any conflict between state laws and federal laws or regulations must be resolved in favour of the federal. At the least, this allows the federal government to impose minimum standards of regulation, for example with regard to air pollution, while allowing the states both to decide on the means by which those standards should be achieved and to set more stringent standards if they so choose. Increasingly, however, Congress has chosen explicitly to pre-empt state action altogether in a variety of fields, notably product liability law, thus preventing any state from imposing more stringent standards than those set by the federal government.

The increase of federal pre-emption has, however, been accompanied by a partial counter-trend—the increasing possibility that a state can be granted a waiver from a particular federal programme. In effect, this is a form of subsidiarity on an *ad hoc* basis, with a particular state allowed to pursue its own method of achieving the federally mandated result—subject to federal approval. Waivers have, for example, been particularly significant in the administration of the Medicaid programme, which provides health care to the very poor. In addition to allowing programmes to be more closely tailored to local needs and circumstances, waivers have also furthered the role of the states as 'laboratories of change', which is one of the more frequently cited justifications of federalism in the first place.

A third mode of federal intervention in what would otherwise be state concerns is through the application of the Bill of Rights or the equal pro-tection or due process clauses of the Fourteenth Amendment to state ac-tions. This has been particularly significant with regard to civil rights and criminal law. Racial integration of schools (including in some cases the mandatory bussing of students to achieve racial balance), strong restric-tions on the imposition of the death penalty, public provision of lawyers for indigent criminal defendants, the so-called 'Miranda warning', periodic reapportionment of legislative districts on the basis of strict population equality all were imposed on the states by the federal courts. Some state regulations of land use have been limited on the ground that they con-stitute uncompensated taking of private property, prohibited by the Fifth Amendment as extended to the states by the Fourteenth Amendment.

The appropriate balance between federal and state power may involve a question of strongly felt political principle, but it also is strongly related to policy preferences. Politicians and citizens alike almost invariably find most convincing arguments that assign the power to make policy in a field to the level of government at which their side of the question is more likely to prevail. Thus, when liberal forces were dominant at the national level, liberals supporting racial integration tended to favour the expansion of national power and conservatives supporting segregation (or attempting to exploit segregationist sentiment to their own advantage) railed about states' rights. With conservatives in control in Washington, however, liberals who support gay rights have become advocates of state autonomy while social conservatives passed the federal Defense of Marriage Act (which would, if found constitutional, relieve the states of their obligation under the 'full faith and credit' clause to recognize same-sex marriages solemnized in other states) and call for a constitutional amendment to pre-empt state action in this field altogether.

In the middle of the first decade of the twenty-first century, a number of questions of constitutional jurisprudence and political choice bear on the evolution of this balance. One question is whether the regulatory powers of Congress concerning the activities of private persons or corporations (for example, to prohibit age discrimination in employment or to set standards for wages and hours) extend to direct regulation of actions of the states themselves. A second is the perennial question of the reach of the Commerce Clause—for example, does the fact that marijuana may be traded (illegally) across state boundaries allow the federal government to pre-empt state laws that would allow personally grown marijuana to be used for medicinal purposes by cancer sufferers?

The implementation of federal programmes through the states by offers of federal funds raises two interrelated problems. On the one hand, the federal funds rarely cover the full cost of the programmes, and on the other hand the federal government often imposes additional requirements on the states that go beyond the original programme but that must nonetheless be satisfied if the states are to receive the original federal payments. The conjunction of these two phenomena has given rise to complaints about 'unfunded mandates'. Although the elimination of unfunded mandates originally was a Republican position, with the intention of reducing Democrat-supported programmes, once they were in power, the Republicans enacted policies that imposed substantial costs on the states (for example, the extensive testing requirements of the No Child Left Behind Act), with the Democrats complaining about the unfunded mandates. This is a continuing point of conflict between the state governors, regardless of party, and the president and Congress, also regardless of party.

Finally, the dependence of the states on federal transfers, and the interconnection of federal and state income tax systems, combine to make state budgets (which generally are required by the state constitutions to be in balance) heavily dependent on federal budgetary policy. On the one hand, it is often far more palatable politically for Congress to cut grants to the states (or fail to raise them, which given inflation is effectively the same thing)—especially so-called 'block grants' that are only loosely if at all tied to specific programmes—than it is to cut specific federal programmes. In this way, the members of Congress get the credit for fiscal restraint, but the state governments take the ultimate blame for reductions in services. On the other hand, because most state income tax systems begin with the federal definitions of taxable income, a federal tax reduction effected by excluding some form of income from taxation will have the effect of imposing a tax reduction on the states, unless they make the politically unpalatable decision apparently to increase taxes.

Relations and diversity among the states

The federal Constitution addresses relations among the states only minimally. No state can 'enter into any Agreement or Compact with another State, or with a foreign power' without the consent of Congress.[4] Disputes between the states are to be resolved in the federal courts. The states are required to give 'Full Faith and Credit to the public Acts, Records, and judicial Proceedings of every other State' and are prohibited from discriminating in favour of their own citizens or erecting protectionist trade barriers against one another. They are required to return persons who have been charged with a crime to the state that has made the charge.

Although these requirements look absolute, in fact there are many exceptions. States may, for example, impose dramatically higher tuition charges at their state universities for students who come from another state. Whether the full faith and credit clause would require states to recognize same-sex marriages performed in other states, and if so whether Congress has the authority to suspend this requirement, is the subject of current legal debate. As well, state governors have on occasion successfully refused to extradite persons accused of crimes where either the justice of the law in question or the ability or willingness to do justice of the state demanding extradition has been in serious doubt.

Subject to these constraints and those discussed in the previous section, the states are free to adopt their own policies. The result is very wide diversity among the states in a host of policy areas, ranging from criminal law and welfare policies to questions of corporate law, environmental and land use policy, and taxation. In creating a single national economy, the Constitution gave the states strong incentives for uniform policies in some areas, while also putting them in economic competition with one another.

Differences in politics and policies among the states stem from a number of sources, of which two may be singled out. The first widely cited source of difference is the 'political cultures' of the states, which is basically a way of summing up differences in historical experiences and in the origins of the people who originally settled there. Daniel Elazar (1966), for example, identified three political cultures: a traditional paternalistic and elitist culture dominant in the states of the confederacy; a moralistic culture particularly strong in the upper midwest; and an individualistic culture that was dominant in the northeast but combined with the moralistic culture in the west and northwest. While one would expect these cultural differences to be mitigated by population mobility, their institutional legacy, for example the association of the moralistic culture with such Progressive reforms as popular initiative and referendum, continue to be significant.

The second source of political difference is that the states are quite different economically and socially, as illustrated in Table 2.1. The problems and interests of a big and empty state like Alaska naturally differ from those of a small and crowded state like New Jersey. The economic resources of the states are quite different, as are the economic activities that produce those resources. Demographically, some states are essentially 'lily white' and native born, while others have substantial minority and immigrant populations (and in Hawaii, it is whites who are a minority group). That cultural differences remain significant is suggested by the enormous contrasts in religious identification among Massachusetts (44 per cent Catholic, 4 per cent Baptist, trace Mormon), Mississippi (55 per cent Baptist, 5 per cent Catholic, trace Mormon), and Utah (57 per cent Mormon, 6 per cent Catholic, 2 per cent Baptist).

Obviously, the substantial economic differences between Mississippi and Connecticut, which has nearly twice the per capita income, translate into substantial differences in the living conditions of their people, which the federal government is under no obligation to equalize, and indeed in some cases exacerbates. These differences are also either mitigated or increased by the policy choices that the states make.

Institutional similarity of the states

Although differing significantly economically and culturally, the basic political institutions of the states are very similar. All are characterized by

TABLE 2.1	Characteristics of the states		
		Maximum	Minimum
Population (in thousands, 2001)		34,501 (CA)	494 (WY)
Land area (thousand sq. miles)		571.9 (AK)	1.0 (RI)
Population per sq. mile (2001)		1143.9 (NJ)	1.1 (AK)
Per cent urban (2000)		94.4 (CA)	38.2 (VT)
Per cent non-white (2000)		75.72 (HI)	3.05 (ME)
Per cent Black or African American (2000)		36.34 (MS)	0.30 (MT)
Per cent foreign born (2000)		26.2 (CA)	1.1 (WV)
Personal income per capita (2001)		$41,930 (CT)	$21,643 (MS)
Percentage below poverty level (1998 to 2000 average)		19.3 (NM)	7.3 (MD)
Toxic releases (million pounds, 2000)		153.4 (TX)	0.2 (AK)
Unemployment percentage (2001)		6.4 (WA)	2.8 (ND)
Union membership (per cent of workers, 2001)		26.7 (NY)	3.7 (NC[1])
Per cent college graduate or more (2000)		34.6 (CO)	15.3(WV)
Per capita non-residential energy consumption (million BTU, 1999)		1,044 (AK)	175 (NY)
Per cent employed labour force in agriculture (2002)		9.0 (ND)	0.7 (AK)
Per cent employed labour force in manufacturing (2002)		20.7 (IN)	2.7 (HI)
Per cent employed labour force in service and finance (2002)		47.3 (AK)	21.2 (AL)
Per cent Catholic		44 (MA)	5 (MS)
Per cent Baptist		55 (MS)	2 (UT)

BTU = British Thermal Unit. State abbreviations come from the US Postal Service and are listed at: http://www.usps.com/ncsc/lookups/usps-abbreviations.html.
[1] North Carolina, along with 21 other states, have 'right to work' laws.
Sources: http://www.bls.gov/opub/gp/pdf/gp02_16.pdf; US Bureau of the Census, Statistical Abstract of the United States, http://www.census.gov/statab/www/; B. Kosmin, A. E. Mayer, and A. Keysar, American Religious Identification Survey (excludes Alaska and Hawaii) (New York: Graduate Center of the City University of New York; http://www.gc.cuny.edu/faculty/research_briefs/asis/asis_index.htm)

separation of powers among independent legislative, executive, and judicial branches. The legislatures of all the states except Nebraska are bicameral. The chief executive of each state is a directly elected governor. Each has a court system headed by a single supreme court (identified here in lower case because it may have another name—indeed, in New York the 'Supreme Court' is the lowest court of general jurisdiction). The legal system of every state except Louisiana is derived from English common law; the legal system of Louisiana, reflecting its history as a French possession, combines this with derivatives of the Code Napoleon. Within this basic similarity, however, there are a number of significant differences. While many of these will be elaborated in later chapters, they can be listed briefly here.

Although no state uses proportional representation for elections to state office (several localities do use single transferable vote (STV), limited vote, or cumulative voting), and the norm is election by first-past-the-post from single member districts, there are exceptions. Louisiana uses a two-round, absolute majority system;[5] many states elect members of at least one house of their legislatures from multi-member districts. States differ in the length of legislative and gubernatorial terms, and in whether these elections are timed to coincide with national elections or not. States also differ in their suffrage requirements—most notably today in their treatment of convicted felons.

With regard to the executive branch, there are two interrelated differences. The first concerns the number of directly elected major executive officers, ranging from only the governor to at least 13 in North Dakota.[6] The second concerns the power of the governor him- (or her-) self. In West Virginia the governor submits a budget that cannot be increased by the legislature, while in Texas the legislature has full power to modify the executive budget; in Minnesota the governor can veto particular items in a bill and it requires a vote of two-thirds of all elected members of each house of the legislature to override the veto, while in Alabama the governor has no item veto power and the governor's veto of a bill can be overridden by a majority.

The most significant difference among judicial branches is in the method of judicial selection. In eight states, the judges of the highest court are selected in partisan elections. In another ten states, they are chosen in non-partisan elections. Nine more states choose at least some judges of inferior courts by popular election. In four states, the judges of the highest court are appointed by the governor, and in two they are appointed by the legislature.

The remaining states use systems generally identified in the United States as 'merit selection', but this should not be confused with the civil service-like career patterns of judges in many European systems. Rather, a nominating commission screens applicants and recommends appointees to the governor, who may (or may not) be given a choice among a few candidates; often judges appointed in this way serve for only a few years and then are subject to a retention election (which in some cases can be contested by candidates who were not nominated through the merit system) to determine whether they will remain in office.

Finally, the states differ dramatically in their use of instruments of direct democracy (initiative, referendum, and recall). Every state except Delaware requires that constitutional amendments be approved by referendum. Twenty-three states (including Delaware) allow, but do not require, the legislature to place ordinary statutes on the ballot for popular approval or rejection. In addition, 18 states allow proposed constitutional amendments, and 21 states allow proposals for ordinary statutes to be put on the ballot by popular petition. Finally, 18 states allow the voters to truncate the term of an elected official by petitioning for a special election to determine whether the incumbent should be removed from office; the 2004 removal of California Governor Gray Davis is the most prominent recent example.[7]

Policy differences among the states

One field in which the states retain great autonomy, and in which differences among the states are particularly obvious, is the criminal law.[8] While all states treat crimes such as murder, rape, or robbery with violence as serious offences—generally punishable by sentences that would be regarded as draconian in most of the rest of the industrialized world (for example, the average sentence for robbery in the United States is more than twice the average in England, while for assault, burglary, or motor vehicle theft American sentences average roughly three times those in England)—the punishments for equivalent crimes may vary widely among the states.[9] Indeed, an act that is considered a serious felony in one state may be regarded as the equivalent of a traffic offence in another; in Georgia the maximum punishment for possession of less than one ounce of marijuana is one year in prison and a fine of $1,000; in Mississippi the maximum is a civil fine of $250. At the other extreme, only 38 of the 50 states allow capital punishment,[10] and of those, by the end of 2004 six had not executed anyone since 1976;[11] of the 944 executions in the United States between 1976 and the end of 2004, over one-third were in Texas, over one half in Texas plus Virginia and Oklahoma, and over 82 per cent were in the south as a whole. (Although federal criminal law allows the death penalty for an increasing number of crimes, at the end of 2004 there had been only three federal executions since 1976.)

Interstate differences with regard to the delivery of public services are also dramatic. In January 2003, the maximum benefit payable to a family of one parent and two children under the Temporary Assistance for Needy Families (TANF) programme ranged between $170 in Mississippi and $923 in Alaska; more than 20 states have established time limits shorter than the federal maximum of 60 months for the receipt of TANF funds, but at the other extreme, Michigan, New York, and Vermont use state funds to continue full benefits indefinitely. In the fall of 2003, spending in public primary and secondary schools ranged between $12,059 per pupil in New York and $5,091 per pupil in Utah. While some of these differences are reflective of differences in the costs of living, and some of the different resources available, part of the difference also reflects different state decisions about programmes to support and levels of taxation to impose. For example, in November 2004 the voters of Alabama rejected a state constitutional amendment to remove (unenforceable) language mandating segregated schools as well as language specifying that 'nothing in this Constitution shall be construed as creating or recognizing any right to education or training at public expense', apparently because opponents convinced many voters that allowing even the implication of a right to public education would ultimately lead to higher taxes. The constitutions of some other states, as interpreted by their own courts, by contrast, not only guarantee a free public education but also that it be 'adequate' or 'effective'.[12]

Although in terms of federalism, education is primarily a state responsibility, in fact control is generally far more local—in the hands of school boards that are in some places directly elected and in others appointed at either the county or even the city or town level.[13] These boards must satisfy state-imposed standards, but within those have significant autonomy regarding curriculum, staffing levels, and so forth. Much of their revenue comes from local (most often real property) taxes, which means that the resources available per pupil can vary very widely even within a state. Moreover, in many places the annual school budget (and in even more places, borrowing, for example, for school construction) must be approved by popular referendum, with the result that the quality of public education may also depend on the willingness of local residents without children to see their taxes increased to support the education of other people's children.[14] Other essential social services, such as police and fire protection, also are generally locally funded and controlled, again with wide disparities in the quality of service within a single state, and often to the disadvantage of central cities with the greatest needs but the lowest local tax base.

Nationally, state tax revenue per capita averaged $1,920, but ranged from $2,986 in Connecticut to $1,372 in New Hampshire. Moreover, the sources of revenue also varied widely. Overall, the greatest source of state tax revenue was sales and gross receipt taxes, making up 46.8 per cent of the total, but while these taxes were 81 per cent of tax revenue in Texas, they were only 12.2 per cent of taxes in Oregon and 9.7 per cent in Alaska. The second largest source of state tax revenue nationally was the personal income tax, accounting for 36 per cent of the total; Oregon was at the top in this category, at 68.9 per cent, while seven states had no personal income tax at all, and two more taxed only income from interest and dividends, which therefore accounted for less than 4 per cent of state tax revenues. Property taxes accounted for only 2 per cent of all state tax revenues, but over 25 per cent of tax revenues in New Hampshire and Vermont. As shown in Table 2.2, when local taxes and non-tax revenue are added, the mix is somewhat different, primarily because real property taxes are the main source of local revenue in much of the United States, but the picture of wide differences among the states remains.

Seen from the perspective of the individual taxpayer, among those states with personal income taxes, the top marginal rate ranged between 3 per cent and 11 per cent, and there were also significant differences among the states regarding the taxability of various sources of income. State general retail sales taxes were imposed in 49 states, ranging between 2.9 per cent and 7 per cent, but when supplemented by local sales taxes, the range (including all 50 states) was between 4 per cent and 11 per cent; moreover, there was considerable variation in whether (and what) food, clothing,

TABLE 2.2	Sources of state revenue		
	National Average	Minimum	Maximum
Property Tax	19	8 AL NM	43 NH
Sales Tax	25	4 AK	43 NV
Income Taxes (including corporate)	18	0 NV TX WA WY	32 MA
Non Tax Revenue	32	19 CT	70 AK

Source: *Who Pays? A Distributional Analysis of the Tax Systems in All 50 States*, Institute on Taxation and Economic Policy, http://www.itepnet.org/wp2000/text.pdf

and services were included. Selective sales taxes (for example, on alcohol, tobacco and motor vehicle fuels) also varied very widely. At the corporate level, there are similarly wide differences, with possible perverse effects. For example, Delaware does not tax corporate profits from intangible assets (such as a trademark); by creating a Delaware corporation that owns a company's trademark and then licenses its use (for a substantial fee) back to the company, income that would have been taxable profits is rendered non-taxable.

The result of these differences is not only that the amount of revenue available varies, but that so too does the incidence of the tax burden. Because of that state's heavy dependence on sales taxes, the average family in the bottom 20 per cent of the income distribution in Washington (income under $17,000) pays roughly 17.6 per cent of that income in state and local taxes, in contrast to a similarly placed family in Delaware (income under $15,000) that pays only about 4.7 per cent of its income in state and local taxes.

As with trade within the European Union, while increased economic development is good for all, the states are also in competition with one another to be the place where that development, with the attendant increases in employment and tax base (although often also in demands for public services), happens. While the Constitution prohibits such trade barriers as interstate tariffs (although the prohibition against bringing citrus fruit into

California from any state except Arizona—identified as an 'external quarantine' but enforced at highway inspection stations that look suspiciously like international customs posts, and indeed the California Department of Food and Agriculture uses the word 'smugglers' to describe those who seek to evade inspection), states have a variety of ways in which they can try to create a 'business friendly' climate. In general terms, 'business friendly' translates into low taxes and weak regulations. In some cases, this means lowering tax rates and weakening regulation generally, but in other cases states or localities offer particular inducements to particular firms in such forms as tax abatements, below market-rate financing, or provision of what are effectively private facilities at public expense.[15]

A second aspect of what has been sometimes characterized as a 'race to the bottom' in both business taxation and regulation has been a fear of encouraging poor people to relocate to a state by providing unusually generous social welfare benefits. While both the importance of being 'business friendly' and the danger of being a 'welfare magnet' have been widely exploited by conservatives interested in reducing taxes and benefits, and indeed have come to be accepted as facts of life by many liberals as well, the evidence—either that states are pursuing these strategies or that the arguments underlying them actually are valid—is rather mixed (for example, Rom 1999: 360).

Although it is customary to think of the United States as a single market, there are a number of respects in which this is not so, as suggested above. Another respect in which the economic integration of the United States is far from perfect concerns the licensing of trade and professional workers. Although there are no restrictions on the movement of people, a licence issued by the state in which one will work is required for many jobs: lawyer, physician, architect, engineer, barber, cosmetologist, plumber, master electrician, etc. Although some states will automatically grant a licence, for some jobs, to someone who is already licensed in another state, both the occupations for which this recognition will be given, and the states whose licences will be recognized, is decided on a state-by-state basis. For example, Pennsylvania will grant a barber's licence without examination only to barbers already licensed in 11 other states which reciprocally will recognize Pennsylvania licences; while Pennsylvania will reciprocally recognize law licences from 30 states, only three of these are among the 11 whose barber licences are recognized. Similarly, a variety of businesses, such as insurance companies or building contractors, must be licensed in each state in which they propose to do business, subject to that state's own requirements.

The limits on the degree to which the United States can be regarded as a 'single market' stemming from the *ad hoc* nature of interstate cooperation with regard to licensing are also evident in other fields, most notably commercial law. The advantages of uniformity of law in many fields that are within the purview of the states led in 1892 to the creation of the National Conference of Commissioners on Uniform State Laws, a non-governmental body composed of lawyers chosen by the states to propose 'uniform laws'. Roughly half of its proposals have not been adopted even by a single state, but a few, most notably the Uniform Commercial Code (UCC), have been widely enacted (in the case of the UCC, in 49 states[16]), although even here 'uniform' is a bit of an exaggeration because each state is free to adopt, and then over time to amend, its own version.

Two further points concerning the 'singleness' of the American market deserve brief mention, if only because these relate to questions that have been contentious with regard to the single European market. The first is that the prohibition of discrimination against 'out-of-state' residents applies only to government action, not to the actions of private individuals or corporations. It is not uncommon, for example, for automobile advertisements offering special terms to end with the tag line 'residency restrictions may apply'. The second is that alcoholic beverages (and to a lesser extent, tobacco) are in a separate category. A very large proportion of the price of these products is excise taxes, which in the United States vary widely among the states. In addition, there are 18 states in which the sale of liquor is a state monopoly, and others in which prices are in some measure controlled. The result can be very large retail price discrepancies across state borders. But carrying alcoholic beverages across state lines can be prohibited, a ban sometimes enforced by sending unmarked police cars to note the licence plates of cars from the high-price state that are parked at liquor stores in the low-price state so that they can be stopped when they return home.

Finally, it should be observed that although the states are nominally equals, in certain fields some states are 'more equal than others'. Businesses can be incorporated in any state, but in fact more than 50 per cent of all publicly traded corporations in the United States, and more than 58 per cent of the 'Fortune 500', are incorporated in Delaware. As a result, the Delaware state Court of Chancery has become the pre-eminent venue for resolving disputes concerning corporate governance, and courts in other states are likely to give great weight to its judgments. Similarly, because Texas is a very large market and requires central approval for all textbooks used in its schools, the Texas Board of Education has substantial influence over what is taught in schools far beyond its borders, as publishers shape content to satisfy the Texas Board's biases. On the other hand, while California clearly sets the standard for the control of motor vehicle-based pollution, the result has simply been the manufacture of special models of cars and special blends of fuel that meet California's higher standards.

American federalism in perspective

The relative importance of the states in comparison to the federal government varies tremendously across policy areas, as does the particular form of shared responsibility between levels. Although there has been a great shift over time in favour of the federal government, the states still are largely autonomous with regard to those government services that most directly affect people's lives: public safety and policing; education; public transportation and highways; provision of hospitals; regulation of insurance; commercial, company, personal injury, real property law.[17] Even where programmes are largely federal (for example, unemployment insurance, Medicaid), they are often administered through the states, with significant state discretion concerning the details of implementation. That said, however, it is clear that beginning with the New Deal in the 1930s, the federal government has become the dominant level of government. Significantly, this shift in the balance of power has taken place without any formal constitutional changes. Rather, what has changed has been political practice and the interpretation of the same text.

The evolving system of regulatory federalism, in which federal authority is in significant measure exercised through the granting or threatened withholding of funds, has two important consequences. The first is that both the quality and the quantity of government service vary from state to state. The schools in some states are better funded and simply better than those in others. Public health or welfare services available to citizens in one state are not available to citizens in another. Rights that are protected in one state are not protected in another. The second is that, as in much of American government, the lines of responsibility are obscured.

Governing is far less centralized in the United States than it is in unitary systems, in which the central government has clear ultimate responsibility even if it has chosen to devolve some (or even substantial) discretion to subnational units. Perhaps surprisingly, however, in some respects the United States is also more decentralized than the European Union, notwithstanding that at least at the nominal level the phrase 'federal Europe' is understood to imply a dramatic increase in central authority over the *status quo*. Certainly the American system is more nationalized with regard to foreign policy, immigration or citizenship, or military affairs (although each state has its own military forces, the 'National Guard', subject to federalization but with the state governor as commander-in-chief and administered by an adjutant general appointed by the governor). The American federal government has an independent income that far exceeds the income of the states, in contrast to the meagre 'own resources' of the EU. On the other hand, the Growth and Stability Pact (to the extent that it is enforced) gives the European level far greater control over national budgets than would be imaginable with regard to federal control over state budgets in the United States. Based on the idea that regulatory harmonization is necessary for the completion of a 'single market', the EU has imposed a wide range of rules (for example, a minimum marketable size for apples) that in the United States would be left to the states or not regulated by government at all. While rates of Value Added Tax are set by the member states and the tax itself is collected by them, the EU imposition of a minimum rate of 15 per cent, and indeed of the VAT system in the first place, is also a greater limitation of second-tier autonomy than would be possible in the United States. Although not always enforced in practice, the EU requires that national (and subnational) procurement policies be non-discriminatory with respect to the nationality of the supplier; it is the policy of many American states to give preferences (in some case amounting to as much as 7 per cent of the contract) to in-state suppliers. Finally, the flip side of the federal monopoly on international relations is that undertakings of the federal government are not necessarily binding on the states. For example, when the United States agreed to limit 'Buy

American' programmes in public procurement in exchange for the EU dropping 'Buy European' programmes, the US government could only try to persuade the states to go along—and with only limited success.

....

KEY TERMS

- block grants
- cooperative federalism
- division of powers
- dormant commerce clause

- dual federalism
- grants-in-aid
- regulatory federalism
- unfunded mandates

....

NOTES

1 The 'dormant commerce clause' is an interpretation of the clause giving Congress the power to regulate interstate commerce. According to this interpretation, the states may not use their otherwise valid police powers in ways that unduly burden interstate commerce.

2 For example, *Wabash, St. Louis and Pacific Ry. v. Illinois*, 118 US 557 (1886), which struck down a state statute forbidding unfair rate discrimination by railroads.

3 *National Labor Relations Board v. Jones and Laughlin Steel Corporation*, 301 US 1 (1937).

4 Examples of such compacts would be the Port Authority of New York and New Jersey or the series of interstate arrangements to share the water of the Colorado River.

5 For reasons that have more to do with uniformity of language than of practice, Louisiana refers to the first round as an 'open primary', but it is in fact the first round of a two-round majority election.

6 In addition to Governor and Lieutenant Governor (elected on a single ticket), North Dakotans also elect the Secretary of State, Attorney General, Treasurer, Auditor, Commissioner of Agriculture, Tax Commissioner, Commissioner of Insurance, Superintendent of Public Instruction, and three Public Service Commissioners. Among the more 'minor' offices filled by election, for example, are the (separate) governing boards of the University of Michigan, Michigan State University, and Wayne State University.

7 The number of signatures required for popular initiatives ranges between 3 per cent and 15 per cent of the vote cast in a previous election (generally, but not always, for governor). Signature requirements for recall elections tend to be much higher, typically around 25 per cent of the vote in the previous election for the office in question.

8 Federal expansionism has taken the form of making many more offences federal crimes. These new laws do not pre-empt the existing state laws, but supplement them, making it possible to be tried in both state and federal courts for the same action under the theory that it constituted two separate crimes. Generally, however, such crimes are tried only in state courts. One notable exception, however, is the federal statute making it a crime to conspire to deprive someone of his or her civil rights. This has sometimes been invoked to try police officers (or others) whose acquittals in state courts have appeared to be the result of racial bias on the part of judges, jurors, or prosecutors.

9 For example, use of a deadly weapon is punishable by a prison sentence of one to five years in Massachusetts but by a sentence of not less than ten years for the first offence (and life imprisonment for a second offence) in Georgia.

10 Although included in the count of 38 states with the death penalty, at the end of 2004 the death penalty statutes in New York and Kansas had been found unconstitutional.

11 In the case of *Furman v. Georgia* 408 US 153 (1972), the Supreme Court ruled that the method by which death sentences were imposed violated the Eighth Amendment, thus ending capital punishment in the United States. The ruling left open the possibility that a state would re-enact a death penalty statute that the Court would find acceptable. In 1976, the Court approved statutes enacted in Georgia, Texas, and Florida—*Gregg v. Georgia* 428 US 153 (1976), *Jurek v. Texas* 428 US 262 (1976), and *Proffitt v. Florida* 428 US 242 (1976). In January 1977, Gary Gilmore was executed by firing squad in Utah.

12 These questions have arisen in the context of the American tradition of funding public education largely through local taxes, which creates tremendous disparities in the resources available in rich and poor communities. While the federal courts have ruled that the equal protection clause of the Fourteenth Amendment does not require that these differences be mitigated, the supreme courts of several states have ruled that their own constitutions require that every school system have sufficient resources to provide an 'adequate' or 'effective' education, even if it means changing the system of school funding.

13 The method of choice is not necessarily consistent even within the same state. For example, in 2005 Maryland had 24 local boards of education, ten appointed and the others elected.

14 This has tended to be a particular problem in cases of suburban and exurban development in areas of very local school finance and control. If large numbers of new residents (sometimes attracted by schools that they believe to be better than those they are leaving) bring a rapid increase in the number of school-aged children beyond the capacity of the existing infrastructure, the only alternative to overcrowding and rapid deterioration of educational quality may be a significant increase in taxes—including the taxes paid by long-time residents, who have little sense of community with the newcomers and who may not be willing to vote for the required increase.

15 In early 2006, the constitutionality of incentives provided to particular firms in order to attract them to a particular state or locality was under challenge. *DaimlerChrysler v. Cuno* and *Wilkins v. Cuno* 126 S. Ct. 36.

16 The exception is Louisiana, whose legal system is rooted in the civil law rather than the common law tradition.

17 Real property law is a technical term in the United States referring to the law related to real estate, as opposed to personal property law.

GUIDE TO FURTHER READING

CONLAN, T. (1998), *From New Federalism to Devolution: Twenty-five Years of Intergovernmental Reform* (Washington, DC: Brookings Institution).

An account of efforts between 1969 and 1995 to reform intergovernmental relations and shift increased power to the states.

ELAZAR, D. (1966), *American Federalism: a View from the States* (New York: Crowell).

Gives a good overview of intergovernmental relations, and of differences among the states.

PETERSON, P. E. (1995), *The Price of Federalism* (Washington, DC: Brookings Institution).

An evaluation of the strengths and weaknesses of the actual operation of American federalism in the 1990s.

3

Elections in the United States

Overview

The United States does not have truly national elections. Rather it has 50 state elections (plus an election in the District of Columbia) that are held on the same day and elect federal officials along with a sometimes dizzying array of state and local officials. These elections are managed by the states, under rules that differ among the states. This chapter discusses the American electoral systems, the selection of candidates, and the conduct of campaigns.

The American electoral systems embody two great ironies. On the one hand, although the United States regards itself as one of the prime movers to bring 'free and fair' elections to the rest of the world, the United States itself would rank rather poorly by the standards international observers generally apply. On the other hand, although the American electoral systems are structured in ways that both assume and re-enforce a two-party system, American elections in practice are more contests between individuals than parties, with the parties themselves playing a secondary, although since 2004 an increasing, role as autonomous organizations.

National elections?

Although it is customary to talk about national elections in the United States, and although certain aspects of the election of federal officials are regulated by federal law (for example, the holding of federal elections on the first Tuesday after the first Monday in November), American national

elections are more properly seen as state events that are held simultaneously than as truly national events. Since 1842, federal law has required
that members of the House of Representatives be chosen from single-
member districts.[1] Although each state has two senators, a state would
elect more than one at a single election only if the election to fill a casual
vacancy were to coincide with a regular senatorial election, in which case
the two positions are considered to be separate offices, each filled from the
whole state as a single-member district. Within this limitation, however,
each state is free to choose its own electoral system. While most use first-
past-the-post, Louisiana uses the two ballot majority system. Any state that
wanted to adopt the alternative vote system (known in the United States
as 'instant run-off') would be free to do so.

Each state also sets its own suffrage requirements, again subject to federal
limitations but not dictation.[2] The right to vote was extended to women by
several states before the ratification of the Nineteenth Amendment in 1920,[3]
and before it was lowered nationally to 18 by constitutional amendment,
the voting age varied among the states. Of greatest current interest, given
both the numbers of Americans convicted of serious crimes and the racial
composition of that group, the states differ in their treatment of convicted
felons. Currently, only Maine and Vermont allow prison inmates to vote; 35
states bar felons from voting while they are on parole; six states effectively
disenfranchise convicted felons for life. Overall, roughly 2.3 per cent of
adults have currently or permanently been disenfranchised as a result of a
felony conviction; for African American men, the overall figure is roughly
13 per cent, while in the states that permanently disenfranchise those with
felony convictions the figure is closer to 40 per cent.[4]

The states also differ widely with respect to the registration of voters,
which is required in every state except North Dakota.[5] Unlike most democracies, the onus to be included on the register rests with the citizen rather
than the election officials. Six states (in addition to North Dakota) allow
citizens to register at the polls on election day; many others require registration as much as 30 days (the maximum permitted by federal law) before
the election.[6] A national postal registration form is widely available, but is
not accepted in Wyoming and is interpreted in New Hampshire simply as
a request for the state's own form. Rules allowing the removal or challenge
of individual registrants, either at the time of registration or at the polls, all
are state-specific.

In order to appear on a party's primary election ballot (see below), a would-be candidate may be required only to file a declaration of candidacy, or the candidate may be required to support that declaration with petitions signed by as many as 5 per cent of the voters eligible to vote in the primary (Oklahoma[7]) or a substantial filing fee (in Florida totalling 6 per cent of the salary of the office in question); independent candidates for a general election may require as few as 25 petition signatures (Tennessee) or as many as 10 per cent of the vote cast in the previous election (North Dakota). In some states, a candidate who is defeated in a party primary is prohibited from standing as an independent in the general election ('sore-loser laws'), but in other states this is allowed. Ballot format, the kinds of voting equipment (for example, punch card, lever machine, touch-screen, paper ballot), the number and location of polling places, the hours of voting, and the conditions under which advance or postal voting will be allowed[8] all are decided by state (or in some cases, local) officials, as are the procedures for verifying, and potentially challenging, the result and resolving any disputes that may arise.

Ballots

Because state and local elections often are held at the same time as federal elections, one of the most distinctive features of American elections is the sheer number of officials to be chosen. In November 2004, for example, voters in Durham County, North Carolina were asked to choose among candidates for: President (and Vice-President), US Senator, US Representative, Governor, Lt. Governor (separately from Governor), eight other statewide officials, state senator, state representative, country commissioners, register of deeds (all partisan offices), plus five separate judgeships and a soil and water district supervisor elected on a non-partisan basis, and to vote on three amendments to the state constitution. Over 111,600 ballots were cast (73.14 per cent of registered voters).

The scale of the process argues strongly for some form of mechanized tabulating and counting, and most Americans who vote at the polls record their votes using some form of voting machine. In the grossest of terms, these fall into four categories: lever machines; punch card machines; optical scanners (similar to machine-scored tests); and electronic touch-screens (similar to automated bank machines). Within each type, however, there are many varieties, which differ in cost (both of acquisition and of maintenance), ease and clarity of use, and reliability (including in some cases, but not others, automated checking for errors that would invalidate the ballot so that the voter can correct them). In some states, the choice of machinery is made at the state level, but in many it is made even more locally. As became clear in the aftermath of the 2000 election, this decision can have a noticeable impact on the rate at which votes are rejected; and in large measure because voting equipment is bought and maintained locally, there is a significant correlation between the affluence of a jurisdiction and the quality of its voting machinery.

As 2000's infamous 'butterfly ballot' demonstrated, the layout of the ballot also involves potentially important decisions. These generally are made at the local level, subject to state law, which, as the Florida example shows, is not always followed. In broad terms, American 'long ballots' (that is, ballots for many offices), are laid out in two possible ways. With the 'office block' ballot, candidates are listed by office, in an order (be it alphabetical or in order of qualifying or randomly) that is specific to the office. With the 'party column' ballot, candidates are listed in a grid, with one dimension defined by office but the other defined by party. Thus all the Democratic candidates would be in one column, all the Republicans in another, etc. In some cases, party column ballots will allow voters to cast a 'straight party ballot' (vote for all the candidates of a single party) by pulling a single lever (or making a single mark or a single punch or a single screen-touch), but even if this option is not available, the party column ballot emphasizes partisanship while the office block ballot emphasizes the individuality of particular candidates.

All of this is illustrated by the ballot for the 2004 election in Durham County, reproduced in Figure 3.1. The first page is basically a party column ballot (for each office, Democrats are listed before Republicans),[9] but the technical limitations of the optical scan ballot do not permit a true grid arrangement. There is a space for voting a straight party ticket, but this excludes the presidential election, for which the voter must make a separate choice; such separations have frequently been adopted when a state's governing party fears a popular presidential candidate of the other party in order to insulate themselves from his 'coattails'. The offices on the second page of the ballot are elected on a non-partisan basis, and so only the office block format is possible.

FIGURE 3.1 **Sample ballot, Durham County, North Carolina, general election of 2004**

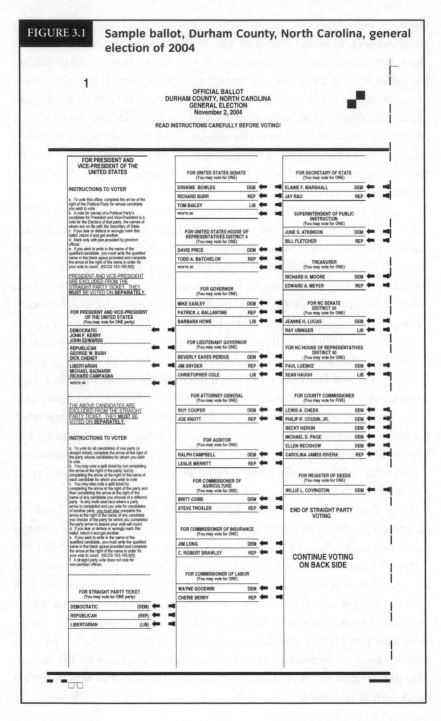

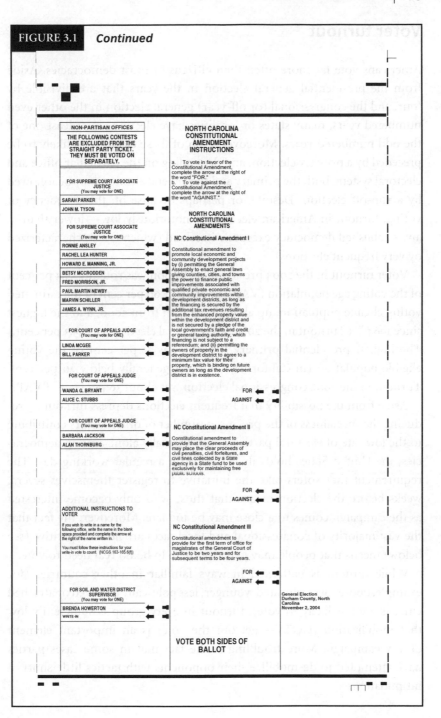

FIGURE 3.1 *Continued*

NON-PARTISAN OFFICES

THE FOLLOWING CONTESTS ARE EXCLUDED FROM THE STRAIGHT PARTY TICKET. THEY MUST BE VOTED ON SEPARATELY.

FOR SUPREME COURT ASSOCIATE JUSTICE
(You may vote for ONE)

SARAH PARKER
JOHN M. TYSON

FOR SUPREME COURT ASSOCIATE JUSTICE
(You may vote for ONE)

RONNIE ANSLEY
RACHEL LEA HUNTER
HOWARD E. MANNING, JR.
BETSY MCCRODDEN
FRED MORRISON, JR.
PAUL MARTIN NEWBY
MARVIN SCHILLER
JAMES A. WYNN, JR.

FOR COURT OF APPEALS JUDGE
(You may vote for ONE)

LINDA MCGEE
BILL PARKER

FOR COURT OF APPEALS JUDGE
(You may vote for ONE)

WANDA G. BRYANT
ALICE C. STUBBS

FOR COURT OF APPEALS JUDGE
(You may vote for ONE)

BARBARA JACKSON
ALAN THORNBURG

ADDITIONAL INSTRUCTIONS TO VOTER

If you wish to write in a name for the following office, write the name in the blank space provided and complete the arrow at the right of the name written in.

You must follow these instructions for your write-in vote to count. (NCGS 163-165.6(f))

FOR SOIL AND WATER DISTRICT SUPERVISOR
(You may vote for ONE)

BRENDA HOWERTON
WRITE-IN

NORTH CAROLINA CONSTITUTIONAL AMENDMENT INSTRUCTIONS

a.   To vote in favor of the Constitutional Amendment, complete the arrow at the right of the word "FOR."
b.   To vote against the Constitutional Amendment, complete the arrow at the right of the word "AGAINST."

NORTH CAROLINA CONSTITUTIONAL AMENDMENTS

NC Constitutional Amendment I

Constitutional amendment to promote local economic and community development projects by (i) permitting the General Assembly to enact general laws giving counties, cities, and towns the power to finance public improvements associated with qualified private economic and community improvements within development districts, as long as the financing is secured by the additional tax revenues resulting from the enhanced property value within the development district and is not secured by a pledge of the local government's faith and credit or general taxing authority, which financing is not subject to a referendum; and (ii) permitting the owners of property in the development district to agree to a minimum tax value for their property, which is binding on future owners as long as the development district is in existence.

FOR
AGAINST

NC Constitutional Amendment II

Constitutional amendment to provide that the General Assembly may place the clear proceeds of civil penalties, civil forfeitures, and civil fines collected by a State agency in a State fund to be used exclusively for maintaining free public schools.

FOR
AGAINST

NC Constitutional Amendment III

Constitutional amendment to provide for the first term of office for magistrates of the General Court of Justice to be two years and for subsequent terms to be four years.

FOR
AGAINST

General Election
Durham County, North Carolina
November 2, 2004

VOTE BOTH SIDES OF BALLOT

Voter turnout

Americans vote far more often than citizens of most democracies. Aside from the presidential general election in the years that are divisible by four, and the congressional (or off-year) general election in the other even numbered years, many states or localities have elections in at least one of the odd numbered years. Moreover, each of these elections is likely to be preceded by a primary election, and depending on the particular office and electoral system, both the primary and the general election may be followed by a run-off election. Despite, or perhaps because of, this frequency of voting, turnout in American elections is notoriously low—lower than in any established democracy except Switzerland (which is also characterized by very frequent elections).

Voter turnout in the 2004 presidential election was roughly 55.3 per cent of the voting age population (VAP), or roughly 60 per cent of the estimated voting eligible population, up about 6 per cent from 2000, and the highest since 1964.[10] (Turnout in the 2003 Swiss general election was 45.3 per cent.) The highest presidential primary turnout was 31 per cent of the voting eligible population (in California), and was generally below 20 per cent. Turnout in the 2002 congressional election was about 36 per cent of VAP.

Aside from the possibility that frequent elections depress turnout by re-ducing the specialness of the process, a number of other factors contribute to the low rate of electoral participation. Virtually alone among democra-cies, the United States holds its elections on a regular working day. The requirement that voters take the initiative to register themselves several weeks before the election means that those who only become interested as the campaign comes to a close may be too late. Moreover, the fact that the vast majority of congressional and local races are not competitive (see below) means that people may perceive there to be no real need to vote.

While turnout is patterned in ways familiar in other countries (for example, poorer, less educated, younger, less politically involved or attached citizens are less likely to vote), turnout in every group is sufficiently low that mobilization (GOTV—get out the vote) is an important element of any campaign. More troubling is the fact that in some cases parties have attempted to de-mobilize their opponents with tactics little short of intimidation.

Congressional elections

Members of the House of Representatives and of the Senate all are elected from single member districts, using the first-past-the-post electoral system (except in Louisiana). In each district (or state, in the case of senators), each voter can choose a single candidate, and the candidate with the most votes is elected, regardless of whether this is an absolute majority of the votes cast. This has several consequences. First, especially when coupled with the direct primary as the virtually universal way of selecting (or de-selecting) candidates, it encourages a personalization of representation, and a disconnection between candidates and their parties. Second, it means that it is possible for a party to win a majority in the House of Representatives with less than a majority of the popular vote, or even fewer votes than the other major party. Third, especially when coupled with the American prejudice in favour of local candidates,[11] this means that the drawing of district lines can have strong influence on the eventual outcome.

Candidate selection

Virtually all major party candidates for office in the United States are chosen in primary elections. Unlike so-called primaries in many European countries, which are conducted by and within political parties, these have been public elections conducted by public officials, under rules set by law rather than by the parties. In recent years, there has been a trend to allow the parties somewhat greater control over their primary elections.

In general terms, there are three major types of primary election in the United States, plus one intermediate type and the special case of Louisiana. In 1998, 12 states chose candidates in a 'closed primary', which restricts participation to those who have, as part of the process of registering as voters, declared themselves to be 'members' of the party. In general this does not even require an (unenforceable) promise of support for the party, and the party itself cannot prohibit any qualified voter from registering as one of its 'members' and participating in its primary. Obviously, a closed primary is only possible in states that have partisan registration. Twenty-one states used an 'open primary', in which any registered voter can participate in the primary election of his or her choice, generally without even the pretence of declaring temporary allegiance to the party. After the Supreme Court ruled in *Tashjian v. Republican Party of Connecticut* (479 US 208, 1986), that the states could not impose a closed primary on a party that wanted to allow independents to participate, several states (ironically, not including Connecticut) adopted a 'modified' system, in which party registrants can vote only in the primary of their own party, but independent or unaffiliated voters can, under various conditions, vote in the primary of whichever party they choose. In 1998, 11 states used the modified primary. Finally, with the 'blanket primary', used in three states, the voter is not restricted to a single party, but can, for example, vote for a Republican candidate for governor, a Democratic candidate for representative, and a Libertarian candidate for senator, all on the same ballot, with the candidate of each party who receives the most votes being declared the nominee of that party. The three other states in 1998 were: Oregon (closed primary for the Republicans and modified primary for the Democrats); West Virginia (closed primary for the Democrats and modified primary for the Republicans); and Louisiana (often identified as having a blanket primary, but strictly speaking not having a primary election at all—notwithstanding the use of that term in the state's election law—since if no candidate obtains an absolute majority of the votes in the first election, a run-off is held between the two top candidates regardless of party). In most states, the candidate with the most votes in the primary becomes the party's nominee, but in seven states (not including Louisiana), an absolute majority is required, and a run-off election is held in the event that no candidate reaches a majority in the first round.

The primary system was introduced in reaction to the perceived power of local party bosses to control nomination, and therefore the representatives ultimately elected. It clearly succeeded in limiting that power, but only at a significant price. On the one hand, it undermined party cohesion and responsibility. Because a party organization cannot assure renomination to its loyal representatives, they have less incentive to be loyal. Rather, they must be concerned not only about challenges from the other party, but about challenges from within their own party as well. Although all but two of them won their primaries, in 2004 only 105 of the incumbent members of Congress seeking re-election did not face primary election challengers. Of the 120 members of the House of Representatives who were 'retired' by the voters in the five elections between 1992 and 2000, nearly one-fourth were defeated in primary elections (231 more failed to seek re-election, at least some of whom presumably decided to retire rather than face likely defeat at the polls). Even those members who face no primary challenger in a particular election must constantly worry about the possibility of an intraparty challenge in the future.

On the other hand, the primary system has made members of Congress even more dependent on financial contributors. Because it is an intraparty contest, a representative cannot rely on party to win the primary. Rather, the candidate needs to build his or her own campaign organization, and be able to mount a primary campaign using non-party resources. Moreover, often the most effective way to preclude a primary challenge in the first place is to have a substantial war chest.

Apportionment and gerrymandering

With the first-past-the-post electoral system, the way in which votes are distributed across districts can have as much impact on the outcome of an election as does their distribution among the parties. Potential distortion in the translation of votes into seats has two sources. The first is malapportionment, having districts of radically different populations each electing one representative. The second is gerrymandering, the deliberate drawing of district boundaries for partisan (or other) advantage.

Although the Constitution requires that congressional seats be reapportioned among the states after every decennial census, it is silent regarding districting within states. Before the reapportionment revolution of the 1960s and 1970s, states that gained a seat might simply divide a large district in two, while those that lost a seat might simply combine two adjacent districts; states whose number of seats remained unchanged might see little reason to alter their district boundaries at all. As a result, malapportionment became a serious problem. For example, in 1960 the population of Michigan's 16th Congressional District was 4.5 times that of the 12th. Many state legislatures were even more dramatically malapportioned. In a series of decisions beginning with *Baker v. Carr* (369 US 186) in 1962, the Supreme Court has established that virtually exact population equality across a state's congressional districts is required. As a result, the difference in official population between the largest and smallest congressional district in Michigan is now exactly one person. On the other hand, because representatives must first be apportioned to the states, the largest congressional districts nationally (the 2nd and 3rd Districts of Utah) have over 1.5 times the population of the smallest (the single district of Wyoming).[12] Given the constitutional mandate of equal representation for each state, the Senate remains massively malapportioned in these terms.

One consequence of the courts' obsession with population equality has been to make respect for local subdivision boundaries in the drawing of district lines impossible. This is illustrated in Figure 3.2, which shows the congressional district and county boundaries in the centre of the state of Maryland. Parts of the city of Baltimore (the inverted 'open box' in the centre of the map) are included in three different districts (the 2nd, 3rd, and 7th), while the 2nd and 3rd Districts each include parts of three counties (two of them the same counties) plus part of the city of Baltimore. This freedom to ignore subdivision boundaries, in turn, has made the ancient art of gerrymandering—the drawing of district boundaries for political advantage—easier than it used to be.[13]

The classic partisan gerrymander works either by *packing* supporters of a party into a district which they will win with an overwhelming majority or *cracking* pockets of their support among districts, in each of which they will be a large minority, while constructing districts which the favoured party will win by modest margins. In 2002, Democrats won 17 of Texas's 32 congressional seats with 43.9 per cent of the vote.[14] By some estimates, the same distribution of support would have produced a 19 to 13 split in favour of the Republicans under the reapportionment plan enacted by the Republican state legislature before the 2004 election, and in 2004 the Republicans in fact won 21 of the Texas seats with 57.7 per cent of the vote (with four districts having no Democratic candidate and three having no Republican candidate). In other cases, districters have engaged in *incumbent protection* gerrymanders, which aim to increase the margins of sitting members regardless of party. In California in 2004, after a bipartisan incumbent protection redistricting in 2002, only one House race out of 53 was competitive. Finally, gerrymanders sometimes are aimed at individuals, either to defeat a particular politician, or to create a safe district for one.

Particularly in the 1980s and 1990s, one additional form of gerrymander—what might be called an 'affirmative action' gerrymander, because its intention is to create districts in which a majority of the voters

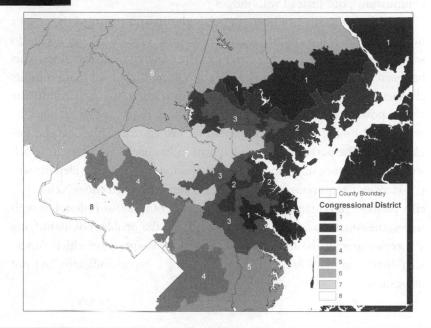

FIGURE 3.2 Congressional District boundaries in central Maryland

are members of a traditionally disadvantaged minority group—became quite significant. The resulting districts had two partially contradictory effects. On the one hand, they increased the number of minority, especially African American, members of Congress and state legislatures. On the other hand, they generally did so by creating districts that were overwhelmingly Democratic, thus 'wasting' Democratic votes and increasing the number of Republicans elected.

Given the potential for partisan mischief in the redistricting process, most countries have given this responsibility to non-partisan or multi-partisan commissions. In the United States, however, redistricting remains largely in the hands of politicians. In all but six states, Congressional district boundaries are drawn by the state legislature, and in all but 14, the legislature draws the districts for its own elections as well. Given the stakes, and the American political culture, by the end of 2004, fully half of the Congressional redistricting plans adopted after the 2000 census had been challenged in court. In many cases, this has meant that the ultimate responsibility for drawing district lines has rested neither with legislators nor with districting commissions, but instead with judges.

In the last decades, two issues in particular have confronted the courts, neither of which has reached a real resolution. The first is the degree to which race can be taken into account in the drawing of district lines. This has been coloured by the provision of the Voting Rights Act that prohibits changes in electoral procedures, including districting, that will 'dilute' the voting power of minorities, and in some cases requires that changes be pre-cleared by the federal Department of Justice before they can be implemented. The particularly vexing question has been the degree to which states can take race into account in anticipation of the Justice Department pre-clearance requirement. The second issue is the degree to which explicitly partisan gerrymanders are permitted under the Constitution. For both issues, the courts have been forced to confront the problem of identifying a gerrymander in the first place, with strange shapes (for which American districting plans are justly famous) being taken as indicative but not dispositive.

Campaigning

In the elections between 1990 and 2000, at least 20 per cent, and in one case over 54 per cent, of the open seats (those in which the incumbent was not a candidate in the general election) changed hands between Democrats and Republicans. In contrast, of the far more numerous districts in which an incumbent was a candidate, it was never the case that as many as 10 per cent of the seats changed hands between the parties, and the figure was more often under 3 per cent. In 2004, 374 of 435 seats were won by margins of at least 55–45, of which 318 were won by margins of at least 60–40; there were more seats won unopposed (32) than were won in competitive races (29), even taking the rather liberal definition of a ten percentage point margin as being competitive. Of the 398 incumbents seeking re-election, only seven were defeated—four of them victims of the Texas redistricting.

In part, the overwhelming success of incumbents seeking re-election is a result of successful gerrymandering. In large measure, however, as demonstrated by the much greater frequency with which open seats change hands, as well as by the frequency with which a district will give a strong margin to its Congressman while voting for the presidential candidate of the other party,[15] party often plays a surprisingly weak role in comparison to the personal support of the candidates. In the United States, a 'safe seat' often is safe not so much for a party as for a particular incumbent. (An alternative interpretation of split-result districts is that the issues that define the parties and their candidates nationally are not those that divide congressional candidates, which localizes, if not necessarily personalizing, these elections.)

Several factors contribute to the personalism of American congressional campaigns. One is the weakness of political party organizations (see Chapter 4), furthered by the crazy-quilt of district lines for different offices (in turn virtually required by the obsession with population equality). A second is the possibility of primary challenges, which requires candidates to maintain support organizations that are independent of party *per se*. Third, the independence of representatives within the Congress (see Chapter 6), itself in part a function of the personal mandate that members have, means that the connection between party label and ideological position or expected behaviour of a candidate can be quite problematic. This, in turn, feeds on a cultural bias, reflected, for example, in newspaper editorial endorsements, that glorifies 'voting for the man, not the party'.[16] Indeed, one of the features of American campaigns that often surprises foreign observers is the difficulty the uninitiated may have even in discovering the partisanship of major party candidates. Richard Nixon's 'Committee to Re-Elect the President' (CREEP), which made no reference to the fact that Nixon was a Republican, is reflected in the general absence of party labels from candidates' campaign posters, TV spots, and leaflets—except, ironically, for things like 'Democrats for Ehrlich' (who was the Republican candidate for Governor of Maryland in 2002), the intention of which is to minimize the importance of partisanship.

The personalism of American electoral politics is also reinforced by the importance of money, and the nature of political finance regulation. Although the parties can campaign as organizations (the 1980 'Vote Republican For a Change' campaign is an example), if they advocate votes for (or against) named candidates, they are regulated as contributors rather than as campaigners unless the spending is *not* coordinated with the party candidate's own campaign. This severely limits the amount of money candidates can hope to receive from their parties. But congressional elections can be tremendously expensive. In 2004, for example, the 1,149 House campaigns

(407 Republican; 402 Democrats; 340 others) raised over $613 million; the fiftieth most expensive campaign spent almost $1.9 million. A big campaign budget not only helps to win elections (only 13 of the top 50 campaigns lost, and six of those losses were to campaigns that spent even more—eight if party independent expenditures are included) and to deter potential challengers, it can also give the candidate increased influence by transferring surplus funds to the party or to other candidates directly. In particular, the rise of leadership political action committees (PACs), through which party leaders, and would-be leaders, raise money, not for their own campaigns but to be re-contributed to the campaigns of their followers, has been one of the factors leading to greater party polarization and cohesion in recent years. On the one hand, one of the complaints often made by members of the House is that they are forced to spend an inordinate amount of time fund-raising; on the other hand, even after contributions from leadership PACs, that the members raised their campaign money themselves both undergirds their political independence and encourages a personal rather than a partisan approach to elections.

This is not to say that the national party organizations are insignificant in financial terms. In September and October of 2004, the two congressional campaign committees made independent expenditures totalling over $82 million. In a few districts, the parties actually spent more than the candidates. Party spending was concentrated in only 47 districts, chosen because they were winnable (or losable), rather than to reward party loyalty. Just over half of the party spending was aimed against the candidate of the other party rather than in favour of the party's own candidate. And as with campaigning by the candidates themselves, the 'product' being sold overwhelmingly was an individual rather than a party. Moreover, over $36 million of the income of the congressional campaign committees came as transfers from the personal campaign committees of congressional candidates; to a significant extent, the candidates are funding the parties, and indirectly each other, rather than the party funding the candidates.

Presidential elections

Reflecting both the reservations of the Framers of the Constitution about giving the ordinary people too much direct electoral power and the problems of communication and transportation in eighteenth-century America, the President of the United States formally is chosen by an electoral college whose members meet in the state capitals in December rather than by the general election in November. Although the electors themselves have been elected by the people in every state since 1880, and with rare (and to date inconsequential) exceptions simply record their votes for the candidate to whom they were pledged before the election, the electoral college method continues profoundly to affect the nature of presidential elections.

Most importantly, because all of the states except Maine and Nebraska choose all of their electors as a block,[17] it is winning states rather than winning votes that counts. This both creates the phenomenon of 'battle-ground states' and raises the possibility that the candidate with the greater number of popular votes will not be elected president — as indeed happened in 2000 (as well as in 1876 and 1888).

The winner-take-all allocation of electors naturally enhances the weight of those states that have a large number of electoral votes, but particularly (or only) if they also are competitive. The allocation of electoral votes on the basis of total representation in Congress (senators plus representatives) also has a significant impact. Most obviously, it gives greater weight to the smaller states than would be justified by their populations alone. In 2004, for example, Alaska had one elector for every 208,977 voting age residents, while California had one elector for every 627,253 voting age residents. Less obviously, but more importantly, this system means that a state's weight in the presidential election is independent of the number of votes actually cast within it. Thus, the effective disenfranchisement of African Americans in the south prior to the implementation of the Voting Rights Act of 1965 did not reduce the electoral college vote of the southern states, nor, for example, does Florida's current policy of disenfranchising convicted felons for life reduce that state's weight in the choice of president (and indeed, if one assumes that the felon vote would make the state less competitive as between Democrats and Republicans, it might even increase Florida's effective weight).

Candidate selection

A sitting president who wants to run for a second term usually has little trouble securing his party's nomination. The most notable exception was

Lyndon Johnson in 1968, who was led to withdraw following a poor (albeit winning) performance in the New Hampshire primary. In this case, one of the candidates generally is known well in advance. For the other party, and for the party of a second-term president, this is not the case, because American parties simply do not have 'a leader' in the way that parties in many other countries do. Thus, the first step in presidential elections is the choice of party nominees, and the contest for the nomination generally begins officially (with the formation of candidate exploratory committees, which are legally allowed to accept donations) as much as two years before the election, and in reality begins immediately after the previous election if not even earlier than that.

Since early in the nineteenth century (1832, in the case of the Democrats; the Republican Party did not exist until 1856), presidential candidates have been chosen by party nominating conventions. Until the 1960s, these were composed primarily of delegates chosen by the state party organizations, and made a real choice of the nominees.[18] Particularly after the reforms instituted by the Democratic Party after 1972, however, the delegates to the conventions have overwhelmingly been chosen in primary elections and local caucuses, beginning in Iowa roughly 11 months before the actual election. Moreover, although it is possible to be chosen as an 'unpledged' delegate, the vast majority of delegates chosen in primaries or caucuses are chosen as supporters of particular candidates. The last year in which a presidential nominee of one of the major parties was not chosen on the first ballot was 1952, and the combination of the number of pledged delegates and the sequential nature of the primary process mean that even post-primary but pre-convention brokerage is unlikely. Although the media often speculate about the possibility of a brokered convention, in reality the likelihood of a national convention doing anything more than ratify the verdict of the primary process is extremely small.

Although both major parties use primaries or caucuses to allow voters to choose the overwhelming majority of convention delegates, the actual rules differ substantially between the parties. Both parties reward states in which they are strong with more convention delegates, but the Democrats base the allocation on the share of the total Democratic vote in the previous three presidential elections, while the Republicans award extra seats to states that have elected Republicans to public office. Both parties stress balance between men and women, although for the Republicans it is an exhortation while for the Democrats it is a requirement, and moreover the Democrats have also sought to secure racial and generational balance. The Democrats make slightly more extensive use of primary elections. Most significantly, whether delegates are selected by primary or caucus/convention, the Democratic Party rules require that pledged delegates be allocated among supporters of presidential candidates in proportion to their support; Republican Party rules allow winner-take-all decisions, so that while all 35 Democratic primaries in 2004 were proportional, only 11 states selected their Republican delegates at least in part through proportional primaries.

From the perspective of a candidate, the primary system has both advantages and disadvantages. On the positive side, the primary contests give the candidate an extended opportunity to build a support coalition of workers and financial backers, which is particularly important given that most of what pass for party organizations in the United States would be more accurately described as the personal support organizations of individual politicians. The primaries also give challengers an extended period of 'newsworthiness' to become better known, so as partially to neutralize the advantage of name recognition generally enjoyed by incumbents. At the presidential level, the extended and serial nature of the process allows a candidate with little national visibility to concentrate his resources in a few places, and use success there to build momentum and thus support for the next round. Alternatively, the primaries allow even a candidate who is effectively unopposed for the party nomination to campaign free of the financial restrictions that come into force once he has accepted his party's nomination and the federal funding that goes with it. With no primary opponents at all, George Bush's primary campaign in 2004 spent over $268 million (and John Kerry's campaign spent over $220 million, much of it after he had effectively secured the Democratic nomination). On the negative side, the winner of a primary contest inevitably enters the general election with the baggage of attacks by his primary opponents and often with a divided party behind him. Moreover, he also enters the general election with the record of positions taken for their appeal within his own party rather than with regard to the electorate as a whole.

The serial nature of the presidential candidate selection process gives great weight to the states that come first in the process, in particular Iowa and New Hampshire. These are widely recognized to be atypical, and in part for that reason a candidate need not come in first in these contests to claim 'victory'. Rather, a candidate must exceed expectations, and thus demonstrate gathering momentum. This often leads to candidates emphasizing their own weakness in order to minimize expectations, a strategy that continues throughout the early primaries.

Presidential campaigns

As with congressional campaigns, presidential campaigns are virtually monopolized by the Democratic and Republican party nominees, but not by the parties as organizations. Although the major parties receive a small subsidy for their national conventions, all other campaign subventions, both matching funds for the primaries and direct grants for the general election (in both cases, limited to candidates who choose to accept spending limits) go to the candidates' own campaign organizations, not to their parties. While there clearly are campaign professionals who are identified as Democrats or Republicans, the organization of each campaign is in the hands of the candidate and his own advisers rather than the party organization as such. (Although there is considerable overlap between the two groups—often brought about by the insertion of the candidate's people into the party organization—and the party apparatus may perform many important tasks for the candidate's campaign, it remains quite marginal as an independent actor.) While the national nominating conventions draft their parties' platforms, both the issues to be emphasized and the positions to be taken on them in the campaign are decided by the candidates' own organization. Indeed, shortly after his nomination in 1996, Republican candidate Bob Dole straightforwardly told the press that he did not feel bound by his party's platform, and indeed had not even read it.

If the party organizations as such are relatively inconsequential actors in presidential campaigns, this does not mean that the presidential candidates are the only actors defining the campaign. As in all democracies, journalists play a large role in defining a campaign. Candidates can, and do, attempt to tailor their campaigns to the needs and prejudices of the media, particularly television, but ultimately the reporters and editors decide what they will emphasize. Even the so-called 'debates' are more accurately described as simultaneous press conferences, with the stimuli (if not the responses), decided by the journalists. The results are well known: careful staging of pseudo-events; campaign messages built around sound-bites rather than analysis; an emphasis on telegenic personality rather than substance; frenetic travel schedules (to allow the candidate to be a local news event in as many places as possible on as many days as possible). The media's tendency to focus on the 'horse race' (which can change constantly, and so fits their definition of 'news'), and their related focus on battle-ground states, both further focus the campaigns and further crowd out substance. Finally, that American candidates are given no free media access, but are limited only by their financial resources in the purchase of air time, has made the 30-second spot ad, with all its emphasis on emotion rather than rationality, one of the dominant forms of campaigning.

Particularly in the 2004 campaign, an additional type of actor came to prominence—the '527 organizations' (named after the section of the tax law that defines them).[19] These groups, which existed before the 2002 Bipartisan Campaign Reform Act (BCRA) changed the political finance rules but grew in importance with the BCRA's banning of 'soft money' contributions to the parties,[20] were active in some congressional campaigns, but were particularly prominent in the presidential race. Excluding transfers among 527s, by 12 December 2004 the 59 Democratic-oriented 527s that raised over $200,000 spent a total of more than $310 million, while the 21 Republican-oriented 527s spent almost $85 million. The best known of these groups, but by no means the largest, was the anti-Kerry 'Swift Boat Veterans and POWs for Truth,' which continued the Republican strategy (used effectively in 2002 against triple-amputee Max Cleland in his bid for re-election to the Senate from Georgia) of attacking-by-proxy the patriotism of their opponents. As this exemplifies, the 527 campaigns tended to be largely negative attacks on the other candidate, which left their own candidate in a position of 'plausible deniability' against charges of mud-slinging.

Another impact of the BCRA was to increase the role of the national party committees as independent actors. Building on the tremendous success of Howard Dean's primary campaign in raising large amounts of money through small contributions over the internet, the Democrats in particular waged a vigorous fund-raising campaign. In the two months before the 2004 election, the Democratic National Committee spent nearly $88 million to oppose President Bush and roughly $4.5 million in support of Senator Kerry. This heavy slant towards negativity was repeated in somewhat weaker form by Republican spending for Bush and against Kerry. Aside from allowing attacks without the newly required tag line for candidate-sponsored ads ('I am . . . and I approved this message'), it is also clearly easier to produce effective negative rather than positive messages without the direct consultation with the candidate's campaign that would convert them into coordinated, and therefore legally limited, expenditures.

Political finance in context

The major party presidential candidates in 2004 raised roughly $500 million each, *federal* spending by the various committees of the two major parties totalled well over $1,300 million in the 2003–04 election cycle, and congressional candidate spending totalled over $900 million. Although there is some double counting because of transfers from candidates to party committees and the reverse, these totals may appear astronomical by international standards. In contrast, total spending in the 2001 British general election was well under $80 million (£ 38.6 million, according to the Electoral Commission).

These figures must be understood in context, however. The scale of politics is an order of magnitude different from that of many other countries. Moreover, many other countries provide candidates or parties with a variety of public goods (TV time, billboard space, meeting halls, etc.), all of which have to be bought by American candidates themselves. The personalism of politics introduces great inefficiencies. For example, a congressional candidate in Baltimore (a medium-sized city) who wants to advertise on a Baltimore television station must buy time at rates based on the station's viewership, but the great majority of those viewers will be in some other candidate's district. At the local level, American campaigning continues to be very labour- and volunteer-intensive—door-to-door canvassing, lawn signs, leaflet mailings, or hand distribution. At the mass level of senatorial races or the presidency, however, only such capital and expertise-intensive techniques as polling, made-for-media event creation, and paid television advertising have the reach necessary.

The primary system also contributes to the aggregate cost of political campaigning. Questions that in most countries would be decided within party organizations, often on a face-to-face basis with little expense and with whatever expenses are incurred charged to intraparty activity, in the United States are decided in public elections and included in the campaign spending totals. Indeed, roughly half of the money spent by Bush and Kerry in 2004 was at least accounted as primary election spending.

However, the most significant reason for the disparity between political spending in the United States and in other countries is the lack of effective regulation in the United States. In large measure, effective political finance regulation has proven impossible because the Supreme Court has defined campaign spending to be a form of political speech given nearly absolute protection by the First Amendment. On the other hand, the Court's approach to contributions has been more flexible, allowing limits in the interest of apparent fairness, but still focused on advocacy of the election or defeat of particular candidates; both spending and contributions ostensibly to advance policy positions, even if they clearly brand a candidate as an opponent, still are protected. As a result, the only spending limits on candidates are those that they accept voluntarily, in exchange for public finance. But since public finance is limited to the presidential race, congressional candidates are effectively unlimited. Moreover, the federal money available to primary presidential candidates in 2004 proved insufficient to 'bribe' either President Bush or Senator Kerry to accept the associated limits.

While the magnitude of political spending in the United States may be understandable, it also raises concerns about undue influence. Numerous studies have found a strong correlation between the interests of big campaign contributors and the actions of members of Congress, although the correlations do not answer the question of whether contributors are buying influence or merely supporting politicians who already support their positions (for example, Bronars and Lott 1997; Kau and Rubin 1982). At the presidential as well as the congressional level, it is clear that large contributors gain easier access, for which reason it is not uncommon to find individuals or groups that contribute (generally in quite unequal amounts) to both candidates or parties. At least since the 1970s, the primary concern was with organized interests (variously created, defined, or regulated by the Federal Election Campaign Act as political action committees, or PACs). In 2004, individual contributors soared in importance, with individual contributions over $5,000 to 527s going from $37 million (from 1,231 individuals) in 2002 to $256 million (from 1,882 individuals) in 2004. Indeed, roughly 15 per cent of all 527 contributions came from exactly three individuals (all Democrats, which also suggests the limits of the political influence of money).

These problems have long been recognized, and attempts have been made to limit the influence of money at least since the Tilman Act of 1907 (which limited corporate contributions to federal campaigns). The BCRA is merely the latest attempt to limit the impact of money on electoral politics. Like previous attempts, it has had a significant effect on the channels through which political money flows, but little success in controlling the ever-growing amounts.

State and local elections

The only generalization about non-federal elections is that no generalization is possible. Subject only to the federal restriction that the system does not demonstrably discriminate on racial grounds, states and, in some states, localities are free to choose their own electoral system, and virtually every electoral system (including list proportional representation (PR), if one includes Democratic presidential primaries) is used somewhere in the United States. While most state and local elections are duopolized by the Democrats and Republicans (occasionally operating under pseudonyms, like the Democratic Farmer Labor Party in Minnesota), sometimes these elections are conducted on a non-partisan basis—either in form (party labels do not appear on the ballot, but parties conduct the campaigns and identify 'their' candidates) or in reality; minor parties (Greens, Socialists, Conservatives, Liberals, etc.) are sometimes not only significant but victorious at the local level. While American citizenship is required for voting in state elections, several localities allow non-citizen residents to vote in local elections.

As noted earlier in this chapter, the states and localities differ widely in their requirements for ballot access for Congress, and this extends with even greater variation to other offices. And, as noted in Chapter 2, the states also differ widely with regard to which offices are elective and with regard to such instruments of direct democracy as initiative, referendum, and recall.

Federal campaign regulations only apply to the elections of federal officials, and each state is free to have its own rules for its own officials. Here again there is wide variation, with some states offering public finance to candidates, and each having its own regulations concerning allowable contributions and reporting of contributions and spending.

Free and fair elections?

Particularly with the increased use of international election observers associated with the third wave of democratization, an international consensus has begun to emerge regarding the standards to which 'free and fair' elections ought to adhere. Of course no one seriously suggests that American elections should be put in the same category of unfreeness or unfairness as elections in the Soviet Union. Nonetheless, given the importance the American government frequently has accorded to the reports of international observers in other countries, it is instructive to ask how American elections would stack up against the criteria those observers apply.

Notwithstanding that the United States is a signatory of the OSCE (Organization for Security and Cooperation in Europe) 1990 Copenhagen Document, which calls for free access for both domestic and international election observers, access afforded in 2004 varied quite widely: in some localities, domestic observers were denied access; in others, international observers were denied access. As in many other fields (for example, assurance of consular access for foreign nationals who are arrested), the decentralization of responsibility means that the federal government is not always able to assure compliance with international obligations.

Decentralization also means that the uniformity of standards generally considered to be essential to free and fair elections is missing—notwithstanding the Supreme Court's insistence on 'equal protection' in ballot counting in Florida in 2000. As already noted, rules regarding the registration of voters, design and casting of ballots, purchases of voting equipment, density of polling stations, permission of postal or early voting, all are decided at the subnational level, and often are correlated with race and class in ways that make it less likely that the votes of people of colour and people without means actually will be effective. While the Help America Vote Act (2002) attempted to address some of these problems, in particular mandating the availability of provisional ballots for those whose names were improperly omitted from the register, the rules regarding whether such ballots would be counted varied widely among states and localities.

Part of the reason for variability was the decentralization of authority, but another was the generally amateurish nature of American election administration. As with the 'Motor Voter' Act (which required states to provide voter registration forms at places where driving licences are issued), the lack of a well-trained staff devoted to electoral administration sometimes creates a very large gap between the spirit or even the letter of the law and what happens in practice.[21] The 'butterfly ballot' of the 2000 election clearly was the result of well-intentioned incompetence. As the OSCE Observer Mission noted in its report: 'It was not clear that poll workers had generally received sufficient training to perform their functions.'

Procedures at polling places to verify the identity of voters and to prevent fraudulent voting often are extremely rudimentary. In some localities, a voter may be asked to sign a card without the original signatures being available for comparison. In others, merely being able to correctly connect one's name with the address listed on the register may be accepted as adequate proof of identity. And there have been numerous reports from places with election-day registration of perfect strangers attesting to a would-be voter's identity simply as a courtesy. The primary check against abuse is the possibility of challenge at the polls either by a party poll worker or by another voter. Not only is this an unreliable method of curbing abuse, it is also, as the OSCE Mission observed, itself subject to abuse or anticipated abuse with the effect of deterring participation by legitimate voters.[22]

The lack of what would for other countries be considered absolute minimum standards of verifiability is also evident with regard to voting equipment. Most Maryland voters in 2004, for example, used touch-screen voting machines, for which the computer source code was considered proprietary information by the machines' manufacturer and therefore unavailable for independent assessment as to its reliability. The machines produced no paper trail or other way in which their accuracy could be checked after the fact, and all this notwithstanding the fact that the machines' manufacturer was a highly partisan Republican who had promised to 'deliver Ohio' to George Bush.

In contrast to the idea of simple and understandable electoral rules, the complexity of the American system, along with the general litigiousness of American society, has spawned a profession of election lawyers. Moreover, the 'cases and controversies' clause of the Constitution (which bars the federal courts from deciding 'hypothetical' cases) means that rules may not be clarified in advance, even if everyone agrees there is a potential problem.

International standards require that election administration be separated from partisan politics. In the United States, the most important decisions, that is the drawing of district lines, are generally made by partisan officials, and generally on partisan (or at best bipartisan) grounds. The officials ultimately in charge of the conduct of elections are usually themselves elected or partisan appointees. (The 'chief electoral officer' in Florida in 2000 was not only herself a partisan-elected official, but was also the co-chair of the Florida campaign of one of the presidential candidates.)

American electoral practice appears to be relatively even-handed as between the Democrats and Republicans, at least in the sense that the decentralization of the process means that partisan control and bias in favour of one party in some places is likely to be compensated by similar bias in favour of the other party in other places. But, notwithstanding the general American confounding of the two terms, 'bipartisan' is not a synonym of 'non-partisan', and American elections are significantly biased against all other parties. Conditions for ballot access and ballot placement generally are more favourable for the established parties; monetary support for presidential campaigns is structured to assure equal treatment of Democrats and Republicans, but is far less favourable for other parties (lesser support for 'minor parties' and support that is both lesser and only given after the fact for 'new parties'). This general rule is best illustrated by the presidential debates. Billed as genuine news events so as to avoid statutory requirements of equal treatment for all legally qualified candidates, these are organized by a commission that is ostensibly non-partisan but in reality is a joint committee of the Democrats and Republicans. Invitations to participate are based on criteria that may appear non-partisan, but in fact will be satisfied only by the two major party nominees (with Ross Perot in 1992 being an exception that is unlikely to be repeated).

Lack of access to the presidential debates compounds the disadvantages suffered by minor parties due to the lack of public provision of media access. The equal access guaranteed to all candidates is, in the United States, merely a guarantee that all candidates will be charged the same rates for equivalent commercial advertising time. But given the rates charged, especially for so-called non-pre-emptable time (which guarantees the ad will be aired at a particular time), this can effectively bar all but the major party candidates from the airwaves.

All this was summarized by the OSCE observers in Florida. As reported in the *International Herald Tribune* on the day after the 2004 election: 'The observers said they had less access to polls than in Kazakhstan, that the electronic voting had fewer fail-safes than in Venezuela, that the ballots were not so simple as in the Republic of Georgia and that no other country had such a complex national election system.'[23]

KEY TERMS

- blanket primary
- closed primary
- electoral college
- gerrymander
- office block ballot
- open primary

- party column ballot
- primary election
- soft money
- sore-loser law
- voter registration

NOTES

1 Although the Constitution gave the state legislatures the authority to decide the 'Times, Places and Manner of holding Elections for Senators and Representatives', it also gave the Congress the power to 'make or alter such Regulations' by law. In terms of contemporary issues, this means that the United States could adopt a system of proportional representation by federal statute, without the need for a constitutional amendment.

2 The original Constitution only required that the franchise for elections of Representatives be the same as for the 'most numerous Branch of the State Legislature', a standard that varied quite widely among the states. Since then, limitations 'on account of race, color, or previous condition of servitude' (Fifteenth Amendment), sex (Nineteenth Amendment), 'failure to pay any poll tax or other tax' (Twenty-fourth Amendment), or age for those 'eighteen

years of age or older' (Twenty-sixth Amendment) have been prohibited by Constitutional Amendment, and tests based on literacy, 'good character', or long periods of residence have been prohibited by federal statute.

3 The first state to have a gender neutral suffrage law was New Jersey in 1776, although the property requirement meant that only unmarried women could vote, and women lost the vote in 1807. More recently, the Wyoming territory granted women the right to vote on the same terms as men in 1869, a practice continued when Wyoming became a state in 1890.

4 'Felon Disenfranchisement Laws in the United States', The Sentencing Project, http://www.sentencingproject.org/ pdfs/1046.pdf.

5 North Dakota municipalities may require voter registration, but only one does so.

6 Strictly speaking, the 30 days maximum applies only to federal elections, but given the administrative problems that would be involved were a state to maintain separate registers for federal and state elections, all states accept the 30-day maximum for their own elections as well.

7 In lieu of petitions, a candidate may pay a fee of $1,000.

8 Federal law requires states to allow military and overseas citizens to cast absentee votes. In three states, these are the only citizens who can do so. At the other extreme, Oregon now conducts its elections entirely by post.

9 The state law requires the major parties (those with at least 5 per cent of statewide registration) to be listed first, and in alphabetical order; the Libertarian candidates for Governor and Lt. Governor are listed third, because the Libertarians did not clear the 5 per cent of registrations threshold. (North Carolina General Statutes, 163–165.6) In other states, the

order might be determined by the parties' strength at the previous election—usually for governor or secretary of state. The two major parties usually are guaranteed more advantageous ballot positions, whether by name or as a consequence of their popularity at the previous election.

10 Because the United States has neither uniform qualifications for voters nor a national register of voters, national voter turnout calculations ordinarily are based on voting aged population (VAP) rather than registered voters. Apportionment of representatives is based on resident population without regard to age.

11 The Constitution requires members of Congress to be residents of the state from which they are elected, but does not require them to reside in the district they represent.

12 The Utah 2nd and 3rd Districts have one more person than the 1st. All of these figures are from the 2000 census, upon which the reapportionments were based. As is well known, the margin of error of the census is many hundreds of times the intrastate population differences.

13 The term 'gerrymander' originated in 1812 with the concatenation of the name of the Governor of Massachusetts, Elbridge Gerry, and 'salamander', used by an opposition cartoonist to describe an oddly shaped district. The practice, however, was clearly evident in the Roman Republic.

14 These figures must be interpreted in light of the fact that one or the other of the major parties did not contest nine of the 32 seats.

15 In the elections between 1960 and 1996, between 23 and 44 per cent of the districts were split between presidential and House candidates. (Norman J. Ornstein, Thomas E. Mann, and Michael J. Malbin (eds.), *Vital Statistics on Congress*, Washington, DC: Congressional Quarterly Press, 1998).

16 Even if they endorse all of its candidates, American newspapers will very rarely, if ever, endorse a party itself. Indeed, it often appears that they go out of their way to endorse candidates across party lines as a demonstration of their objectivity.

17 In Maine and Nebraska, the two electors corresponding to the state's two senators are elected together statewide, and consequently go to the presidential candidate with the most votes in the state as a whole, while the electors corresponding to the state's members of the House of Representative are elected individually at the district level. In 2004, the voters of Colorado rejected by referendum a proposal to divide that state's electors among the candidates on the basis of proportional representation.

18 Even when the conventions 'chose' the nominees, this did not mean that the delegates made a free choice. Rather, they were the 'units of influence' with which party oligarchs negotiated among themselves to choose a nominee.

19 A 527 organization is defined as 'a party, committee, association, fund, or other organization (whether or not incorporated) organized and operated primarily for the purpose of directly or indirectly accepting contributions or making expenditures, or both, for . . . [the purpose of] influencing or attempting to influence the selection, nomination, election or appointment of an individual to a federal, state, or local public office or office in a political organization'. 26 United States Code 527 (e).

20 'Soft money' contributions were funds given to the political parties but were not to be used in federal campaigns. Because of the legal definition of campaigning as advocating a vote for or against a particular named candidate, however, many campaign related activities, like 'get out the vote' drives or party building activities, did not count as campaigning. Soft money was not subject either to contribution limits or to reporting requirements under the old Federal Election Campaign Act (FECA).

21 It was discovered (after it was too late), that in some states the registration forms completed at Motor Vehicle offices never were delivered to voter registration officials or entered by them into the actual register of voters.

22 A particularly egregious example was the purging from the Florida voter rolls of individuals whose names were identical (or similar) to those of convicted felons without any attempt to verify that they were indeed the same people.

23 Thomas Crampton Wednesday, 3 November 2004, http://www.indybay.org/ news/2004/11/1702712.php.

....

GUIDE TO FURTHER READING

Jacobson, G. C. (2004), *The Politics of Congressional Elections* (New York: Pearson Longman).

A classic study frequently updated of how congressional elections are contested and of how electoral politics shapes other aspects of the political system.

Mann, T. and B. E. Cain (eds.) (2005), *Party Lines: Competition, Partisanship, and Congressional Redistricting* (Washington, DC: Brookings Institution).

An assessment of party attempts to manipulate the rules of the electoral game to their own advantage.

Polsby, N. W. and A. Wildavsky (2004), *Presidential Elections: Strategies and Structures of American Politics* (Lanham, MD: Rowman and Littlefield).

A data-rich account of presidential elections from the pre-primary positioning of potential candidates through to the end of the election.

Wolfinger, R. E. and S. J. Rosenstone (1980), *Who Votes?* (New Haven, CT: Yale University Press).

An analysis of turnout in American elections from both individual behavioural and institutional perspectives.

4

The American Party System

Overview

The organization of American parties parallels both the division and the separation of powers in the structure of government. American parties also are characterized by informal, candidate-centred organizations, in place of any real party membership organizations. The formal party organizations act as a service organization for candidates, and while the campaign industry tends to be organized along partisan lines (very few consultants are equally willing to work for candidates of either party), this is a far cry from actually having these individuals as part of party organizations. While partisan attachments and identifications structure much of American politics, parties as organizations (with the partial exception of the caucuses of the parties within legislative bodies) have almost no capacity to direct politics. Although on the one hand the United States is virtually a pure two-party system, on the other hand, in the way political parties are understood in most other countries, the United States has no parties at all.

The American party system is characterized by one of the great ironies that was seen in Chapter 3 with regard to the electoral system. On the one hand, the United States has one of the purest two-party systems in the world. Although there are many minor parties, they rarely win more than a few per cent of the vote, and even more rarely elect one of their candidates to office.[1] The last time the Democrats and Republicans did not hold at least 95 per cent of both houses of Congress was in the 56th Congress (1899–1901); the last time a party other than the Democrats or Republicans elected a president was 1848 (Whig, Zachary Taylor), six years before the Republican Party was founded. Moreover, at least for the past many decades, on those few occasions when an independent or minor party candidate is elected to Congress or to a state legislature, that person is effectively 'annexed' to one of the two major parties.

On the other hand, in the way in which citizens of most other countries understand the word 'party', one might argue that the United States actually has no political parties at all. Of course, like most similarly provocative statements, this would be an exaggeration, but one that contains an important element of truth. While the party caucuses and their leaders in each House of Congress and in each house of the state legislatures (the 'party in public office') to a large degree (albeit one that varies, both over time and among venues) dominate the legislative arenas, there is often very little coordination across venues. The extra-governmental apparatus (the 'party central office') of each party is both extremely weak and extremely fragmented, with little or no independence or influence over the traditional party functions of policy formulation, candidate selection, or campaign coordination. Party as an organization of citizens ('the party on the ground') is virtually non-existent in the United States: while there are many Democratic and Republican clubs, they generally have no formal connection to the parties that nominate candidates or organize legislative bodies, and their members have no special rights or privileges within the party; while party registrants have many of the privileges associated with membership of parties in most countries (for example, the right to participate in candidate selection through the primary election process—although in states with open or blanket primaries, even this right is not restricted to party registrants), on the one hand they incur none of the obligations like the payment of fees or doing party work typically associated with membership, while on the other hand the party has no control over who chooses to register as one of its 'members' (for example, it is literally impossible for the party to expel one of its registrants). While it is customary to talk about 'the party in the electorate', this refers only to the amorphous body of regular party supporters, not to any formal, let alone comprehensive, organization.

From the perspective of parties as 'bod[ies] of men united, for promoting by their joint endeavours the national interest, upon some particular principle in which they are all agreed', the picture has been variable. At times, there have been issues that have sharply divided one party from the other. At other times, the joke that American parties are like 'two bottles on a shelf... one labeled "milk" and the other labeled "whiskey"... but both

[are] empty' has been nearer the mark. But no matter how vacuous they have been in terms of policy, parties have been the basic organizing units of the government and politics. And no matter how great the division over one or more crucial issues, American parties have never exhibited the level of disciplined unity of action that is taken for granted in most other countries.

The evolution of the American party system

Notwithstanding the distaste of the Founders for political parties, which by their nature embody the spirit of 'faction' against which they warned in *The Federalist*, parties in the United States, as in other countries, emerged as the natural response to the universal fact that those who are able to coordinate their actions are more effective than those who are not. One venue for such coordination is among officials with relatively compatible views within government, both within legislative assemblies (i.e., Congress or the state legislatures) and across branches and levels of government. The roots of parties (or factions) in this sense were evident in the colonial assemblies, and in Congress by the mid-1790s. A second venue is in the conduct of electoral campaigns, which because the franchise was much broader much earlier in the United States than in most other countries meant that proto-parties in this sense also developed earlier, and in some states also predate the Constitution. The third venue in the United States was the election of the president. This was the stimulus for the formation of national parties that would link, at least every four years, the state and local 'parties on the ground' and the caucuses in the national and state legislatures, and particularly in the electoral college, and indeed for more stable and coherent parties at the state level as well. The question of presidential elections did not arise until the Constitution was in place, and indeed until the problem of a successor to the first president, George Washington, had to be faced, and became even more pronounced with mass suffrage and with the choice of presidential electors in an election rather than by the state legislatures.

In the terms in which political party systems conventionally are described, the United States both has a strong two-party system, and has structured its political institutions in ways that maintain not just a two-party system, but a system of precisely the two parties that currently dominate. In fact, however, the current party system actually is the third American two-party system, and moreover one that has undergone dramatic transformation over time.[2] Further, within the context of the current system of Democratic versus Republican parties, there have been times when third parties, although not serious contenders for power at the national level, have had a significant impact on national politics, as well as individual presidential elections that were significantly influenced by the presence of a third party or independent candidate (Mazmanian 1974; Rosenstone 1996).

The first party system emerged out of the questions attendant upon the initial institutionalization of the new government after the ratification of the Constitution. The first Washington administration represented what would today be called a 'government of national unity'. Washington him-self—'first in war, first in peace, and first in the hearts of his countrymen', in the words of Richard Henry Lee's congressional eulogy—was elected president by a unanimous electoral college, and appointed a cabinet that included representatives of both sides of the debate about the appropriate strength and the appropriate policies of the national government (although it did not include any hard-core anti-Federalist opponents of the new Constitution). The first to organize nationally were the Federalists, led particularly by Alexander Hamilton. They were the party of a strong central government, sound money, and commerce, based primarily in New England. In re-sponse, the advocates of more limited government (especially at the central level) and policies that would benefit debtors, the interests of small farmers in the west and plantation owners in the south formed a coalition under the label of Democratic–Republicans, with Thomas Jefferson as their most prominent leader, and allied themselves with urban interests represented particularly by Aaron Burr and the Sons of Tammany in New York.

Although the Federalists elected John Adams as president in the first post-Washington election, he was the last Federalist president, although the Federalists remained a significant party into the second decade of the nineteenth century. There was, then, a period of one-party dominance (the so-called Era of Good Feeling) after 1816 (the year of the last Federalist presidential candidacy, and the last full year in which the Federalists held as many as one-third of the seats in the House of Representatives) that led to factionalism within the Democratic–Republican Party, with two significant Democratic–Republican candidates in 1820 and four in 1824. In 1828, the Democratic–Republicans were dominated by supporters of

Andrew Jackson and, by 1832, became simply the Democrats. The rival factions ultimately coalesced into the Whig Party, representing the northern commercial and southern agricultural elites, held together by their opposition to Jacksonian democracy. As with the first party system, the Democrats favoured inflationary policies (epitomized by Jackson's opposition to the Bank of the United States)[3] and low tariffs (both to provide cheaper imported industrial goods from Europe and to discourage retaliatory tariffs against American agricultural exports), while their opponents (first the Federalists and then the Whigs) favoured sound money and tariff protection for industry. The Whigs won the presidency in 1840 and 1848, both times having nominated a war hero. In the 1850s, however, the issue of slavery both split the Democrats and led to the collapse of the Whigs.

The Republican Party, formed in 1854, nominated its first presidential candidate, John Frémont, in 1856. It was explicitly anti-slavery, although that stand was more significant in the east than in the west, and pro-business. In 1860, the Republicans nominated Abraham Lincoln, who was elected in a four-candidate race with an electoral college majority but only 39.8 per cent of the popular vote. That election precipitated the secession of the southern states, and thus the Civil War. The post-war period of Reconstruction (military occupation of the south and attempted forced social transformation) firmly identified white southerners (which, after Reconstruction was brought to an end, allowing the southern states to disenfranchise their black populations, in politics effectively meant the south as a whole) with the Democrats. The Republicans also became the party of big business, the industrial economy (including industrial labour), and heavily subsidized 'internal improvements', in particular the transcontinental railroad.

The Democrats, however, were torn between the interests of the conservative upper classes in the south, and their Jacksonian clientele of small farmers in the west. One result was the rise of a series of 'third' parties, including the Greenback (that is cheap money) Party and the Populists.[4] While these parties had an impact on the terms of national political debate, their medium-term effect was to cement Republican dominance at the presidential level. The perception that the Republicans were in the pocket of monopoly capital, coupled with the corruption of urban Democratic machines, led in the 1910s and 1920s to the rise of the Progressive Movement, and in some places a Progressive Party. Again, they influenced national politics—in particular with such 'party breaking' reforms as the direct primary—without ever achieving significant national representation.[5] The Democrats won only four presidential elections between 1860 and 1932 (1884 and 1892 under Grover Cleveland, and 1912 and 1916 under Woodrow Wilson, whose 1912 election was made possible by Republican former President Theodore Roosevelt's decision to run as the Progressive (Bull Moose) Party candidate).

The Great Depression saw a fundamental realignment of the parties' support, but left the party organizations intact. The New Deal realignment forged the Democratic coalition that dominated national politics from 1932 into the 1960s, although it was a coalition with deep internal conflicts. In the south, the Democrats were the party of the socially conservative whites (particularly white Protestants) whose primary concern was the maintenance of racial segregation. On the other hand, many of these southern conservatives were prepared to support policies that benefited the poor, so long as they did not threaten to undermine the subservient position of the southern black population or the persistence of a patriarchal society more generally. Indeed many of the peculiarities of American social policies dating from the New Deal are the result of compromises between moderate economic liberalism and extreme racial conservatism on the part of southern Democrats in the 1930s.[6] In the rest of the country, the Democrats became the party of economic liberals and the economically and socially disadvantaged: organized labour, Catholics (as immigrants, against whom primarily Protestant 'nativists' frequently discriminated), Jews, blacks, urbanites. Particularly among urban immigrant populations, for whom partisanship was likely to reflect the integrative and service providing activities of local organizations rather than national policy preferences, the existence of two large rival groups that were 'normally' both within the Democratic coalition, might lead one to identify primarily with the Republicans in a particular city. For example, '[b]y the early 1930s first- and second-generation Irishmen comprised 13 per cent of a sample of 1,000 family heads in New Haven [Connecticut], but they held 49 per cent of all government jobs. The Italians suffered most of all from Irish exclusiveness: there were *no* government employees among the Italians in the sample' (Wolfinger 1974: 37, citing McConnell 1942: 214). This exclusion from the Democratic Party was exploited by the leaders of the Republican Party,[7] who recognized an untapped source of potential Republicans, which was cemented by the defeat of Italian Republican Mayor William Celentano by ostentatiously Irish Democrat Richard Lee in 1949.[8]

Developments beginning in the 1950s undermined the New Deal Democratic coalition. In the mid-1960s, Lyndon Johnson's replacement of the Kennedy administration's cautious approach to racial questions with strong support for civil rights legislation opened the door to the Republicans' 'southern strategy' of covert appeal to racism. Such an appeal moved many white southerners and, notwithstanding the long-overdue enfranchisement of southern blacks, the south as a region in national politics from the Democrats to the Republicans, while solidifying the Democratic allegiance of African Americans, to the extent that they became the most politically monolithic group in the country. The economic emancipation of women also undermined traditional social roles in ways that many found threatening, and from which they sought refuge in socially conservative institutions, such as churches. The rise of issues such as abortion rights and the rights of homosexuals altered the meaning of 'social liberalism' and challenged conservative religious beliefs. This furthered the mobilization of fundamentalist Protestants into politics while also redefining the political relevance of Catholicism (and to a lesser extent of Judaism) from being attributes of ethnic identities to being instead politically relevant ideologies. Both of these changes in the realm of religion benefited the Republicans, with the first further cementing their hold on the south while the latter weakened the ties of traditionally socially liberal groups to the Democratic Party. Economic progress led to an explosion of the self-defined middle class, and a corresponding shrinking of groups identifying themselves as working class, while the shift from a manufacturing to a service economy dramatically weakened the organizational grip of the union movement. A succession of issues, including especially the conjunction of inflation and economic stagnation ('stagflation') in the 1970s and the failure of questions of race to 'go away', undermined public confidence in the ability of government to solve problems at all.

The outline of the coalitions represented by the two parties have in general been set by 'realigning elections', so-called because they have redefined the basic structure of political conflict in ways that have durably altered political allegiances, and in doing so also changed the balance of support between the parties. One such realignment occurred in conjunction with the Civil War, and created a strong link between white southerners and the Democratic Party. Another was reflected in the election of 1896, which cemented a Republican coalition of business, industry (including large elements of industrial labour), and 'modernity' against a Democratic coalition of sectional interests, farmers, and religious conservatives.[9] There was also a realignment between 1928 and 1936 associated with the Great Depression. Whether the developments since the 1960s should be classified as another realignment has been a subject of debate. On the one hand, both the demographic characteristics of the groups usually supporting the two parties at the presidential level and the distribution of party identifications (and consequently the 'normal' winner), and the major policy questions dividing the parties, have changed substantially. On the other hand, unlike previous realignments, these changes have taken place over decades rather than years. Moreover, whereas previous realignments (re)defined large groups of apparently committed partisans, the changes of the late twentieth century appear to have created large numbers of weak party identifiers and non-partisans who, while ordinarily supporting Republican presidential candidates, have proven extraordinarily willing to cast split-ticket votes.

The party coalitions

Although, as just described, the Democrats and Republicans have been in continuous existence as the two dominant parties in American politics for over 150 years, the nature and social composition of their supporting coalitions have changed substantially. In part, this simply reflects changes in society and in the issues to be addressed, but it has been facilitated by the fact that, in contrast to parties in many other countries, American parties never have had formal links to organizations of particular segments of civil society. The American labour movement, for example, explicitly decided in the nineteenth century not to cast its lot with either party. Hence, while there have been times when the unionized working class overwhelmingly supported one party, there has not been a major labour party.[10] Similarly, although there have been times when the great majority of Catholics or evangelical Protestants have been on one side of the political fence, the United States has never had a significant Christian Democratic or Protestant party, although in a (probably misguided) effort to force American parties to fit into the categories of European party families, there have been some suggestions that the Republicans might now be identified as Christian Democrats (Petrocik 1998). Other (similarly misguided) efforts might identify the Democrats with the European Social Democratic family and the Republicans with European Liberals, although a fair assessment of the policies of the two parties would put them both to the right of most European Liberal parties on the economic left–right dimension.

While no election is really typical, some sense of the current demographics of American partisanship can be inferred from exit polls conducted at the 2004 presidential election. As Table 4.1 suggests, the Republicans have become the party (or at least George Bush was the candidate) of white,

TABLE 4.1	2004 presidential vote by demographic characteristics of exit poll respondents	
	Democrat (Kerry)	Republican (Bush)
Gender		
Male	43.9	54.6
Female	51.3	47.8
Ethnicity		
White	40.9	58.1
Black	88.3	11
Hispanic/Latino	53.2	44
Mexican descent	56	41.5
Cuban descent	16.9	83.1
Asian	56.1	43.4
Party identification		
Democrat	88.7	10.8
Republican	6.3	93.2
Independent	49.8	47.4
Religion		
Protestant	36.8	62.2
Catholic	46.8	52.1
Jewish	74.3	25.3

continues

Table 4.1 continued

	Democrat (Kerry)	Republican (Bush)
Muslim	92.6	5.9
None	67.2	31.1
Frequency of church attendance		
At least once a week	38.5	60.4
A few times a month/year	52.5	46.6
Never	62.2	35.9
Born again or evangelical Christian		
Yes	34	65
No	55.1	43.7
Union family		
Yes	59.2	39.7
No	43.9	54.9
Income		
under $50,000	54.8	44.3
Over $50,000	42.5	56.3
Region		
East	55.3	43.3
Midwest	47.9	51
South	41.5	57.5
West	49.6	48.7
Size of place		
City over 500,000	59.7	39
Smaller city and suburban	47.7	51.2
Rural	39.5	59.2
Education		
Did not complete high school	50.2	48.8
High school or college	46.2	52.9
Postgraduate	54.4	44.0

Source: Inter-University Consortium for Political and Social Research study 4181, 'National Election Pool General Election Exit Polls, 2004'. Neither the Consortium nor the original investigators bear any responsibility for the analysis or interpretations presented here

southern, religiously committed, rural, Protestants of moderate education. The Democrats (or Kerry) were the party of blacks, Asian Americans, and non-Cuban Hispanics, big cities (most of which are near the east and west coasts), the traditional unionized working class, non-Christians and the non-religious. Although Table 4.1 suggests that the Democrats were also the party of women (although not so heavily as they were when Bill Clinton was the Democratic candidate), in fact this difference primarily reflects the overwhelmingly (74.8 per cent) Democratic support of non-white women—the majority of white women voted for Bush. Looking instead at the way in which votes divided among respondents who cited particular issues as being the most important in determining their votes, Table 4.2 suggests that the Democrats are the party of those who would be on the left of the traditional, economic, left–right dimension, while the Republicans have become the party of the right (that is, of the opponents of change) on what would usually be described as a 'new politics' or 'social' dimension. This is repeated with regard to personal qualities of the candidates identified as particularly important. Indeed, looking at the overwhelming differences in party support associated with issue priorities and preferred personal qualities shown in Table 4.2, one might conclude with only some exaggeration that the Republicans have become the party of the scared, the self-righteous, and the simple-minded. In the age of terrorism, increasing religiosity, and sound-bite news media, all three groups appear to be growing.

Notwithstanding increasingly bitter conflict between Democrats and Republicans, and some clear and growing differences in general party orientation, it appears easier to identify core demographic constituencies for each of the parties than it is to identify core policy positions—in part because the standards are lower. A demographic group that splits 75–25 will be considered a core constituent group (for example, Jews and the Democrats), whereas a party legislative caucus that splits 75–25 on a policy will be considered disunited. Beyond this, however, it is hard to identify core positions because, given the lack of significant party discipline and the absence of any party agency with the authority to speak definitively about party policy, there is a wide range of opinion (and action) within each party on virtually every significant issue. It is also because the fragmented and personal nature of American electoral campaigns and the diffusion of authority within governmental institutions do not encourage candidates, let alone parties, to

TABLE 4.2	2004 presidential vote by most important issue and most important personal characteristic of a presidential candidate as reported by exit poll respondents

	Democrat (Kerry)	Republican (Bush)
Most important issue		
Taxes	42.7	56.4
Education	72.7	26.3
Iraq	73.1	26.2
Terrorism	13.9	85.8
Economy/jobs	79.8	18.5
Moral values	18.1	80.1
Health care	76.7	23.1
Most important candidate quality		
Cares about people like me	74.5	24.4
Has strong religious faith	7.9	91.6
Is honest and trustworthy	28.7	70.1
Is a strong leader	12.2	86.7
Is intelligent	90.7	8.5
Will bring about needed change	94.6	4.6
Has clear stands on the issues	20.2	78.6

Source: Inter-University Consortium for Political and Social Research study 4181, 'National Election Pool General Election Exit Polls, 2004'. Neither the Consortium nor the original investigators bear any responsibility for the analysis or interpretations presented here

take clear positions. And further, the increasing dominance of the electronic media means that there is less room for fully articulated policy statements. On the other hand, even if their meaning is unclear and variable, it is possible to identify a party with particular sound-bites or catchphrases, sometimes chosen by the party itself and sometimes imposed on it by its opponents.

Significantly contributing to their national dominance, the Republicans have proven considerably more skilled at identifying themselves with positive phrases, and their opponents with negative ones, than have the Democrats. In this, they have been aided by an array of conservative 'talk radio' programmes, for which there is no significant liberal counterpart, and by a far greater willingness to call names (or to sit by while their supporters call names) without worrying that some groups will find those names offensive. Perhaps nothing is more illustrative of this than the degree to which conservative Republicans, with the acquiescence of some moderate Democrats, turned the word 'liberal' from a simple description of an ideological tendency into a term of opprobrium.[11]

In these terms, the Republicans have become the party of 'family values', as a code phrase for conservative Christian morality. They are also the 'pro-life' (that is, anti-abortion) party and the party of 'personal responsibility'. They are identified as the party of 'low taxes', 'smaller and less intrusive government', and 'national security'. The advantage of these labels, aside from the fact that they are all positive valence phrases, is that they are sufficiently abstract that one can think positively about the Republican Party because one thinks positively of 'family values', even when one disapproves of specific policies being advanced under that label (for example, denying hospital visitation rights to homosexual partners in long-term committed relationships), when the phrase and the reality are not entirely consistent (for example, many Republican tax cuts at either state or federal levels have had the effect of shifting the tax burden to lower levels of government rather than significantly lowering the overall rate of taxation, or of shifting the source of government revenue from general taxation to charges that can plausibly be identified as 'fees', again without substantial aggregate reduction), or when putting the policies associated with one phrase into practice undermines the values associated with another (for example, when 'personal responsibility' means cutting the welfare benefits that allow the poor to practise 'family values').

The Democrats, on the other hand, while generally accepting identification as the 'pro-choice' party or the party of 'social responsibility', have also been identified in the public mind (by their Republican opponents) as the party of 'special interests' and 'big government' and as the 'tax and spend' party. As with the Republican phrases, the first two of these have the advantage for the Democrats of being positive valence and somewhat ambiguous. 'Pro-choice' shifts the emphasis from one's attitude about abortion to the question of government interference in decisions that many who oppose abortion nonetheless feel should be private and personal; 'social responsibility' appeals to the ideas of community and that government ought to 'solve' problems, while leaving all the specifics to the imagination. In many respects, the 'special interests' epithet is simply an accurate description of the nature of both parties as coalitions of groups with 'special' interests. The Republican genius has been to identify 'their' special interests with broader categories (for example, to serve right-wing evangelicals while claiming to speak for all nominal Christians (and Jews), or to serve the rich while claiming to speak for the broad middle class). While Republicans in power have tended to shift the areas in which government intrudes from the economic to the social or cultural, they have done little if anything actually to reduce the size of government; while the Democrats might justly be accused of taxing and spending, the Republicans have avoided the equally accurate epithet of 'borrow and spend'. In these terms, the Republicans and Democrats have been playing the same game—but the Republicans have played it more effectively (see Lakoff 2004).

Party organization

American party organizations reflect both the federal structure of the American polity and, particularly at the federal level, the separation of powers that underlies the structure of government. In one sense, as suggested above, one could argue that the United States has no political parties, or at least no strong political parties, at all. In another sense, one could argue that there are at the national level not two parties but six: three Republican parties (presidential/national committee; Senate; House) and three Democratic parties. In yet a third sense, the two-party system is really a 102 party system, with the national Republican and Democratic parties, respectively, being no more than loose and at times transient alliances of 50 independent state Republican and 50 independent state Democratic parties.

The national parties

In organizational terms, each of the two major parties is really three semi-independent entities. Of these, the 'senior partner' is the 'presidential' party, headed by the party's national committee. Although differing in detail, both national committees reflect the federal nature of both the country and of the parties themselves, and are composed of representatives of the state parties.

For the Republicans, the national committee members are the state party chair plus one national committee man and one national committee woman from each state; for the Democrats, in addition to the state chair and the highest-ranking state party official of the other gender plus 200 members apportioned among the states, there are also representatives of various status groups (for example, women, college Democrats), office-holder associations (for example, Democratic governors, mayors, and municipal officials), and the Democratic leadership in Congress.

The national committees, which meet twice a year, are responsible for calling and organizing the parties' quadrennial national conventions. These conventions nominally choose the presidential and vice-presidential candidates, although as noted in Chapter 3, in reality they merely ratify the outcome of the primary process. They also draft the parties' electoral platforms (manifestos), but since the platforms themselves are of little importance, platform 'planks' are often used as symbolic consolation prizes for the supporters of candidates who did not win the nomination. Rather than being party decision-making or policy-debating bodies, the national conventions are essentially party rallies, intended to energize the local activists, and made-for-television campaign spectaculars. They no longer choose candidates, and never decided policy or chose the party central office executive.

The primary function of each national committee is to elect the national chairman. When the party controls the White House, the chairman is effectively named by the president, and the job is of relatively low visibility or influence. When the party has lost the previous presidential election, the chairmanship becomes a token in the competition for party leadership, and *faute de mieux* the chairman has some, albeit limited, visibility as the public face of the party—a position from which the chairman is in any event deposed as the contenders for the next presidential nomination are identified. In either case, the position is more concerned with organization than with policy. And, as in much of American politics, the primary organizational concern is fund-raising. The national party organizations have become increasingly significant as providers of services and funds for state parties (Herrnson 1988), which increases the significance of the national chairman as the 'chief operating officer' for the national committee, without necessarily translating into substantive influence. Moreover, regardless of who is in the White House, between the time the party's presidential candidate is chosen and the time when the election is either won or lost, the national chairman clearly works at the direction of the candidate, and not the other way round. Indicatively, although it is common to refer to federal campaign subsidies as going to the parties (and eligibility is determined on the basis of the votes received by each party's candidate in the previous election), except for the relatively small amount that is allocated for the national conventions, the subsidies all are given to candidate organizations, and not to the parties themselves.

In many ways paralleling, rather than being subordinate to, the national committees, as well as being independent of each other, are the party organizations in the two Houses of Congress. The leaders of these party organizations are the minority and majority leader in the Senate, and the minority leader and Speaker in the House. (In contrast to the presidents of many parliamentary chambers, the Speaker of the House of Representatives is clearly the leader of the majority party rather than a neutral presiding officer.[12]) These leaders are elected by their respective caucuses.

Unlike parliamentary parties in other countries, however, the American congressional parties also have their own fund-raising and campaign-assisting organizations: the National Republican Congressional Committee (NRCC), the National Republican Senatorial Committee (NRSC), the Democratic Congressional Campaign Committee (DCCC), and the Democratic Senatorial Campaign Committee (DSCC). The first such committee, the Union Congressional Committee (the predecessor of the NRCC), was formed in the wake of the Civil War to assist northern Republican members of the House (senators still were chosen by the state legislatures) to campaign independently from the nominally Republican president, who after the assassination of Abraham Lincoln in 1865 was the southerner Andrew Johnson. While relations between a congressional caucus and a president chosen under the same party label have never since been as poisonous, the desire of members of Congress to preserve their independence from the presidential wing of the party has maintained these committees in both parties and both chambers as both legally (for example, with regard to campaign finance regulation) and politically separate entities. The congressional campaign committees have been active in candidate recruitment (which, given the primary election system, is not to be confused with candidate selection), in assisting candidates in raising funds, identifying issues and opposition weaknesses, hiring consultants, and in providing training. In allocating resources, they tend to strike a balance between supporting all incumbents (who are their constituency) and concentrating on marginal races. What they have not done is to apply anything beyond the most minimal tests of party loyalty (for example, voting for the 'correct' candidate for Speaker of the House) or ideological compatibility in deciding whom to support.

While the six national party committees do some political work in-house, they serve primarily as brokers and service providers for the party's candidates and as fund-raising agencies. Most of the actual work of American politics is done by volunteers (at the most local levels) and by independent professionals hired by the candidates themselves. Although these professionals are independent in the sense that they have no formal relationship with either party, most are clearly (and generally highly) partisan. Working in one of the national committee offices is often the first step on the career ladder to independent consultancy, and the party offices are often the brokers between a would-be candidate and campaign professionals within that party's family.

Although they are not formally part of the national parties, each party has two varieties of loosely affiliated organizations. One type is associations of partisan officials at various levels of government, for example, the Conference of Democratic Mayors and the Republican Mayors and Local Officials or the Democratic, and Republican, Governors' Associations. These both serve as party 'caucuses' within the ostensibly non-partisan bodies at the same level of government (US Conference of Mayors; National Governors' Conference) and work to advance the interests of 'their' governments at higher levels. While some of these are formally represented on the Democratic National Committee, their Republican equivalents do not have *ex officio* seats on the Republican National Committee. The other variety is at the same time more explicitly political and more disconnected from the parties as organizations. These include 'think tanks' like the Progressive Policy Institute or the Heritage Foundation, and groups of partisans who want to shift the direction of policy within their own party. The most obvious example of the latter is the Democratic Leadership Council, which describes itself as 'not a political committee, and . . . not organized to influence elections', but which has tried to move the Democratic Party towards what they perceive to be the political centre, and was the springboard for Bill Clinton's rise to the presidency.

Finally, and even more distant from the formal party organizations, are a penumbra of organizations that are part of the 'party in the electorate', but are not connected with the party even as closely as groups like the Heritage Foundation or the Democratic Leadership Council. These include groups like the 527 organizations cited in Chapter 3, and groups like labour unions, the National Association for the Advancement of Colored People (NAACP), or the National Rifle Association (NRA). Although they may claim to be non-partisan, and although in some cases their tax status may require them to keep their distance not only from the parties but from individual candidates as well, their particular ideological orientations make them the natural supporters of only one party. Particularly at the congressional level, this rarely means blanket support for the party, however, but only support for particularly congenial candidates, and indeed in primary elections may translate into active opposition to incumbents who have strayed too far from the organization's idea of what the party line should have been.

State parties

American parties in the nineteenth and early twentieth centuries, particularly but not exclusively in the urban areas, were often political machines, dominated by a 'boss' and his cronies, and supported by the exchange of patronage, ranging from wholesale graft to the provision of a job sweeping the streets or a turkey at Christmas, for political support. While these machines were predominantly local, the boss of a major urban machine might also control politics in his state. At the national level, however, there would only be a temporary coalition every four years to support a presidential candidate, in return for local control of federal patronage. Although the majority of these machines were aligned with the Democrats, there were enough Republican machines (for example Pittsburgh and Philadelphia in Pennsylvania, or Rochester in New York) to make this a legitimately bipartisan phenomenon. Nomination, and the possibility of election (which was not always determined by the numbers of citizens voting for the various candidates—'the votes didn't make the result, the checker made the result', as one machine operative is reputed to have testified), was in the hands of the machine, and therefore they controlled many of the holders of public office. When corruption became too rampant, or a particularly zealous judge or prosecutor successfully sent the machine's leaders to jail, reformers might take control temporarily, but while in office they frequently tried to ensure the perpetuation of 'good government' by imposing legal restrictions on the parties.

Although some political machines (for example, the Daly machine in Chicago and the O'Connell machine in Albany) clearly lasted into the 1960s or even later, the Progressive reforms of the late nineteenth and early twentieth centuries had three major consequences for understanding American party organization. First, in establishing a merit-based civil service system and competitive bidding for government contracts, they dramatically reduced the significance of patronage, although it is still common to find many local party activists on the public payroll in one way or another and the largest contributors to local politicians still are often found in the construction industry. This process was later furthered by the rise of federal welfare programmes that turned many of the discretionary 'favours' of local politicians into 'entitlements' and reduced (along with rising standards of living more generally) the relative desirability of the kinds of low wage jobs that had been in the gift of 'ward heelers'. Second, to a great extent they transformed parties at the state and local levels from purely private organizations for the selection of candidates and conduct of campaigns, into quasi-state organizations for the administration of elections with their structures and procedures largely controlled by statute rather than party rules. Only at the end of the twentieth century did the federal courts begin to recognize the associational rights of parties as assuring them some rights to control their own nominating procedures (for example, allowing parties to decide for themselves whether voters who were registered as independents would be allowed to vote in the party's primaries), although those rights still are severely limited in the name of the state's interest in honest and orderly elections. Third, because virtually all of the regulation is at the state level, there is no uniform model for state and local party organization. That being the case, the rest of this section describes what might be called 'typical' state party organization rather than the organization of any particular state party.

The first respect in which the legal regulation of parties has an obvious impact is with regard to the idea of party membership. Legally, at least to the extent that the law recognizes the idea of party membership at all, the members of American parties are those who have registered as such—not with the party, but with the public body in charge of the electoral register. The party itself has no control over who may register as one of its 'members', and the 'member' assumes no responsibility to the party. In states without partisan registration, the definition of 'membership' may be even more vacuous: the Virginia Democratic Party, for example, defines as a member 'Every resident of the Commonwealth of Virginia who believes in the principles of the Democratic Party . . . '.[13] By this definition, many, if not most, 'members' of the Virgina Democratic Party must be presumed to be ignorant of their own 'membership'.

Alongside this legal definition of party membership, there is another kind of membership—membership in the various Democratic or Republican 'clubs' that exist at the local level. While some of these are territorially defined (for example, the Central Baltimore County Democratic Club or the Eastside [Detroit] Republican Club), others are defined by a combination of geography and special interest (for example, local branches of the Log Cabin Republicans or Stonewall Democrats, both organizations of gay and lesbian partisans). These are genuine membership organizations, for which application and dues payments or other contributions are required, and from which expulsion is a theoretical possibility. Although club membership rates, even among committed party supporters, are far lower than party membership rates in most European democracies, when active these clubs may perform some of the functions of more typical mass party organizations: discussing political issues; supporting particular candidates for nomination; raising funds and organizing volunteers for campaigns—although rarely enough to be significant except in the most local races. What they lack, however, is any formal rights within the party as a legal entity: they are not represented in party conventions; they do not elect party leaders (for example, the state or county chairman); they have no place in the process of candidate nomination beyond their ability to aid, as any organization might aid, in the campaign of a candidate they support.

The legal party organization itself is headed by a state central committee and a state chairman who is chosen by the central committee. Members of the central committee themselves are chosen in primary elections or district conventions, which means that they are chosen by the party members, but only in the sense that all party registrants or self-proclaimed supporters are party members—and given generally low turnout in primary elections, and that many of those who do vote in primaries do not bother voting for members of the party committees, generally a quite small proportion of these 'members'. Like the national committees, the state committees and their chairs are primarily involved in fund-raising, organizational maintenance, and the provision of some public visibility for the party when it does not control significant public offices. From the point of view of a news producer interested in partisan balance, the state party chair is better than no one—but not much better. State party committees (and the party national committees) generally maintain websites advancing the party's agenda, which at the state level is defined as support for the policies of that party's governor or opposition to the policies of the other party's governor, and send out a steady stream of e-mails with talking points, morale-boosting reports, and solicitations for contributions, but of course only to those who have already indicated that they are supporters, most commonly by having contributed money in the past.

Formally below the state central committee, but more accurately in a relationship of cooperative or affectionate independence described some decades ago as 'stratarchy', are an array of county, town, city, district, and ward committees. Because of the American obsession with population equality in legislative districts, particularly the district committees rarely nest neatly either within one another (for example, state legislative districts within rather than cutting across Congressional Districts) or with respect to towns or counties. Again, fund-raising and maintaining a network of volunteers and political connections upon which individual candidates can attempt to draw are the primary functions of these more local committees. They often have the power to replace a candidate who dies or withdraws between the primary and general elections, and may even have the power to name a successor to a public official who is unable to complete his or her term,[14] but most of the time it is doubtful that the average citizen is even aware of the existence of these committees.

Parties in American politics

Party affiliation is central to the political identity and careers of politicians. With the exception of the many conversions of southern Democrats to the Republican Party in the wake of the civil rights revolution, very few politicians have 'crossed the aisle' and even fewer have done so and remained in office after the next election. At the core of each 'party in the electorate' is a group of intense 'party identifiers', in the strong sense that they think of themselves as *being* and not merely supporting Democrats or Republicans.

Lifelong affiliation with a party, whether by politicians or by core supporters in the electorate, is not the same as strong party coherence, and indeed is supported by lack of coherence. A politician rarely, if ever, is forced to choose between deference to constituents or conscience, on the one hand, and party affiliation, on the other; in virtually all cases he or she can simply act in accordance with the former while retaining the latter. Particularly given the primary system, partisan voters can almost always find someone to support within their own party, and given the diversity within each party, the personalism of American politics and the number of candidates for different offices generally on the ballot at any election it is easy to rationalize disagreement as being with particular people rather than with the party *per se*. Even the strongest of partisans cannot be counted upon to vote for every candidate standing under the party's banner, even as their partisanship remains intact.

Within American politics, party is the most common starting point for the building of coalitions both within government and in the electorate. There is a presumption of party unity—that senators of the president's party will vote to confirm his nominees to high office; that party registrants will vote for the party's candidates; that a governor whose party has a majority in both houses of the state legislature will get his or her programme enacted—but it is a presumption that is easily overridden in particular circumstances. The coalitions supporting particular pieces of legislation often cut across party lines. Similarly, the coalitions supporting the election of individual candidates—contributors and campaign workers, as well as voters—are often put together in parallel to party organizations, and draw from normal supporters of both parties. It is uncommon, but not shockingly so, for an elected official of one of the major parties to support the election of a candidate of the other; even in what one might expect to be the most partisan of venues, the rules of the two parties' national committees only demand support for the presidential candidate, leaving the national committee member free to support whomever he or she would like for other offices without regard to party.

At the heart of all of this is a deep ambivalence concerning parties, or at least concerning partisanship. This was well expressed in comments made by former President Jimmy Carter on a morning television show during the 2004 presidential race, when he opined not only that the campaign was too bitter, but also that it was *too partisan*. In a culture that values bipartisanship primarily as an indicator or even, incorrectly, as a synonym for non-partisanship, parties must have an ambiguous place. There is no doubt that they are essential to the functioning of democratic government. As E. E. Schattschneider (1942: 1) wrote in a book about party government *in the United States*, 'political parties created democracy, and modern democracy is unthinkable save in terms of the parties'. It is largely the capacity of political leaders, organized into parties, to mitigate the intentionally instilled antagonisms between legislative and executive (and to a lesser extent judicial) branches of government and among the different levels of government that prevents the separation and division of powers, which are at the heart of the American constitutional system, from leading to paralysis. On the other hand, party government, as the term is understood in other countries—politicians competing for office primarily as representatives of their parties; voters choosing primarily on the basis of party; parties behaving as cohesive teams that take collective responsibility for government—has never existed in the United States, if only because the kinds of party required do not exist. The American 'big tent' parties have done well in integrating the tremendous diversity of culture, interest, and condition that characterize American society into a functioning political community, and in channelling the diverse demands of that society into the governmental arena. They play a central role in structuring politics, and in putting particular individuals in positions of power or influence. The parties do not, however, govern in the sense implied by the phrase 'party government'. Nor, given the emphasis placed on the individual accountability of politicians to their individual constituencies, and the value placed on consensual rather than simple majoritarian decision-making, do most Americans want them to.

....

KEY TERMS

- congressional campaign committee
- national chairman
- national committee
- national convention
- realigning election
- Reconstruction

NOTES

1 According to the National Conference of State Legislatures, fewer than two dozen of the 7,382 state legislators are independents or members of third parties.

2 More commonly, scholars distinguish five or six stages of development of the American party system. The first two correspond to, although they are not perfectly coterminous with, the Federalist versus Democratic Republican and the Democrat versus Whig party systems. The final four, however, are all characterized by systems in which the Democrats and Republicans were the two major parties, and are distinguished by changes in the dynamics of party competition, the bases of party support, and the structures and activities of the parties rather than a change in which parties are competing or in their leadership—beyond the natural changes brought about over time by retirement and death. In this characterization, the third party system ends around 1896, the fourth around 1932, and the fifth in the 1960s (see Chambers and Burnham 1975; Aldrich 1995).

3 As with the question of federal assumption of state revolutionary war debts that divided the Federalists and Jeffersonian Democrats, three issues were conflated: the balance between federal and state levels of government; protection or reduction of existing economic and political privilege; and likely inflationary results into the future.

4 The Populists peaked nationally in 1896, winning 22 (of 357) seats in the House of Representatives.

5 Their peak was nine (of 435) House members, elected in 1912.

6 Southern Democrats were generally anti-union, but favoured aid to farmers, old-age insurance, and government pork-barrel spending.

7 Ironically, given that Jews in general identify with the Democrats, the Republican leaders were Jewish brothers.

8 At 'a Knights of Columbus function [Lee] used a brogue that was not noticeable in other circumstances.' (Wolfinger 1974: 40, citing Fred Powledge, 'The Flight from City Hall', *Harper's Magazine* (November 1969): 77.

9 Indicatively, the Democratic candidate, William Jennings Bryan, who in 1896 made his famous 'Cross of Gold' speech (so-called for its final phrase, 'you shall not crucify mankind upon a cross of gold'), calling for bimetallism and the free and unlimited coinage of silver (an expansionary monetary policy which would favour indebted farmers), volunteered to serve as an assistant prosecutor in the 1925 'Scopes Monkey Trial', in which a Tennessee teacher was accused of the crime of teaching 'any theory that denies the story of the Divine creation of man as taught in the Bible'.

10 Another reason for the absence of an American labour (or socialist) party is that the United States effectively had universal (white) manhood suffrage before there was a significant industrial working class. Hence, the demand for voting rights could not be exploited to organize such parties.

11 Somewhat less pervasive in its impact, but more extreme in its content, is the coining of the word 'feminazi' by conservative radio host Rush Limbaugh—without any of the demands for apology and retraction that accompanied Democratic comparisons of the treatment of prisoners at Guantanamo Bay or Abu Ghareb to the Nazi regime.

12 The majority party in the House also has a majority leader, but this person is second in the leadership to the Speaker.

13 The Virginia Republicans also require an open, but obviously unenforceable, statement of intent to support all of the party's nominees at the ensuing general election.

14 For example, if a seat in the Maryland General Assembly (the state legislature) becomes vacant, the district committee of the departing member's party suggests a replacement to the governor. If they can agree on a single suggestion, the governor is obliged to appoint that person.

GUIDE TO FURTHER READING

ALDRICH, J. (1995), *Why Parties? The Origin and Transformation of Political Parties in America* (Chicago: University of Chicago Press).

An analysis of the role parties play in American politics, focusing on their importance to candidate selection, voter mobilization, and ultimately governing.

BECK, P. A. and M. R. HERSHEY (2001), *Party Politics in America* (New York: Longman).

Considers party organization, policy positions, and activities—looking at the party as an organization, the party in the electorate, and the party in government.

HERRNSON, P. S. (1988) *Party Campaigning in the 1980s* (Cambridge, MA: Harvard University Press).

An analysis of parties as providers of services to candidates.

MILLER, W. E. and J. M. SHANKS (1996), *The New American Voter* (Cambridge, MA: Harvard University Press).

A comprehensive study of American voter behaviour by one of the authors of the seminal book *The American Voter* and one of their foremost students.

THURBER, J. A. and C. J. NELSON (eds.) (2000), *Campaign Warriors: Political Consultants in Elections* (Washington, DC: Brookings Institution).

What difference does it make that politics has become increasingly professionalized, and that functions once performed by volunteer parties are increasingly performed instead by paid consultants?

WATTENBERG, M. (1998), *The Decline of American Political Parties* (Cambridge, MA: Harvard University Press).

A study of how individual candidates have displaced parties as the primary focus of voters' loyalties and attention.

5

....

The Chief Executive

Overview

The President of the United States is both ceremonial head of state and political head of the executive branch of the federal government. Both roles contribute to giving him a variety of political resources. Some are formal, like his role as commander-in-chief of the armed forces and his power to nominate the principal officers of government. Others are informal, like his role as the head of his political party. The actual power of the president depends on how effectively he can mobilize those resources in trying to manage an enormous executive branch, some of which has been intentionally structured to insulate it from direct presidential control, and in his relations with the Congress.

In contrast to the Congress, to which the Constitution gives an extensive and detailed list of powers, the powers of the president are barely sketched. 'The executive Power' is vested in the president; he is named as commander-in-chief of the army and navy (and of the state militias, 'when called into the actual Service of the United States'); he is charged with taking 'Care that the Laws be faithfully executed'; he may require the principal executive officers to give their opinion concerning their own duties in writing; he can grant pardons and reprieves for 'Offenses against the United States' (but not for offences against an individual state, which is to say not for most 'ordinary' crimes);[1] he has the power to appoint judges, diplomats, and executive officers, and to make treaties—all with the 'Advice and Consent' of the Senate.

At least in conjunction with the American nuclear arsenal and the economic power of the United States, these powers are sufficient to lead some to identify the president as the most powerful person on earth. They are, however, precisely the same powers (less, of course, the global economic and military might of the country) held by presidents in the late nineteenth century, when the president clearly was not the most powerful person in the government, let alone the country or the world. In fact, rather than conferring power (the ability to prevail against opposition), the Constitution gives the president great power resources: whether he is able to convert those formal resources, and the range of informal resources that accompany them, into power, and whether that power is adequate actually to prevail, depends on his political skill, the strength of his political support in the country, the extent of authority granted by law, and the context in which he is operating at any particular time.

Head of state

The president fills two roles in the American system that in the great majority of democratic countries are filled by two different people. On the one hand, he is the political head of the federal government: a politician who has climbed to the top of Disraeli's 'greasy pole', but still merely a politician. In parliamentary systems, the most closely analogous position is that of prime minister. Most of this chapter is concerned with the president in this capacity, and with the presidential, and the 'political' levels of the executive, establishment through, or in spite of, which the president tries to lead the government. (The bureaucracy more generally is the subject of Chapter 7.)

On the other hand, the president is also the American head of state, the personal embodiment of the sovereign nation. In monarchies, this role is played by the monarch, and the American presidency has over time acquired many of the trappings of royalty. The president has his own 'theme song' (*Hail to the Chief*) and flag, everyone stands when he comes into the room, even his close family members refer to him as 'the President' when talking in public. The president is the centre of major ceremonies and state occasions, offers comfort and encouragement to the nation in times of crisis, and in what for other people would be his private life represents the sophistication, culture, and values (or lack thereof) of the country.

These trappings of royalty that surround the president as head of state convey enormous political advantages that can be exploited by the president as head of government. As the experience of Bill Clinton shows, the president is not insulated from personal attack, but clearly is a politician who must be treated with deference, who will not be called a liar even when he obviously is not telling the truth and who cannot ordinarily be called upon to give testimony under oath, who can command media attention in circumstances in which he appears to be above politics, and who is in a stronger position than one who does not share these opportunities. The president can deploy a range of symbolic resources that are his as head of state—the presidential seal, the White House, Air Force One, the honour guards and military bands—in the service of his political objectives.

The aura surrounding the presidency can also prove a liability, however. Not only the president, but his wife, children, and siblings all become the subject of intense public scrutiny. The personal peccadillos that would not even be noticed in a senator's family can be a major embarrassment in a president's family. Certainly, the fact that some of Bill Clinton's indiscretions occurred in the Oval Office greatly magnified the political damage done. The president may also suffer from a kind of splendid isolation, constantly surrounded by courtiers who allow him to believe that his every statement is profound, and who only tell him what they think he wants to hear.

The president as political leader and head of government

The mystical exaltation of the presidency is not the only basis for deference by those surrounding the president. He is also the boss, as epitomized by the apocryphal story of Abraham Lincoln polling his cabinet: after the cabinet secretaries had unanimously voted 'no', he is said to have announced, 'the ayes have it!' The Constitution does not grant power to the executive branch or to the presidential establishment, but to the president himself as the incumbent of a singular, constitutionally defined, office. While a number of independent agencies have been established, which have executive functions but to which the president cannot simply give orders, and although legislation often limits the range of options that can be considered and establishes procedures that must be followed by members of the executive branch in reaching decisions (as well as establishing the authority to make the decisions in the first place), the president is generally understood to be the CEO of the government, in principle able to determine most decisions, even when he does not have the legal authority simply to give orders that will be obeyed—if he has, and is willing to expend, sufficient political capital.

Presidential power and influence in the legislative process

Notwithstanding the rhetoric of separation of powers, the American system is really characterized by an overlap or mixing of powers. This is particularly evident with regard to the legislative process. A simple reading of the Constitution would suggest taxation, allocation of spending, and general legislation all to be the prerogatives of Congress. While this formally is true, however, increasingly initiative in these matters has shifted to the executive branch, which submits the 'first draft' of the budget with detailed proposals for both taxation and spending. The executive also increasingly sets the primary agenda for legislation in other areas. While Congress remains free to amend, supplement, ignore, or simply replace executive proposals, and while it is free to legislate in any field in which the Constitution grants the federal government authority, the president largely determines the congressional agenda.

The first tool of presidential influence is the annual State of the Union message, delivered in January, shortly after the opening of each new session of Congress. Although presidents from Jefferson (for whom it smacked of a Speech from the Throne) to Taft simply delivered this constitutionally required message in writing, it is now delivered in person, and nationally televised in prime time before a Joint Session of Congress with the members of the cabinet and the Supreme Court in attendance. Aside from showing the president 'clothed' in the full majesty of his office, the State of the Union allows the president to put his legislative programme at the forefront of political consciousness—of Congress, the news media, and the attentive public at large.

Because virtually everything government does costs money, the budget is a policy statement of central importance, and the White House is the primary initiator of the budgetary process with the executive budget, submitted to Congress on the first Monday in February for the federal fiscal year that will begin on 1 October. (For the budgetary process after the executive budget arrives in Congress, see Chapter 6.) Over time, the construction of the executive budget has become increasingly centralized in the Office of Management and Budget (OMB) in the Executive Office of the President, making the budget an even more powerful instrument of the presidential agenda and policy control. Moreover, on the theory that everything has budgetary implications, Congress has given the president the authority to require agencies to get OMB clearance for all executive requests for legislation, further broadening the general policy significance of the president's budgetary powers.

Executive branch involvement is also evident as Congress considers legislation in committee. Executive departments provide much of the information on which members of Congress can base their decisions, and both the White House and the executive agencies maintain legislative liaison offices (which, if outside the government, would simply be identified as lobbyists), to promote their views.

The most obvious presidential involvement in the legislative process comes at the end. Every bill passed by both houses of Congress goes to the president, who has a number of options, depending on whether Congress remains in session. If Congress is in session, then the president either can sign the bill or take no action for ten days (excluding Sundays), in which case the bill becomes law, or he can veto the bill (return it to Congress together with a statement of his objections), in which case it becomes law only if Congress again passes the bill, but now with roll call votes and a two-thirds majority (of those voting, a quorum being present) in each house required. If Congress is not in session, the president's options are to sign the bill into law or to let it die through inaction (the 'pocket veto').

As Table 5.1 shows, presidents have varied enormously in their explicit use of the veto power (not surprisingly, it has been used most frequently when the White House and Congress are controlled by different parties), and only a tiny proportion of vetoes have been overridden by Congress. Table 5.1 actually understates the potency of the veto power, however. The president's ability to threaten a veto is at least as significant as his actual use of this power. By announcing in advance that an extraordinary majority will be required, he may force compromise or even a withdrawal of the

TABLE 5.1	Presidential vetoes

President	President's party	Majority party in Congress	Regular vetoes	Pocket vetoes	Total	Vetoes over-ridden
F. D. Roosevelt	D	D	372	263	635	9
Truman	D	1947–48: R	42	33	75	6
		1945–46; 1949–52: D	138	37	175	6
Eisenhower	R	1953–54: R	52	31	83	0
		1955–60: D	21	77	98	2
Kennedy	D	D	12	9	21	0
L. B. Johnson	D	D	16	14	30	0
Nixon	R	D	26	17	43	7
Ford	R	D	48	18	66	12
Carter	D	D	13	18	31	2
Reagan	R	1981–86: HR–D; S–R	20	28	48	6
		1987–88: D	19	11	30	3
G. H. W. Bush	R	D	29	15	44	1
Clinton	D	1993–94: D	0	0	0	0
		1995–2000: R	36	1	37	2
G. W. Bush (1st term)	R	2001–02: HR–R; S–D[1]	0	0	0	0
		2003–04: R	0	0	0	0
Total, 1789–2004			1,484	1,066	2,550	106

HR = House of Representatives; S = Senate

[1] The Republicans controlled the Senate from 20 January to 6 June 2001 by virtue of the vice-president's casting vote (because the Senate was tied with 50 Democrats and 50 Republicans). On 6 June, James Jeffords of Vermont left the Republican caucus and became an Independent who caucuses with the Democrats, giving them a one-seat majority. The Republicans regained the majority on 12 November 2002 due to the election of Republican James Talent to replace Democrat Jean Carnahan, who had been appointed by the Governor of Missouri to replace her husband who had been elected in 2000, notwithstanding that he had died before the election.

Source: Clerk of the House of Representatives (http://clerk.house.gov)

proposals that he opposes. Still, this is primarily a negative power, and so it is far more useful for a president who wants to prevent action than it is for a president who wants the law changed.

The conduct of foreign and military policy

The power to 'receive Ambassadors and other public Ministers' coupled with the explicit power to appoint (and the implicit power to remove) American diplomatic representatives and the authority to 'make Treaties, provided two-thirds of the Senators present concur' make the president the nation's 'chief diplomat'. The president's power in foreign affairs (and in some areas of domestic policy as well), has been expanded by the use of 'executive agreements' with other countries. These do not require Senate ratification, but like treaties become part of 'the supreme Law of the Land', even if they involve the exercise of powers not granted to the federal government by the Constitution. An additional increase in presidential power has come from the granting of 'fast-track' authority to negotiate tariffs: when granted by Congress (which is not always the case, again with the partisanship of president and Congress coming into play), this allows the president to negotiate tariff agreements that, although they alter tax rates, which should be the prerogative of Congress, will be subject only to an up-or-down vote with no amendment possible.

Although a straightforward reading of the Constitution might suggest that Congress would have considerable authority in military affairs— Congress has the power to 'make Rules for the Government and Regulation of the land and naval forces' as well as to declare war—the president's position as commander-in-chief has made him the prime architect of military policy. His formal position has been buttressed by the tendency of citizens to look to a single leader in times of crisis, and by the need for rapid response in the fast-moving modern world. The last time the United States Congress declared war was June 1942,[2] but that has not prevented presidents taking military action in Korea, Vietnam, Grenada, Panama, Bosnia, Somalia, Afghanistan, Iraq (to name only some of America's undeclared wars), either with or without the sanction of the United Nations. The president has often sought congressional approval for these interventions only after the troops are already in the field. Congress attempted to reassert its authority with the 1973 War Powers Resolution (passed over a presidential veto), but with little significant impact on presidential claims of virtually unlimited discretion (indeed, obligation) to defend American interests abroad as they see fit.

Particularly during the unrest in the south surrounding the civil rights movement of the 1950s and 1960s, the power of the president to call the National Guard into federal service was significant in domestic politics, because it allowed presidents to use the local 'militias' to enforce federal court orders against their neighbours, rather than bringing in 'outsiders' in the form of federal troops. During the Iraq War, this power allowed much of the burden of foreign military operations to be shifted to the states, and the incompatible policies of an all-volunteer army and long-term military intervention to be reconciled.

While Congress can intervene in the conduct of foreign and military policy through the requirement that the Senate ratify treaties and confirm appointments, through the power of the purse, and through congressional control over the legislation required to implement policies or agreements, these policy areas have become nearly the exclusive preserve of the executive branch. Given the weight of the United States in world affairs, this makes the president a very powerful man. It is not an unmixed blessing, however. Because foreign relations and defence are policy areas in which only the president can act with authority, in a dangerous and interdependent world they become policy areas to which the president *must* give high priority, whether he wants to or not. The danger, particularly from the perspective of a president who has an ambitious domestic agenda, is that so much of his energy and political resources will be pre-empted by foreign and military affairs that he cannot pursue his domestic goals effectively. On the plus side, however, is the possibility that political capital gained from foreign policy or military successes, or even from popular rallying around the flag when the result is not a clear success, can be applied in other areas.

Power to appoint

The president can also exercise control through the power of appointment (and in some cases, of removal). Excluding judges and military officers, in November 2004 there were 1,438 'Policy and Supporting Positions' subject to presidential appointment, 1,118 requiring Senate confirmation and the other 320 at the president's sole discretion.[3] In addition, roughly 700 members of the senior executive service were non-career (at least in part political) appointees, with no security of tenure.

Personal loyalty and ideological compatibility (plus some modicum of technical competence) naturally play a role in presidential appointments, but the president's choices are constrained by many other considerations. His appointments must pay some deference to the range of opinion within his party, and its supporting coalition more generally. When the official to be appointed will serve outside Washington, the senators from the area in which the appointee will work, especially if they are of the president's party, may expect to be consulted, or even to name the official themselves. First-tier appointees (for example, cabinet secretaries) may exercise some control over the appointment of their subordinates (for example, deputy and assistant secretaries), although the president may also want to use such second- and third-tier appointments to assure that there is someone loyal to his programme in a department whose head has been appointed for party-balancing reasons. The law often requires partisan balance for 'independent' regulatory agencies (for example, the Federal Election Commission, the Federal Communications Commission), which may require the president to appoint members who are not from his party. Increasingly, presidents have felt constrained to make their administrations 'look like America', with an increasing range of demographic groups claiming entitlement to their share of the appointments.

Appointments can be used to reward individuals or groups for their support, as well as to put loyal lieutenants in key positions. At the same time, however, presidents often face the same problem as Louis XIV: that every time they make an appointment, they get ten malcontents and one ingrate.

Informal power resources

In addition to his formal powers, and the advantages that accrue from his status as head of state, the president has a number of additional resources upon which he can draw to advance his objectives. The most obvious of these is democratic legitimacy: he is the only one with a mandate from the country as a whole. The value of this resource initially depends on the magnitude of the president's electoral victory and the success of the congressional and senatorial candidates on his party's ticket with him, and then increases or decreases with his popularity and approval, as indicated in opinion polls.

In deferring to a popular president, other officials are combining democratic principles with self-interest. A Democratic party official in the 1930s is reputed to have shown the debris pulled in with an arriving ferry to a local candidate who was concerned about his own campaign. 'Franklin Roosevelt is your ferry boat [he said,] and you come in with him.' While no longer true to the same degree, it clearly is good for a candidate's own election chances to be on the same ticket as a successful president. Moreover, the president can choose whether or not to support the election (appear at events, encourage contributions, provide photo opportunities) of candidates who have, or have not, supported him, with the value of such support directly reflective of the president's own popularity. The significance of this political resource is multiplied by the president's role as the head of his party and ultimate 'boss' to the national committee headquarters, but this is also one reason why the congressional parties maintain their own, independent, campaign support committees.

The president also has wide discretion over policy and patronage: not only which policies to emphasize but also where to locate the economic advantages (for example, jobs) or environmental disadvantages (for example, nuclear waste facilities) that will result from them. These too can be used to reward or punish members of Congress, governors, mayors, etc.

The president benefits from the absence of any tradition of principled resignation. Although some lower-ranking officials have resigned in protest of policies they could not support, it is essentially unheard of for top officials to air policy disagreements with the president. Instead, they will hold their tongues, or resign because of 'ill health' or 'to spend more time with my family', and then possibly write a book detailing their objections to the presidential policy. By the time the book appears, however, the policy may no longer be topical, and its author is no longer a member of the administration, both of which reduce the political cost to the president of the resignation.[4]

Perhaps most significantly, the president has media access and agenda control. Although the president cannot count on all-network pre-emption whenever he asks for it, the president remains automatically newsworthy. He is in a unique position in that, simply by making an important announcement, he can move other, and potentially embarrassing, stories to the back pages or off the reportorial agenda altogether. There is a corps of White House correspondents who are virtually guaranteed time on the broadcast media and space in the press, and for the most part all they have to report is what the administration, through speeches and press briefings, tells them. While there is some independent investigative reporting, to the extent that the administration can limit itself to a single 'message of the day', it usually determines what will be covered, thus allowing the executive to supplement the obvious advantage of control over information in general, with control over the subjects and themes of the news as well.

A fixed term

So obvious that it is easily overlooked, another important resource of the president is that he has a fixed term. Prime ministers can be deposed at any time, either from within their own party should the party lose confidence in the prime minister's ability to lead the country or to win the next election, or because of the collapse of a coalition. The loss of a motion of no confidence in parliament effectively ends the tenure of a prime minister. While in some countries and under some circumstances this may result in a premature election (and possibly the return to office of the same individual), the result is a new prime minister with nearly the same legitimacy as the one replaced. The American president, however, can only have his four-year term abbreviated by death, resignation, or impeachment. And in any of these cases, the result is that the vice-president becomes president. The vice-president, however, has no real electoral mandate or national supporting coalition. While the country may rally around the new president in trying to recover from the 'national nightmare' (as Gerald Ford described the events of the Watergate crisis that ultimately made him president), this is not the basis for strong and active leadership.

Security of tenure means that the president can weather downturns in popularity, personal or political scandals, or failures of policy than might unseat a prime minister. It also gives others a strong incentive to cooperate with the leader whom they cannot replace and so must live with. On the other hand, the constitutional limitation of presidents to two terms of four years (plus up to two years of his predecessor's term, in the case of a vice-president who 'inherits' the presidency through death, resignation, or impeachment)[5] creates the phenomenon of the 'lame duck' president, who cannot run again and has therefore lost many of his long-term and campaign-related political resources. Rather than being obliged to live with him, opponents may choose simply to wait him out.

The president, cabinet, and executive agencies

The president, as chief executive, is the head of an executive establishment that in September 2004 had more than 2.6 million civilian employees. Of these, almost 1.7 million worked for the executive departments: an increase of 5.7 per cent from 2001 under a 'government-shrinking' Republican president that wiped out a 10 per cent decrease between 1995 and 2001 under a 'tax and spend' Democrat. The other civilian executive employees worked for the Executive Office of the President (1,792) and the independent and regulatory agencies (roughly 75 per cent of them for the US Postal Service).

The cabinet

The traditional core of the executive branch is the now 15 executive departments, each headed by a cabinet member (all titled 'Secretary of...' except the Attorney General, who is the head of the Department of Justice).[6] Of these, by far the largest is Defense with over 650,000 civilian employees, while the smallest is Education, with fewer than 4,500. Measured by spending, the largest departments are (in order) Health and Human Services, Defense, and the Treasury, each with annual outlays well in excess of $350,000 million, while the smallest are Commerce, Interior, and State, each spending less than $12,000 million. Departmental importance can also be assessed in terms of closeness to the president and centrality to his agenda. By this standard, the State, Defense, Treasury, Justice (especially because of its role in the selection of federal judges), and Homeland Security (since its creation in 2002) are always first-rank departments, while other departments move up and down the pecking order depending on the particular president.

Collectively, the heads of the executive departments, along with the vice-president and a number of other officials designated by the president to be 'of cabinet rank' (in 2005: the White House Chief of Staff, the Director of the Office of Management and Budget, the Administrator of the

Environmental Protection Agency, the United States Trade Representative, the Director of the Office of National Drug Control Policy), form the president's cabinet. In fact, the cabinet as an institution has no legal standing. While the Constitution refers to 'the principal Officers of the executive departments', it treats them as individuals, and there is no requirement that they meet or act collectively. Notwithstanding the story of President Lincoln, the cabinet meets relatively infrequently (under President George W. Bush, roughly every 45 days), and certainly is not a body in which votes are taken. First, it is too big for intensive discussion. Second, whatever the subject at hand, it would be outside the bailiwick and expertise of most cabinet members. Third, on most important questions, the power to decide ultimately rests with the president alone. While all presidents have small coteries of advisers (a 'kitchen cabinet'—some in the formal cabinet and others not) with whom they consult regularly, and will meet with individual cabinet members as the need arises, meetings of the full cabinet are, in President Kennedy's words, 'a waste of time'.

Cabinet departments are created, and their responsibilities defined, by Congress. Their budgets ultimately are decided by Congress. Congress passes, or not, the legislation desired by the departments, and exercises oversight through hearings, before which both cabinet secretaries and subordinate political and civil service executives may be called to testify. All of these both limit the president's authority to control the organization and the activities of the executive departments, and entail divided loyalties for them and their heads.

Cabinet secretaries have three essential roles. First, they are members of the president's team, responsible for the elaboration and implementation of his programme within their particular areas of responsibility. Second, they are the heads of and spokespersons for executive departments that have their own institutional programmes and interests, and are responsible for advancing those interests both with Congress and with the White House. It is often said in Washington that 'where you stand [on policy questions] depends on where you sit [in the organizational structure]'. A cabinet secretary whose job requires that she spend most of her time interacting with departmental officials is likely before long to start seeing their ideas as her own. Third, many were selected in part because of their demographic or ideological identity, and many executive departments were created to represent particular interests (for example, agriculture, business, labour), and the cabinet secretaries are expected to represent those interests as well. While these roles are related, they are not always compatible.

Further complicating the task of a cabinet secretary is the fact that he or she is not the only political appointee at the head of a presumably loyal and neutral civil service establishment. Even the Department of Education in 2004 had eight Assistant Secretaries plus a Chief Financial Officer, a General Counsel, an Inspector General, and a Commissioner for the Rehabilitation Services Administration, all appointed by the president with Senate confirmation, plus four more officials appointed by the president without Senate confirmation and 20 non-career Senior Executive Service positions. While all looking like subordinates on an organization chart, however, particularly in the less central departments like Education, some of them may have been appointed to represent groups that are not in sympathy with all of the president's programme, or, alternatively, to serve as a check on a cabinet secretary who was appointed for that reason.

Independent regulatory agencies

If one accepts Harold Lasswell's (1950) definition of politics as being the answer to the question 'who gets what, when, and how', everything that government does, and a lot besides, is political. Notwithstanding this fact, however, there has been a strong tendency in the United States to want to get politics (meaning primarily, but not exclusively, party politics) out of government. This is particularly reflected in the independent regulatory commissions. Although generally listed as part of the executive branch in simple tripartite categorizations, they are deliberately insulated from direct presidential (and congressional) control.

The first of these agencies, the Interstate Commerce Commission (ICC), was established in 1887 in response to perceived abuses by monopoly transportation providers, particularly railroads.[7] It was followed by the Federal Trade Commission (1915), the Federal Power Commission (1920—since 1977, the Federal Energy Regulatory Commission), the Federal Radio Commission (1927—succeeded by the Federal Communications Commission in 1935), and then a large number of additional agencies beginning in the New Deal. These agencies combine quasi-legislative (rule making) and quasi-judicial (licensing and penalty assessing) functions with more traditionally executive functions. They also deal with highly complex fields in which technical expertise rather the ideology might be seen to define the public interest, and in which frequent review and adjustment of rules are likely to be necessary. Moreover, many of them are responsible for fields with enormous economic implications.

The independent regulatory commissions are headed by boards appointed by the president subject to confirmation by the Senate, for staggered fixed terms (which vary among commissions, but generally are either five or seven years). The commission chairs are also designated by the president. No more than half (rounded up) of the members can be of a single political party. The commissions do not report to the president, and their members cannot be removed by him, but over time a president will have appointed a majority, or even all, of a commission's members.

More significant than the possibility that a single president will come to dominate commissions that are supposed to be insulated from partisan politics has been the danger that a commission will be 'captured' by the interests they are supposed to be regulating—through expectations of future employment in those industries; payment of lecture fees, transportation and hotel costs at conferences; in private meetings (limited, but not eliminated, by the Government-in-the-Sunshine Act of 1976, which requires that most agency meetings be held in public). Even when procedural regularity is maintained, however, it remains the case that an industry with billions of dollars at stake is almost always better able to present its case than are the representatives of an amorphous public interest. Obviously, all of this is a greater problem for a president who wants strong regulation than it is for one who favours deregulation in the first place.

Although not strictly a regulatory commission, the Board of Governors of the Federal Reserve system is a particularly important agency in this mould. The Board has seven members, appointed for an unusually long term of 14 years, from whom the president designates a chairman (with a four-year term)—a position held by Alan Greenspan from 1987 to 2005. 'The Fed' is the American central bank, and is responsible for American monetary policy. Thus a major policy instrument is out of the hands of the president and Congress (unless they were to amend the law), and given different time horizons and different preferred trade-offs among inflation, unemployment, economic growth, a rising stock market, etc., this has sometimes led to conflict between the Fed and the 'political' branches of government. Beyond the independence granted by long and fixed terms of office, the Fed is more financially independent than most agencies because it generates roughly $800 million in income, mostly interest on the government bonds in its portfolio.

A second variety of independent agency are those headed by presidential appointees who are responsible to the president in the same way as cabinet secretaries, but are not attached to any cabinet department. Examples include the Environmental Protection Agency (EPA), the Central Intelligence Agency, and NASA.

A third type is government corporations, of which by far the largest is the United States Postal Service (USPS), which replaced the cabinet-level Post Office Department in 1970. Other examples include the Federal Deposit Insurance Corporation and the Tennessee Valley Authority. Like the regulatory commissions, these are headed by presidentially appointed boards and are subject to congressional oversight, but basically are expected to operate according to normal business practices. In a somewhat different category, the Corporation for Public Broadcasting (CPB, which describes itself as 'a private corporation funded by the American people') is structurally similar to other government corporations, but (unlike the BBC or the now-defunct Independent Broadcasting Authority in the UK) does not operate either broadcasting or production facilities, and indeed is specifically prohibited from doing so; instead of being run like a business, the statute governing the CPB identifies it as a 'nonprofit corporation . . . which will not be an agency or establishment of the United States Government', although it is hard to see how an agency whose directors are appointed by the president and confirmed by the Senate, and whose income comes overwhelmingly (85 per cent in 2003) in the form of a federal appropriation could reasonably be called anything else.

The presidential establishment

Early presidents had very few staff members working directly for them, and with the exception of a single secretary to sign land grant patents during the administration of Andrew Jackson, until 1857 they paid for these staff members from their own resources. By 1930, the publicly provided White House staff consisted of little more than the Secretary to the President, two other secretaries, and an administrative assistant.[8] Additional presidential confidants might be placed in other government positions (for example, assistant secretary in some cabinet department) or simply give advice informally. A number of agencies (Committee on Public Information, War Industries Board, National Defense Council) were created during the First World War, but allowed to lapse in the return to 'normalcy' of the 1920s. Early in his first term, Franklin Roosevelt created an Executive Council, but it consisted of the heads of other agencies, and had only one professional staff assistant.

The unsatisfactory nature of these arrangements led Roosevelt to name a committee, which had been selected so that it would say what Roosevelt wanted to hear, to recommend reforms, and in 1939 resulted in the establishment of the Executive Office of the President (EOP) by an executive order authorized by Act of Congress. The actual organization of the EOP is largely at the discretion of the president. Originally, it consisted of four units; by Roosevelt's death in 1945, there were six; and by the end of Truman's second term in 1953, there were 11. In 2004, the EOP included the Office of Management and Budget, the Council of Economic Advisors, the Council on Environmental Quality, the Office of the US Trade Representative, the Office of Science and Technology Policy, the Office of National Drug Control Policy, the National Security Council, the Domestic Policy Council, the Office of Faith-Based and Community Initiatives, and the Foreign Intelligence Advisory Board. It also included the White House Office and the Office of the Vice-President, plus a number of smaller units.

Some of these agencies, like the National Security Council, formally consist of cabinet members or other high officials. In these cases, the real addition is their professional staff. These staffers, like members of the Council of Economic Advisors, are supposed to improve policy by providing the president with expert advice and options. How effective they are in this largely depends on the president; not all presidents want options rather than validation of preconceptions, and they can choose their advisers based not only on the quality of the advice, but also on the substance of the advice they expect.

Other agencies, particularly the Office of Management and Budget, are intended to further presidential control and coordination. In addition to its role in preparing the executive budget, and in clearing departmental proposals for legislation and overseeing executive agency testimony before Congress (ostensibly with regard to their budgetary implications, but in reality for their conformity with presidential objectives more generally), OMB is also the 'central regulatory reviewer' and oversees the collection and dissemination of information within and from the executive.

Agencies like the Office of the US Trade Representative, the Office of Global Communications, or the Office of National Drug Policy Control are intended both to unify control over activities that cut across department lines and to provide more direct presidential control over activities that would normally be separated from the White House by many layers of bureaucracy. Their location in the EOP is also meant to signal their importance to the president.

As the EOP has grown, many of the problems of coordination, conflicting objectives and loyalties, and bureaucratic infighting that made presidential control of the executive branch problematic before the EOP was created have come to afflict the EOP itself. The president still needs a corps of aides whose only loyalty is to him and his programme. For this reason, increasingly, real influence has shifted not only from the executive departments to the EOP, but from the EOP in general to the White House staff in particular. According to a *Washington Post* report, on 12 June 2004 the White House staff included roughly 430 people, topped by 16 people with the title 'Assistant to the President' (plus one 'Senior Advisor to the President'—Karl Rove) with annual salaries of $157,000 (86.5 per cent of the vice-president's salary of $181,400, and just under the salary of a rank-and-file member of Congress). Altogether, the White House Office includes roughly 100 policy staff appointed by the president without Senate confirmation.

More than any other group of high officials, the senior White House Staff tend to be people with long-time personal connections to the president who appointed them; seven of the 17 top advisers in June 2004 had direct ties to George Bush when he was Governor of Texas.

Aside from Karl Rove, widely regarded as the president's chief political strategist, whose position epitomized the pre-eminently political nature of the White House staff, the positions of the other 16 most senior staff underscore what is important for a president. Five—the Chief of Staff plus his deputy, the Chief of Staff to the vice-president, and a Staff Secretary (since appointed, but not at the time of writing confirmed, to a circuit judgeship), and the Assistant to the President for Presidential Personnel—were in charge of coordination within the White House and the executive branch more generally. Two were concerned with economic and domestic policy (within a year the domestic policy assistant was Secretary of Education). Three were concerned with security policy: the National Security Advisor (within a year Secretary of State), her deputy (who succeeded her as National Security Advisor), and Homeland Security. One was in charge of Legislative Affairs, that is, Congress. Two were concerned with legal matters: the White House Counsel (within a year Attorney General), and his deputy. Finally, three were in charge of presenting the president to the outside world: the Assistant to the President for Speech Writing and Policy Advisor, the Press Secretary (whose primary responsibility is the White House Press Corps), and the Assistant to the President for Communications (responsible for the rest of the media).

The moves from the White House staff to cabinet positions are not entirely matters of promotion. In part, they reflect instead the increased ability of a second-term president to place his own loyalists in these positions without as much concern for balance. In areas in which the president chooses or is forced to be involved, the greatest political assets are proximity to the president and 'face time' with him, and these make the White House staff central actors in the policy-making process.

Presidential inexperience and transition

The presidency of the United States, combining world military and diplomatic leadership with responsibility for domestic security and governance, is a job for which there probably could be no adequate preparation. Nonetheless, as is evident in Table 5.2, which lists all 41 men who have served as President of the United States, a review of recent incumbents suggests that American presidents come to the White House unusually ill prepared in comparison to the leaders of many other countries.

Except for George H. W. Bush, who had been vice-president and held a number of appointive offices, including the directorship of the Central Intelligence Agency (CIA), the last president elected who had any significant experience in national government or in foreign affairs was Richard Nixon in 1972. Every other president in the last thirty years has been a former state governor. While this has given them executive experience, it means that

TABLE 5.2	Presidents of the United States		

President	Party	Served	Most recent prior government position
George Washington	nd	1789–1797	President of the Constitutional Convention
John Adams	F	1797–1801	Sitting Vice-President
Thomas Jefferson	D–R	1801–1809	Sitting Vice-President
James Madison	D–R	1809–1817	Secretary of State
James Monroe	D–R	1817–1825	Secretary of War
John Quincy Adams	D	1825–1829	Secretary of State
Andrew Jackson	D	1829–1837	Senator
Martin Van Buren	D	1837–1841	Sitting Vice-President
William Henry Harrison	W	1841	Ambassador
John Tyler	W	1841–1845	Vice-President; succeeded on death of the President
James K. Polk	D	1845–1849	Governor
Zachary Taylor	W	1849–1850	General
Millard Fillmore	W	1850–1853	Vice-President; succeeded on death of the President
Franklin Pierce	D	1853–1857	Representative
James Buchanan	D	1857–1861	
Abraham Lincoln	R	1861–1865	Representative
Andrew Johnson	D	1865–1869	Vice-President; succeeded on death of the President
Ulysses S. Grant	R	1869–1877	General
James A. Garfield	R	1877–1881	Representative
Chester A. Arthur	R	1881–1885	Vice-President; succeeded on death of the President
Grover Cleveland	D	1885–1889 1893–1897	Governor
Benjamin Harrison	R	1889–1893	Senator
William McKinley	R	1897–1901	Governor
Theodore Roosevelt	R	1901–1909	Vice-president; succeeded on death of the President
William H. Taft	R	1909–1913	Secretary of War
Woodrow Wilson	D	1913–1921	Governor

continues

Table 5.2 continued

President	Party	Served	Most recent prior government position
Warren G. Harding	R	1921–1923	Senator
Calvin Coolidge	R	1923–1929	Vice-president; succeeded on death of the President
Herbert Hoover	R	1929–1933	Secretary of Commerce
Franklin D. Roosevelt	D	1933–1945	Governor
Harry S. Truman	D	1945–1953	Vice-president; succeeded on death of the President
Dwight D. Eisenhower	R	1953–1961	General
John F. Kennedy	D	1961–1963	Senator
Lyndon B. Johnson	D	1963–1969	Vice-president; succeeded on death of the President
Richard M. Nixon	R	1969–1974	Former Vice-president
Gerald R. Ford	R	1974–1977	Vice-president; succeeded on resignation of the President[2]
Jimmy Carter	D	1977–1981	Governor
Ronald Reagan	R	1981–1989	Governor
George H. W. Bush	R	1989–1993	Sitting Vice-president
Bill Clinton	D	1993–2001	Governor
George W. Bush	R	2001–	Governor

Parties: nd, no designation; F, Federalist; D–R, Democratic–Republican; D, Democrat; W, Whig; R, Republican

[1] Arthur is the only president of the United States never himself elected to any office, including the presidency.

[2] Gerald Ford was appointed vice-president by President Nixon under the terms of the Twenty-fifth Amendment, following the resignation of Spiro Agnew on his conviction on tax charges.

they come to the White House without experience in the most important policy areas of presidential responsibility, and without experience in dealing with Congress.

This lack of national experience may partially explain why senators have often been chosen as running mates. (Another reason is undoubtedly that with a six-year term, senators often can run for vice-president without risking their Senate seats.) The question is why senators have not made particularly successful presidential candidates: the last person to go directly from the Senate to the White House was John Kennedy in 1960, and the only other senator to do this in the twentieth century was Warren Harding in 1920.

Rather than being a paradox, it appears that precisely the experience with a range of policy that makes a senator an attractive vice-presidential candidate, and would prepare him or her to be president, has proven a liability as a presidential candidate. Senators have to have taken positions on a range of national issues that can come back to be used against them in a presidential campaign. On most of these questions, an ex-governor has no record at all, and can tailor his positions to the national constituency of the moment.

One consequence of this combination of inexperience with national, and particularly international, affairs and the fact that a governor (and in many respects a senator as well) will have made his prior political career almost entirely within a single state—that a successful candidate for the White House will have spent at least two years building a national support coalition to the contrary notwithstanding—is to make the roughly 11 weeks between election day and inauguration day extremely important. On the one hand, even if many posts can be left vacant until after the new president has taken office, many hundreds of key posts must be filled immediately—and for reasons described above, many, if not most, of them will be filled by people the president-elect does not know. And given the now-standard practice of FBI background checks on potential appointees, the time pressure under which these decisions must be made is only increased. This gives tremendous power to the president's transition team, who, even if they do not make the final decisions, will be instrumental in constructing the short-lists from which appointments are made. On the other hand, the president-elect, who until election day has had to speak in oversimplified and distorted campaign rhetoric, must prepare to face the reality of problems in areas about which he has not previously had any experience. The degree to which he uses the transition period to discard the ideological blinkers which may have been useful on the campaign trail but are likely to be disastrous as guides to real policy—even if it means discarding, or at least supplementing, his long-time advisers—bears mightily on his likely success as president.

The vice-presidency

Although the vice-president is only 'a heartbeat away' from the White House, and although five of the 12 presidents since 1940 had been vice-president (two succeeding to the presidency on the death, and one on the resignation, of the president, and two elected in their own right), the constitutional position of the vice-presidency is still well summarized in Daniel Webster's reputed reason for declining nomination to the office: 'I do not propose to be buried until I am dead.' The only constitutionally prescribed duty of the office is to preside over the Senate (and except on ceremonial occasions, the vice-president rarely does that), and the only power is to cast the deciding vote in case of ties.

Traditionally, the vice-president's primary contribution to the presidency was electoral: to 'balance the ticket' by representing a different section of the country and perhaps also a different wing of the party than the presidential nominee. Naturally, selection on the basis of difference was not conducive to a close working relationship. The dual role of the vice-president, with one foot in the executive and the other in Congress, also inhibited presidential confidence, as perhaps did the role of the vice-president as a living reminder of the president's own mortality.

In the years since Harry Truman became president without ever having been told about the atomic bomb project while he was vice-president, the position of the vice-presidency has been significantly increased by statute and practice. In 1949, the vice-president was made one of the four statutory members of the National Security Council. The escalating demands on the president's time have led to greater use of the vice-president as a stand-in for the president on second-order occasions ('attending a lot of funerals in funny little countries', as George H. W. Bush put it when he was vice-president), although Richard Nixon famously turned one such trip to his advantage in his 'kitchen debate' with Soviet Premier Nikita Khrushchev at the US Trade and Cultural Fair in Moscow in 1959. The vice-president may also be used as a spokesman or hatchet-man, able to say things that would be impolitic from the president himself.

While senators have become frequent running mates for presidential challengers (Quayle in 1988, Gore in 1992, Edwards in 2004), vice-presidents have taken on the role of natural successors to presidents who have reached their two-term limit (G. H. W. Bush in 1988, Gore in 2000). However, whether this is a cause (the president has an incentive to try to vicariously hold the White House through his vice-president, and having a 'natural' successor minimizes intraparty conflict) or an effect (the vice-president is in a more prominent position to seek his party's nomination) of the vice-president's greater role, it remains true that the vice-presidency is what the president makes of it.

State governors

The chief executive of each of the 50 states is a directly elected governor. In the most general of terms, the governors occupy a position in their states that is analogous to that of the president at the federal level. In detail, however, both their constitutional and their political positions differ significantly, both from those of the president and from one another.

In the mid-1960s, Joseph Schlesinger proposed a five-part 'index of formal powers of the governorship' (Schlesinger 1965). The average scores for the 50 states, updated to 2002, are shown in Table 5.3, along with comparable measures for the presidency. Although neither president nor the average governor is more 'powerful' on each measure, for all but tenure potential the differences are quite large. Moreover, some of these figures actually

TABLE 5.3	Institutional powers of the president and state governors	
	President	Governors (2002)
Separately elected executive branch officials	5	2.9
Tenure potential	4	4.1
Appointment power	4	3.1
Budget power	1	3.1
Veto power	2	4.5

Source: Council of State Governments, Book of the States 2002 (Lexington, KY: Council of State Governments, 2002), p. 142

understate the differences between presidential and gubernatorial powers, as well, of course, as saying nothing about differences among the states.

The president looks most powerful with regard to separately elected executive branch officials. While a few states share with the federal government the characteristic of having only one independently elected executive official, most have a directly elected secretary of state, attorney general, and treasurer and/or comptroller, plus a variety of other elected officials, commissions, and boards. In 17 of the 45 states that have lieutenant governors (roughly the equivalent of the vice-presidency, although also with powers that vary widely among the states), that person is not elected jointly with the governor. In some cases, the result is a partisan division within the executive branch, and in any case, a governor has far less authority over a directly elected executive official than the president has with regard to an official whom he appointed.

With regard to tenure potential, the gubernatorial average masks enormous variation. At one extreme, the governors of seven states may serve an unlimited number of consecutive four-year terms. In 2005, New York Governor George Pataki was in the middle of his fourth consecutive four-year term. At the other extreme, the governor of Virginia has a four-year term, but cannot serve two consecutive terms, while the governors of New Hampshire and Vermont can be re-elected to an unlimited number of consecutive terms, but those terms are of only two years.

In Schlesinger's terms, the appointive power of governors is noticeably lower than that of the president because it is often shared with other elected officials, although in some cases governors can make appointments with no further approval required where the analogous appointment at the federal level would require Senate confirmation. On the other hand, Schlesinger's (1965) index excludes judicial appointments. While all federal judges are appointed by the president, simple gubernatorial appointment of state judges is a minority option. Quite aside from the fact that the sheer number of presidential appointments exceeds that available to a governor, their scope is greater as well.

With regard to budget power, the governors on average are more powerful than the president, but again there is wide variation. In Maryland, whose governor has the most extensive budgetary powers in the country, the legislature may reduce or restrict proposed spending in the executive budget but may not increase it, and may only authorize but not require the transfer of funds from one item to another. In Nebraska, increases in the executive budget require a three-fifths vote. At the other extreme, however, in Arizona, Colorado, and Texas, the legislature often simply ignores the governor's budget and produces one of its own.

The veto power of state governors also is usually stronger than that of the president, although until 1996 the governor of North Carolina had no veto power at all, and in a few states only a simple legislative majority is required to override the governor's veto. In at least 20 states, for example, a veto override requires a vote of two-thirds of the legislators elected, rather than two-thirds of those present and voting. Most significantly, however, in all but eight states the governor has an item veto, either over appropriations bills or more generally, which allows the governor to strike out particular appropriations or (in somewhat fewer cases) statutory sections, while signing the rest of the bill into law. While the president was given this power with respect to appropriations by the Line Item Veto Act of 1996, in 1998 the Supreme Court overturned the Act, ruling that line item veto power could only be granted through a constitutional amendment. In one respect, however, governors (and state legislatures) have weaker budgetary powers than the president and Congress; most state constitutions require that the state's operating budget be in balance and many require referendum approval for the sale of state bonds. As the perennial federal debt attests, the national government operates under no such restrictions.

As with the president, the political power of governors depends on the partisan composition of other branches of the government and their own charisma or popularity, as well as on their formal powers and the opportunities that those either give them or foreclose. It also depends on the institutional strength of legislative leaders; for example, a state assembly speaker with particularly extensive powers and long tenure may prove a strong challenge to the authority, even of an institutionally strong governor, of his or her own party.

The political power of governors is highly situational, and thus impossible meaningfully to track over time. Their institutional power, however, has in general increased since the 1960s, the one exception being with regard to budgetary powers, where legislative reforms over the last forty years have given some legislatures greater capacity to counterbalance extensive gubernatorial powers.

KEY TERMS

- commander-in-chief
- Executive Office of the President
- fast-track tariff negotiations
- head of government
- head of state
- independent regulatory commissions
- item veto

- lame duck
- Office of Management and Budget
- pocket veto
- State of the Union
- veto
- War Powers Resolution
- White House Office

NOTES

1 In particular, while foreign protests against capital punishment in the United States often are directed at the president, and ask him to take action to stop an execution, except for federal executions—which are extremely rare—the president has no legal authority to do anything.

2 A state of war with Japan was declared on 8 December 1941, the day after the Japanese attack on Pearl Harbor. War was declared against Germany and Italy after they declared war on 11 December, and against Bulgaria, Hungary, and Romania in June 1942.

3 Confirmation of presidential appointments requires a simple majority vote of the Senate. If an appointment that normally requires confirmation is made while the Senate is not in session, the president can make a 'recess appointment', which allows the nominee to serve for up to one year without confirmation.

4 Similarly, high officials are rarely fired because of policy disagreement or administrative failure—they, too, resign after a decent interval to spend more time at home. However, criminal indictment, personal scandal, or public statements that make the official an embarrassment may lead to more immediate departure from office. Somewhat lower in the hierarchy, both more direct firings or demands for resignation (for example, Michael Brown as head of the Federal Emergency Management Agency) and resignations on matters of principle (for example, the 2002 resignation of the Director of the Office of Regulatory Enforcement at the Environmental Protection Agency over (non)-enforcement of the Clean Air Act; a judge's resignation from the Foreign Intelligence Surveillance Court over President Bush's authorizing of domestic spying; a US diplomat who resigned to protect the administration's Iraq policy) occur somewhat more frequently.

5 This limitation was introduced by the Twenty-second Amendment, ratified in 1951, which was adopted in reaction to Franklin Roosevelt's election to four consecutive terms (although he died early in the fourth term). Until Roosevelt, whose third election took place in 1940, after war had broken out in Europe, although before the United States entered the war, even very popular presidents had followed the precedent set by George Washington and retired after two terms in office.

6 The departments, in the order of their achieving cabinet status (which is significant only in that it determines the order in which cabinet secretaries would succeed to the presidency in the event of simultaneous vacancies in the offices of Vice-President, Speaker of the House of Representatives, and President Pro Tempore of the Senate) are: State (1789); Treasury (1789); Defense (1947, but the successor of War 1789 and Navy 1798); Justice (1880, but ranked in presidential succession on the basis of the creation of the office of Attorney General in 1789); Interior (1849); Agriculture (created in 1862, but achieved cabinet status in 1889); Commerce (1913, successor of Commerce and Labor 1903); Labor (1913, successor of Commerce and Labor 1903); Health and Human Services (1979, but the successor of Health, Education, and Welfare 1953); Housing and Urban Development (1965); Transportation (1966); Energy (1977); Education (1979); Veterans Affairs (1988); Homeland Security (2002).

7 The ICC lost many of its functions in 1966 to the newly created Department of Transportation. Its functions were further reduced as part of the move towards deregulation, and the agency was abolished in 1995, with many of its (few) remaining functions transferred to the National Transportation Safety Board (created in 1967 and made entirely independent of the Department of Transportation in 1975).

8 The three secretaries were to be paid $10,000 per year each, and the total authorized spending for other members of the White House staff was $93,520 (45 Stat. 1230).

....

GUIDE TO FURTHER READING

ABERBACH, J. A. and M. A. PETERSON (eds.) (2005), *The Executive Branch* (Oxford: Oxford University Press).

A major collection of essays on the institutions of the executive branch.

BARBER, J. D. (1992), *The Presidential Character: Predicting Performance in the White House* (Englewood Cliffs, NJ: Prentice-Hall).

How the personal psychology of presidents affects their performance in office.

NELSON, M. (ed.) (2003), *The Presidency and the Political System* (Washington, DC: Congressional Quarterly Press).

A collection of essays on various aspects of the presidency.

RUDALEVIGE, A. (2005), *The New Imperial Presidency: Renewing Presidential Power after Watergate* (Ann Arbor, MI: University of Michigan Press).

How measures adopted after the Nixon administration to restrain presidential aggrandizement have been eroded to reconcentrate largely unchecked authority in the White House.

6

The Legislative Branch

Overview

The major topics of this chapter are the organization of Congress with particular reference to bicameralism, and the differences in composition and rules of the House of Representatives and Senate. Other major topics include: the importance of committees and subcommittees, both in the legislative process and with regard to oversight of the executive; the paradox of weak parties in chambers that are organized entirely along partisan lines; the basics of 'how a bill becomes a law,' emphasizing the importance of multiple veto points (including the possibility of a presidential veto) and of conference committees; and the strengths and limitations of the leaders of the congressional parties. Notwithstanding the intensification of partisan rancour within Congress, with regard to the overall control of legislation, it is still largely the case that 'there's no one in charge here'. This has important consequences for strategies of influence by interest groups, coalition-building by the administration, and the content of policy that ultimately is adopted.

If space in the Constitution is a valid indicator, then the Framers expected that Congress would be the dominant branch of the federal government. While there were strong and activist presidents—Jefferson, Jackson, Lincoln, Theodore Roosevelt, Wilson—until the presidency of Franklin Roosevelt with the Great Depression and the Second World War, both initiative and power lay primarily in the Congress, and the president was often more like chief clerk than chief executive. Although that clearly has changed, the American Congress remains an unusually strong and independent national legislature.

The organization of Congress

The Congress consists of two chambers: the Senate with 100 members, two from each state chosen for six-year terms with one-third coming up for election every two years; and the House of Representatives (henceforth the House) with 435 members apportioned among the states on the basis of population and chosen for two-year, non-overlapping, terms.[1] These differences have four significant consequences. First, because the electoral basis of the two chambers differs both with regard to the time of election and with regard to the weight accorded to different areas (in particular, with large urban areas more heavily represented in the House, and largely rural and less populous states more heavily represented in the Senate), it is possible for different parties to have majorities in the two houses, which has happened in four of the last 30 Congresses (1947–2006). Second, while the House must formally be reorganized after every biennial election, the Senate is a continuing body.[2] Third, at least in part because of its larger size, the House is more strictly organized and rule bound, whereas the Senate's rules are more flexible and the Senate generally proceeds by unanimous consent. Fourth, and again because of size, each senator serves on more committees, and therefore is in a position to be intimately involved in more policy areas, and to choose what those areas will be, than are members of the House.[3]

The presiding officer of the House of Representatives is the Speaker, who is elected by the full chamber, but since party unity on the resolution to organize the House is absolute, in fact the Speaker is chosen by the majority caucus.[4] Unlike the presiding officer of many parliaments, the Speaker is the leader of the majority party, and although he is expected to enforce the rules fairly (an expectation that is not always met), he is also expected to use his prerogatives in the interests of the majority party, and of the president *if* the president's party is the majority party in the House. Formally, the presiding officer of the Senate is the vice-president. In his absence, which is the norm, the formal presiding officer is the president pro tempore, who by tradition is the member of the majority party with the longest continuous service. In fact, reflecting that the presiding officer in the Senate has far less power than the Speaker of the House, the Senate chair usually is occupied by a junior member of the majority party as part of a process of apprenticeship into the Senate's norms and procedures.

Congress deals with four basic types of proposal. A *bill* is a proposal for a law; if approved by both houses and signed by the president (or allowed to become law without his signature), it becomes a statute. Most *joint resolutions* are similar to bills in that they have the force of law if approved by both houses and the president, but they generally deal with much more limited matters. What is often called the War Powers Act was actually a joint resolution enacted over the veto of President Nixon in 1973. Congress also uses a joint resolution to propose a constitutional amendment, in which case the president's approval is not required, but three-fourths of the states must ratify the proposal before it becomes part of the Constitution. A *concurrent resolution* does not require presidential approval, and does not have the force of law; it does require the approval of both houses. Concurrent resolutions are used to settle procedural matters internal to Congress (for example, to set the date for adjournment) and to express the sentiment or opinion of Congress as a whole. The annual budget resolution (see below) is a concurrent resolution. Finally, a simple resolution is internal to a single house, and is used to amend the rules of that house or to express its sentiment, for example to extend condolences to the family of a member who has died, or to give advice to the administration regarding some matter of policy.

Party unity in Congress

The traditional norm for parliaments is for there to be a clear demarcation between government and opposition. A party or coalition with a majority of the seats would expect to win all important votes with its own unanimous votes, and to be opposed unanimously by the other parties. Except for occasional free votes of conscience or with regard to issues of intense local concern, even minor breaks in party unity would be considered significant.

Although these norms of strict party discipline were always stronger in some parliaments than in others, and have weakened somewhat in recent decades, the contrast between them and the norms of the American Congress is stark. Except for procedural matters like the election of the Speaker, there are at most a handful of votes that see a majority made up exclusively of members of one party opposing a minority made up exclusively of the members of the other party. Indeed, only about half of the roll-call votes in Congress qualify as 'party unity votes,' meaning that majorities of the two parties were on opposite sides of the issue, and only about 45 per cent of the party unity votes in the 107th Congress (2001–02) saw as many as 90 per cent of the Democrats voting in the House on one side and 90 per cent of the Republicans on the other, and that was the highest proportion of 90–90 votes since before the First World War.[5] The proportion of 90–90 party votes in the Senate was a bit lower than in the House in the 107th Congress, but a bit higher in the 106th. During the entire period from 1950 to 1990, however, the proportion of 90–90 party votes in both houses hovered around (and more generally below) 10 per cent. While party has always been a significant predictor of the votes of members of Congress, and has become far more powerful as a predictor since the ideologically more united and more motivated Republicans regained control in the 1990s, there is only sparse evidence of party discipline of the sort common in parliamentary systems. To a very great extent, party unity is the result of agreement, loyalty, and negotiation rather than direction.

The significant increase in party unity since the 1990s, but also the degree to which disunity continues to be tolerated, are reflected clearly in the distribution of individual party unity scores.[6] In 1983, no member of the Senate had a party unity score as high as 95; in 2003, 62 senators had party unity scores at least that high. With top party unity scores of 97 in 1983, there was not much room for members of the House in 2003 to exhibit higher party unity than the most 'loyal' representatives in 1983, yet 94 members in 2003 did so with party unity scores of 98, 99, or 100 (Speaker Dennis Hastert, who generally only votes to break a tie or to emphasize the importance of a measure). At the other end of the scale, in 1983 there was one senator of each party with a party unity score below 50, indicating that he voted with the other party on more than half of the party unity votes; for the House, there were eight Republicans and nine Democrats who voted with the other party on at least 60 per cent of the party unity votes. By 2003, the most 'disloyal' Democrat in the House voted with the Republicans on 'only' 49 per cent of the party unity votes, while the corresponding figure for the Republicans was 'only' 35 per cent. In the Senate, the most disloyal Democrat was Zell Miller of Georgia, who voted with the Republicans on 91 per cent of the party unity votes (a higher level of Republican voting than five Republican senators) and ultimately was invited to give the keynote address at the

2004 Republican convention. Ignoring him, the lowest party unity scores in the 2003 Senate were 57 for the Democrats and 65 for the Republicans. Even those with the lowest scores remained members-in-good-standing of their caucuses. The most senior 'disloyalists' among the House Republicans were denied committee chairmanships to which their seniority might have entitled them, but they continued to chair subcommittees. Not only did the Republican 'disloyalists' in the Senate not lose their committee chairs, but the most disloyal among them (Lincoln Chafee of Rhode Island—the 'missing Linc' as some of his colleagues described him) in 2000 actually had a television campaign spot funded by the Republican Senatorial Campaign Committee which stressed his votes *against* important legislation that the Republican leadership had supported.

The key point here is that while party unity is valuable to the leadership, being the leaders of the majority (rather than the minority) party is even more valuable. Given that some disunity is the norm, and therefore not regarded as a serious sign of party weakness, and given the candidate-centric nature of many congressional election races, this may encourage leaders to allow, or even to encourage, members to vote against the party line when it is electorally expedient, and unlikely to affect the ultimate outcome anyway. Chafee voted against the Republican position, but this did not cause that legislation to be rejected. In part, this is so because defections from the majority party can be compensated by defections from the minority party, but it also encourages the majority leadership to maintain good relations with at least some members of the minority party. This incentive to be able to reach across party lines is particularly strong in a closely divided House, and is especially strong in the Senate, where 60 votes are needed to end a filibuster (that is, holding the floor for the purpose of obstructing business). Neither party has had such a majority on its own since 1979.

Another indicator of the permeability of the boundary between the parties in Congress is the frequency with which bills are co-sponsored by members of both parties. While this is unlikely on the most partisanly divisive legislation, the point here is that much legislation does not divide the parties. Indeed, even members who appear to be ideologically 'poles apart' (for example, arch-conservative Senator Orrin Hatch and archetypically liberal Edward Kennedy) will not infrequently collaborate on legislation, sometimes precisely in order to remove it from the realm of partisan division.

The roles and powers of congressional leaders

If there is an overarching principle of congressional leadership, it is fragmentation rather than concentration of power. This reached its heights in the 1950s, with committee chairmanships determined strictly by seniority (length of continuous service on that committee), and each chairman operating largely as an independent oligarch within his jurisdiction. Since then, there has been a significant reconcentration of power as the party caucuses have exercised more control over chairmanships. This reconcentration has been particularly evident in the House of Representatives, where the authority of the Speaker has been very significantly increased, although the Speakership still is weaker than it was in the days of 'Czar' Reed at the end of the nineteenth century, in the sense that the Speaker now exercises his powers less as an independent oligarch and more as the leader of the majority party. Moreover, although the ability to set the agenda can be very important, and the party leaders have the power to do a variety of things for members that can make their lives (both personal and political) more pleasant, much of the power exercised by the leaders is negative—the ability to prevent a bill from being considered or reported by a committee or to prevent it from coming to the floor—although failure to block a measure often can be traded for affirmative support on other questions.

In contrast to the leaders of many parliamentary parties, the leaders of the parties in Congress have few real sanctions at their disposal. Even if executive office were not constitutionally incompatible with membership in Congress, it would be in the gift of the president rather than congressional leaders. Although congressional leaders may be able to influence the flow of money (for example, through the use of leadership PACs[7]), and may have some celebrity value in campaigning for individual members, most members are already in a strong position to raise funds on their own. Most clearly in contrast to other countries, renomination and the right to use the party's name is won in primary elections, again limiting the ability of congressional leaders or formal party organizations to affect the re-election chances of individual members, although the Republican leadership in the House has shown some willingness in recent years to channel money to the primary campaigns of conservatives who want to challenge sitting

Republican members who have not been sufficiently loyal, thus giving some credibility to a threat that re-election chances will be adversely affected by indiscipline. Even within their own chambers, the range of rewards and punishments is limited: leaders may influence assignments to committees and the choice of committee chairmen[8] (far more so in the House than in the Senate), and even the allocation of offices and parking spaces, although most of these decisions are formally made either by committees or by the party caucuses acting on the recommendation of committees. While neither party any longer adheres strictly to a seniority rule, and indeed the Republicans have imposed a six-year cumulative term limit for holding the chairmanship of any individual committee, the value of the seniority system as a means of replacing internal conflict with a more or less automatic way of filling chairmanships remains apparent in both parties. Generally, party leaders are expected to use their powers first and foremost to 'keep peace in the family', which limits their use as weapons to impose decisions on the unwilling.

In the absence of the real ability to command, the greatest assets of the leaders of congressional parties are their power to control the agenda—a power that is substantially greater for the leader of the majority party, but which can be exercised to some extent by any member who is particularly skilful in exploiting the rules of the chamber—and their central position as brokers in the construction of majorities for particular pieces of legislation. Knowledge of what will be valuable to whom, and who might be willing to compromise on that question in exchange for something else, frequently gives the leadership the capacity not just to broker a coalition, but to choose which coalition to build and on what terms.

The most important leader in the House is the Speaker, who is both presiding officer and leader of the majority party. The Speaker determines the committee(s) to which bills are referred and also appoints his party's members of the Rules Committee and of conference committees (usually in consultation with the chairman of the committee that originally considered the bill). The Republican imposition of term-limits on committee chairmen has increased the relative power of the Speaker, by limiting the ability of committee chairmen to entrench individual power bases. The power to refer a bill to more than one committee has increased the Speaker's power by allowing him (or potentially her) to choose which committee will consider which parts of the bill, and to impose deadlines for committees to report on the bill, thus obviating the power of a committee chairman to kill a bill through inaction. In addition, conflicts between versions of the bill reported by different committees are resolved in the Rules Committee, which the Speaker effectively controls. When the other party controls the White House, the Speaker also becomes the principal national face of his own party. The Speaker has a range of opportunities to do good turns for the members of his party (appointments to special committees or task forces that will generate favourable publicity in the member's district, introductions to potential sources of financial support, practical advice from an experienced politician). The Speaker's task as party leader is obviously easier when the members of his party are in fundamental agreement and when they feel that they owe their positions to him.[9] Thus, Newt Gingrich was a very powerful Speaker at beginning of the 104th Congress, when the Republicans in the House felt that they owed their new majority status to him and his 'Contract With America'. When his confrontational style and ethical lapses led some members of his caucus to see him as a political liability, he was much weaker as Speaker, and after he led his party to a much poorer than expected result in the 1998 mid-term election, he was replaced.

The other principal leaders of the majority party in the House are the majority leader, the Whip, the chairman of the party caucus, and the chairman of the party congressional campaign committee. The majority leader is the Speaker's principal deputy in managing the schedule of the House, consulting with members, and representing the party before the public. The Whip is the communications director for the leadership. Along with a staff of assistant whips, the Whip is responsible for knowing what members want, and what they will tolerate, as well as keeping the members informed of party priorities and the schedule of the House. The minority party leadership structure is basically the same (absent, of course, the Speakership, which means that the minority leader is the top of the minority leadership hierarchy). The Senate leadership positions also are essentially the same as those in the House, except that there is no position equivalent to that of Speaker, so that the majority leader is, in fact, the leader of the majority party. This is not just a difference of title, however, in that the power of the Senate majority leader is far less than that of the Speaker—more akin to a 'herder of cats' than the commander of an army. Thus, for example, while the Speaker largely controls the agenda of the House, the majority leader in the Senate is more the central negotiator seeking an agreed schedule of action on the floor: a senator with great responsibilities, but rather less real power.

All of the party leadership positions are filled by election by the relevant party caucus. These elections have tended to be more hotly contested, particularly between the 'conservatives' and 'moderates', in the Republican caucuses, while the Democrats have had a more institutionalized pattern of succession from Whip to Leader, to Speaker (in the House, when they were in the majority). That each of the positions is elected individually means that there can be significant differences within the leadership, as illustrated by the election in 2006 of John Boehner as House majority leader over Roy Blunt (the Republican Whip, who had been acting as majority leader since the indictment of Majority Leader Tom DeLay had forced him to step down), who had been supported by Speaker Hastert.

Committees

As Woodrow Wilson observed, 'Congress in its committee-rooms is Congress at work'. In the 106th and 107th Congresses (1999–2002), 11,448 bills (plus 129 joint resolutions, 968 concurrent resolutions, and 1,296 simple resolutions) were introduced into the House of Representatives, and 6,468 bills (plus 109 joint resolutions, 322 concurrent resolutions, 761 simple resolutions) were introduced into the Senate. In contrast, between January 2001 and May 2004, only 1,119 bills were introduced into either house of the 37th Canadian Parliament. In even greater contrast, on 15 October 2005 there were only a total of 68 public bills to be considered during the 2005–06 session of the British Parliament, 32 of which were government bills. The obvious solution to what would otherwise be massive overload is to divide the work through the use of committees. Committees perform two additional functions. On the one hand, they divide the power as well as the work, allowing a large number of individual members to occupy significant positions as chairs of committees or subcommittees, while allowing even junior members at least to be little fish in a little pond. On the other hand, they encourage members, and by extension the Congress as a whole, to develop expertise in particular areas of policy, thereby putting themselves on a more equal footing *vis-à-vis* the executive.

There are three basic varieties of committee in Congress: select (or special); joint; and standing. Select committees are normally temporary, although, as its name implies, the House Permanent Select Intelligence Committee is not. They also generally do not have legislative authority. Select committees are used to study problems, to conduct investigations, to provide more intensive and continuous oversight of the executive than the schedule of a standing committee would allow, to provide a point of access for some interest groups, and to provide a platform for individual members.

Unlike select and standing committees, which are committees of either the House *or* the Senate, joint committees have members from both houses, and the chairmanship rotates between them. Joint committees are used for investigations (which in congressional parlance generally means drawing attention to an issue and putting information and positions into the public domain rather than truly investigating), and also where the House and Senate have a common administrative interest. In the 109th Congress, there were four more or less permanent joint committees: Library (overseeing the Library of Congress); Printing (overseeing the Government Printing Office); Economic (which undertakes studies and conducts hearings on a range of economic questions); Taxation (which provides a venue for coordination and cooperation of the highly specialized committee staffs of the two chambers, as well as expert staff from the Treasury Department). The other variety of joint committee is a House–Senate conference committee, appointed to reconcile differences in House and Senate versions of a specific bill, and dissolved after they make their report.

By far the most significant committees, however, are the standing committees. Authorized either by legislation or by the rules of the individual chambers, these committees consider legislation, both reducing the large number of bills introduced to a manageable number for consideration on the floor of the chamber and often substantially altering (or explicitly deciding not to alter) the content of the bills reported to the floor. They also conduct oversight hearings with regard to the executive agencies within their jurisdiction, and through the processes of authorization and appropriation control their ultimate budgets. In the 109th Congress (2005–06), there were 20 standing committees in the House (plus the Select Intelligence Committee) and 16 in the Senate (plus three select or special committees, and the Committee on Indian Affairs). These are listed in Table 6.1, along with the number of subcommittees of each.

TABLE 6.1	Committees and subcommittees of Congress		
House		**Senate**	
Agriculture	5	Agriculture, Nutrition, and Forestry	4
Appropriations	10	Appropriations	12
Armed Services	6	Armed Services	6
Budget	0	Banking, Housing, and Urban Affairs	5
Education and Workforce	5	Budget	0
Energy and Commerce	6	Commerce, Science, and Transportation	10
Financial Services	5	Energy and Natural Resources	4
Government Reform	7	Environment and Public Works	4
Homeland Security	5	Finance	5
House Administration	0	Foreign Relations	7
International Relations	7	Health, Education, Labor, and Pensions	4
Judiciary	5	Homeland Security and Government Affairs	3
Resources	5	Judiciary	8
Rules	2	Rules and Administration	0
Science	4	Small Business and Entrepreneurship	0
Small Business	4	Veterans' Affairs	0
Standards of Official Conduct	0	Indian Affairs	0
Transportation and Infrastructure	6		
Veterans' Affairs	4		
Ways and Means	6	Select Committee on Ethics	0
Select Committee on Intelligence	4	Select Committee on Intelligence	0
		Special Committee on Aging	0

Both the size of standing committees, and the ratio of majority to minority members, is decided at the beginning of each Congress. These reflect both the popularity and importance of the committee (adding committee slots can be a cheap way for leaders to satisfy their followers) and the party balance of the chamber as a whole.[10] The majority party in the chamber is assured a majority on every committee and subcommittee, as well as all of the committee (and subcommittee) chairmanships.

Standing committee membership is also decided at the beginning of each Congress, but starting from the presumption that all returning members will stay on the same committees unless they ask to be transferred or are forced off by a change in the party ratio. Newly elected members, or returning members who wish to transfer (generally to a more powerful or prestigious committee) apply to the appropriate committee of their own party (the Steering Committee for the House Democrats and Republicans; the Committee on Committees for Senate Republicans; the Steering and Coordination Committee for the Senate Democrats). All of these committees, but especially the House Republican Steering Committee, are institutionally biased in favour of the leadership.[11] These committees make recommendations to the full caucus, which ordinarily (but no longer as 'automatically' as in the past) approves them. They then go to the full chamber, which formally elects all committee members. The party committees try to balance four basic criteria (within the constraints of number of slots and limitations on the number of 'plum' committees on which a member may serve). The most obvious is the interests and abilities of the applicants. Although the numbers may require that some members be given assignments that they do not want, the committees try to satisfy their clienteles. A member with particular expertise (a physician, a retired military officer, an industrialist, a farmer) will be favoured for a committee where that knowledge will be valuable. The second is re-election value. Members generally want, and to the extent possible will be given, assignments to committees that will allow them to serve their constituents in particularly visible ways. The combined effect of these two criteria creates significant biases in the composition of committees. For example, although agriculture committees deal with legislation that may have profound, if diffuse, impact on consumers, they are dominated by members from farm states (in 2005, 14.7 per cent of the members of the House, but only 2.2 per cent of the House Agriculture Committee, came from New York, New Jersey, or New

England). Similarly, members from localities with large military bases are over-represented on the military affairs committees, and so forth. The third criterion is seniority. Other things being equal, a member with longer continuous service in the chamber will be given priority over a more junior member. Finally, attention is given to balance, balance among ideological wings of the party (in some cases to assuring balance, but in others to assure the loyalty to the party and its leadership of those put on the committee), among regions of the country, and to some extent also to counteracting the substantive biases that result from the first two criteria.

That the majority party controls all of the chairmanships does not assure uniformity of political orientation, however. Aside from the paucity of effective means, or will, to impose discipline, the committee assignment process results in a strong selection bias. Moreover, while long service on a committee allows a member to develop expertise in a field, it also leads to established relationships with bureaucrats, interest organizations, and other members that tend to entrench particular priorities and ways of thinking. Additionally, each committee chairman brings his or her own orientations and priorities to a position of considerable power.

Finally, one other type of 'committee' deserves mention—the various congressional caucuses, not of the parties but of members who share an ethnicity (for example, Congressional Black Caucus, Congressional His-panic Caucus) or concern about a particular set of issues (for example, Women's Issues, Arts, India and Indian-Americans, Rural [issues], or Rural Education). Except for the Black Caucus, which is generally aligned with the Democrats simply because there have been almost no Black Republicans, they are almost always bipartisan, and co-chaired by a Democrat and a Republican. Aside from occasionally coordinating demands to be made on the leadership of the parties, these caucuses serve as fora for sharing information and developing cross-party legislative proposals.

How a bill becomes a law

Only members of Congress can introduce a bill or resolution for consider-ation. Executive agencies often provide a draft of proposed legislation, but they must find a senator or member of the House to introduce it form-ally. Although many important bills are understood to be central to the president's programme and to have been drafted in the White House, there are no 'government bills' in the sense in which the term is used in many other countries. The nearest equivalent are so-called presidential support votes, which are votes on bills on which the president has taken a public position. Except that bills relating to taxation must be introduced in the House, the legislative powers of the two chambers of Congress are equal.[12]

After a bill is introduced, it is immediately referred to committee. In the House, bills are referred by the Speaker; in the Senate, the referral is generally made by the parliamentarian, subject to (rare) appeal to the floor.[13] Particularly in the House, a bill may be sent to more than one committee (multiple referral), either sequentially or in parts. Because a bill's fate can be importantly determined by the choice of committee to which it is referred, members may try to package bills in ways that will steer them to one committee rather than another. For major legislation, this is impossible since the content is well known. Most proposed legislation, however, is not in this category, so that, for example, calling a payment by truckers a 'fee' rather than a 'tax' could affect whether it is sent to Ways and Means (tax) or to Transportation and Infrastructure (fee).

For many bills, committee referral is the end of the road; the committee chairman never schedules consideration, and the bill dies. Indeed, some bills are introduced with no expectation that they will be considered, but merely to allow the member to claim credit with some constituency. If the bill is to be considered, the chairman may schedule hearings, at which bureaucrats, group representatives, and other interested parties can express their views and offer advice, or the chairman may refer the bill to a subcommittee whose chairman may, or may not, schedule hearings. The subcommittee and the full committee then consider the bill in detail, frequently changing it substantially, or even rewriting it entirely, vote on the bill, and, if a majority approves, the committee returns it to the full chamber along with a written report, possibly including a minority report as well. Throughout the committee process, the committee staff, who effectively work for the chairman and the ranking minority member, can play a crucial role by arranging witnesses, providing information, framing issues, drafting amendments—and sometimes slipping them in at the last minute (either with or without the connivance of the chairman).

Once reported out of committee, a bill must compete for time before the full chamber. The procedures used by the two houses are quite different.

In the House of Representatives, the norm is for the bill to go to the Rules Committee, which reports a special rule, setting the conditions for debate, including the amount of time allowed (usually one or two hours, but for particularly important or controversial legislation as much as ten hours) and who will control that time (generally, the chairman and ranking minority member of the substantive committee that considered the bill), and either allowing (open rule), limiting (modified rule), or prohibiting (closed rule) amendment of the bill once it goes to the floor. Because the majority members (of which there are a disproportionate number) of the Rules Committee are appointed by the Speaker, it is effectively controlled by him. Most rules, which technically are resolutions of the House, begin '. . . at any time after the adoption of this resolution the Speaker may . . . declare the House resolved into the Committee of the Whole House on the state of the Union for consideration of the bill . . . ', thus giving the Speaker the authority to decide when, and if, the bill actually will be debated. Almost all debate on the bill and proposed amendments takes place while the House is constituted as the Committee of the Whole, with a quorum of 100 rather than 218. Once the time allotted to the bill by 'its rule' has expired, the bill as amended goes back to the House *per se*, which must approve it, generally by a majority of those present and voting, and generally using a recorded vote.

The Speaker also controls the other major route to the floor of the House—suspension of the rules—through his power to recognize members. Under this procedure, debate is limited to 40 minutes and there can be no amendments. While generally used for minor and uncontroversial legislation, it can also be used as a way to avoid unfriendly amendments or for the Speaker to facilitate the defeat of a bill that he opposes but is required by political exigencies to call to the floor, since passage under suspension of the rules requires a two-thirds majority.

Senate procedures are much less formal, and tend to a much greater degree than those of the House to favour the rights of the minority over the prerogatives of the majority. 'Some commentators say the Senate has only two rules (unanimous consent and exhaustion) and three speeds (slow, slower, and slowest)' (Davidson and Oleszek 2000: 247). Most bills come to the floor under unanimous consent agreements, which are the equivalent of special rules in the House in that they set limits on debate and amendment in the interest of expediting the conduct of business. The Senate majority leader, like the Speaker and chairman of the Rules Committee in the

House, plays a central role in drafting these agreements and in scheduling business on the floor. But unlike the House leadership, who can impose their decisions by majority vote (assuming that they can hold their caucus together, which on procedural matters tends to be relatively easy), the Senate leader can only 'impose' his decisions with the acquiescence of all of the other 99 senators. As a result, advance negotiation and compromise, including especially with the minority leader, are essential.

As in the House, where a bill can be forced from a committee through a discharge petition signed by 218 members (although bills subject to discharge petitions have almost never been passed, the threat of a petition can be a useful spur to committee action), the Senate has a variety of ways to force a committee to act, or to by-pass it altogether. The most common is simply to attach a stalled bill as an amendment to another. Unlike the House, the rules of which require that amendments be germane (relevant to the subject of the original bill), the Senate has no germaneness rule.

Senators have a variety of ways in which they can obstruct business, some formally enshrined in the rules and others equally enshrined in the 'folkways' of the Senate. By tradition, any Senator can put a 'hold' on any floor action simply by asking his or her leader not to schedule action.[14] It is, however, up to the majority leader to decide whether a hold will, in fact, be honoured. A filibuster (holding the floor for the purpose of obstructing business) is in the rules in the sense that, unlike most bodies, the Senate cannot shut off debate by a simple majority vote. Rather, cloture requires the votes of 60 senators (67 for proposed changes to the rules), allowing 41 senators effectively to prevent the Senate from doing its business.[15] In practice, rather than allowing the Senate to grind to a halt, business that would be subject to a filibuster and which lacks the necessary support for cloture to be invoked, will simply be postponed indefinitely or withdrawn. Moreover, the Senate has also developed a system that allows other business to proceed 'in parallel' with a filibuster. In effect, by lowering the stakes for the leadership, and so making them less likely to devote the time and resources required to invoke cloture, this actually increases the likelihood that the filibuster ultimately will be successful in getting the matter withdrawn.

As with any social system that gives individual members such wide latitude to be obstructionist, the Senate depends on its members not to abuse their position. Just where 'hard ball politics' ends, and abuse begins, however, often is in the eye of the beholder. Generally, holds and threatened filibusters have been used to force the majority to make some accommodation to the minority, not to thwart it altogether. Particularly as the conservative wing of the Republican Party have become more aggressive in their attempts to reshape constitutional jurisprudence by reshaping the federal judiciary, Democratic use of these procedures to block the confirmation of judicial appointees that the Democratic minority find too extreme (as the Republicans had used them to block many of President Clinton's judicial nominees when the Democrats controlled the White House) has become a flash point. Rather than withdrawing objectionable nominees in favour of more 'moderate conservatives', the Republicans in 2005 accused the Democrats of illegitimate obstructionism, and threatened what was dubbed 'the nuclear option' of using a procedural ruling from the chair (which would be occupied by the vice-president, in his role as President of the Senate) to bar filibusters of judicial nominations altogether. Typically for the Senate, after considerable posturing on both sides, a compromise—heavily weighted in favour of the majority—was reached.

Once a bill is approved in the chamber in which it was introduced, it is sent (in amended form) to the other chamber, where the whole process is repeated. Unless the second chamber passes the bill sent to it in exactly the same form as the first, the bill must either shuttle back and forth between the two chambers until they agree, or, in the case of the most significant legislation (less than 20 per cent of the legislation actually passed by Congress), it is sent to a conference committee. The members of this joint committee formally are named by the Speaker and the presiding officer of the Senate, but usually are chosen by the chairman and ranking minority member of the standing committee that considered the legislation in the first place. These appointments can be crucially important, and in recent years have become increasingly politicized. Ostensibly, the purpose of a conference committee is to reach a compromise on the differences between the two versions of the legislation, but it is not bound to do so. Conference committees may adopt provisions that had been explicitly rejected in one house, or add provisions that were not even considered.[16] While either house can use the resolution creating the conference committee to instruct its conferees, these instructions are not binding. When the conference committee has finished its work, its report is returned to both houses as a privileged motion, on which a simple yes or no vote is taken without the possibility of further amendment.

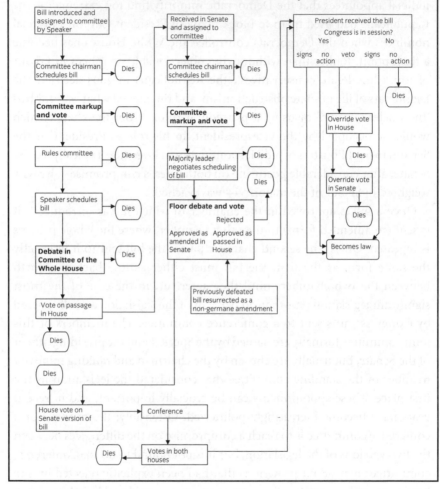

FIGURE 6.1

Path of a bill introduced in the House of Representatives. (Bold face indicates points at which substantial amendment is likely. This is a highly simplified schematic, which in particular omits the possibility of multiple committee referral in the House as well as alternative routes to the House floor, such as suspension of the rules or special calendars)

If the bill is passed in both houses of Congress, it is sent to the president for signature or veto. If vetoed, it is returned to the house in which it originated for a vote on whether or not to override the veto, and, if successful there, to the other house for its own override vote.

Although, as illustrated in Figure 6.1, this is a system with many dead ends and many veto players, the ultimate output (like the original input) is prodigious in comparative terms. The 106th and 107th Congresses produced 987 laws. The 37th Canadian Parliament, sitting for almost as long, only produced 127 laws—about the same number as the British Parliament produces in a comparable time period. Of course, raw numbers of enactments tell only a small part of the story. At least as significant is the fact that American legislation tends to be far more detailed, for example establishing detailed rules that legislation in other countries would merely authorize administrative officials to make, or allocating funds to a long list of specific projects where the parliaments of other countries would merely appropriate money to broad classes of activity, and allow the administration to allocate it to particular projects.[17]

The budgetary process

All money spent by the federal government must be appropriated by Congress. At the level of individual appropriations, this is a two-step process. First, legislation is passed that *authorizes* the appropriation. This is generally part of the legislation dealing with the substantive policy, and so is dealt with by the substantive policy committees, which are, therefore, usually identified as authorizing committees. After the expenditure of money is authorized, the funds then must be appropriated in separate legislation, dealt with by the appropriations committees of the two houses. There is no requirement that money authorized actually be appropriated, which makes the appropriations committees extremely powerful, a power enhanced by their capacity to add 'strings' to appropriations, for example requiring that money authorized for highway construction be used for specific road projects. Although not all such earmarked appropriations are properly identified as 'pork barrel', and not all 'pork' comes in the form of earmarked appropriations, this is a major method of providing particular benefits for a member's district or state, for which he or she will later take credit. Aside from the great policy power wielded by the appropriations committees, this ability to direct funds to one's own district or state (or to those of one's colleagues in return for support on other matters) explains why these are such sought after committee assignments.

That individual members of Congress can often claim credit for appropriations, particularly locally popular 'pork barrel' spending, while Congress as an institution takes the blame for higher taxes or deficits, is one of the reasons for the phenomenon of even quite senior members campaigning for re-election by 'running against Congress'. Along with the division of authorizing authority among many different committees and having different committees responsible for appropriations and taxation, it helps explain why Congress has been notoriously unable to control its own profligacy. From time to time, fiscal conservatives have proposed amendments to the Constitution that would require a 'balanced budget', but given the history of creative accounting both by Congress and the president to make the budget appear closer to balance than it really is, it is unlikely that these would be any less damaging or more effective than the European Union's 'growth and stability pact'.

Although balanced budget amendments have died in Congress, the Congress has taken less drastic steps to try to limit, or at least to rationalize, spending. While these have gone through a number of iterations, there have been two basic thrusts. The first was to require Congress to set an overall spending target in a budget resolution to be adopted early in the budgetary process, establish budget committees in each house to oversee the process and reconcile (subject to enactment by Congress as a whole) appropriations with the budget resolution, and create the Congressional Budget Office (CBO) to provide Congress with its own source of professional expertise. The second was to enact provisions triggering automatic spending cuts, thus allowing reductions to be made without members of Congress having to take direct responsibility for them.

The first step of this process came with the Budget and Impoundment Control Act of 1974. This was followed by the Gramm–Rudman–Hollings Act, which attempted to force deficit reduction through across-the-board spending cuts (although only after taking nearly 70 per cent of the budget off of the board), and then the Budget Enforcement Act (BEA) of 1990. Through this process, rules were gradually relaxed. For example, the 1974 Act envisioned two budget resolutions each year, one to set targets and the second to reconcile actual appropriations with those targets. In 1982 the second resolution was dropped because of time pressures. In 1988, Congress failed to adopt a budget resolution at all because of irreconcilable differences between the two houses, notwithstanding that both had Republican majorities. The original BEA plan of separate caps on domestic, defence, and international discretionary spending (intended to protect the defence budget from diversion to domestic projects) was dropped in favour of a single cap. The budget committees also represented a significant centralization of power within each house of Congress, while the CBO has increased the ability of Congress at least to question the fiscal projections of the White House.

The 'normal' appropriations process requires passage of 11 bills, each relating to a group of federal agencies. Sometimes work has not been completed on some, or all, of these bills by the start of the federal fiscal year on 1 October. In that case, the normal practice is to pass a 'continuing resolution', which is a short-term appropriation as a pro-rata portion of the previous year's appropriation. In 1995–96, however, the Republican majority in Congress attempted to force President Clinton to accept their budget priorities by allowing spending authority to lapse (thus effectively shutting the government down), and by failing to raise the federal debt ceiling (thus threatening default on federal bonds).[18] Both of these attempts failed: the public blamed the Republicans for intransigence rather than rewarding them for resolve, and Secretary of the Treasury Robert Rubin borrowed from the federal employee retirement fund in order to avoid default.

The typical appropriations bill runs to hundreds of printed pages and is an important policy document in at least two respects. On the one hand, appropriations are often very specific: not $86.587 billion for the Department of Agriculture, but $10,046,000 for the office of the Secretary of Agriculture, $7,544,000 for the Office of Budget and Program Analysis, $2,981,000 for the purpose of providing Bill Emerson and Mickey Leland Hunger Fellowships through the Congressional Hunger Center, $100,000 for a pilot programme in the State of Alaska to assist communities with community planning, etc.[19] On the other hand, appropriations often have quite detailed strings attached, so that they specify not only how much is to be spent, but precisely how (and, as often, precisely how not) it is to be spent. These restrictions may be as trivial as limiting the amount that may be spent on entertaining, or as substantive as eliminating an entire programme or agency. This detailed use of the 'power of the purse' is one of the primary ways in which Congress can attempt to control the use of executive discretion. And because authorization is not a guarantee of appropriation, and because many of the strings attached to appropriations—especially those tying the spending of money to particular projects and particular places—originate or can be eliminated in the subcommittees of the Appropriations Committees, these are particularly prized assignments.

Congressional staff

Although the level of staff and other support given to members of parliaments to allow them better to carry out their official duties has increased significantly in many countries, the support afforded to members of Congress is of a different order of magnitude. Beyond an individual suite of offices in Washington, in 2001 each member of the House of Representatives was allotted between $980,699 and $1,469,930 as a 'representational allowance', while each member of the Senate was allotted between $1.9 million and $3.2 million, plus the rental for offices in his or her state of between 5,000 and 8,200 square feet.[20]

These allowances translate into a large corps of staff assistants, both in Washington, and in the members' districts. In 2001, the 435 members of the House employed 7,209 members of personal staff, roughly 42 per cent in their districts and 58 per cent in Washington. The 100 senators had 3,994 members of personal staff (about 69 per cent in Washington). While the law prohibits the use of these staff members for 'political' purposes (for which read 'electoral'), and members are quite careful to keep their campaign staff separate from their congressional staff, it is inevitable that the presence of a staff committed to constituency service, and the regular distribution of 'news from your Congressman' printed and mailed at public expense, gives incumbents a significant advantage in name recognition and in a reservoir of favours done.

The personal staff given to members as members are not the only staff members, however. First, leaders of the House have an additional 166 staff members and the leaders of the Senate an additional 221 staff members. Then, the committees, which is largely to say the committee chairmen and ranking minority members, have their own staff: 1,201 (ranging from 148 for Appropriations to 26 for Veterans' Affairs and 11 for Standards of Official Conduct) in the House, and 889 (from 91 for Appropriations to 16 for Veterans' Affairs) in the Senate. And, on top of these, the Congress as a whole employed 3,155 people in the General Accounting Office (Congress's fiscal watchdog agency vis-à-vis the executive), 722 people in the Congressional Research Service (located in the Library of Congress and devoted to satisfying the information requests of members of Congress), and 228 people in the Congressional Budget Office.

While these figures are, of course, dwarfed by the staff available to the president, they give the Congress a real capacity to challenge information provided by executive agencies and to formulate their own proposals.[21] In particular, the staff of committees that deal with highly technical matters, either in their capacity as technical experts, or in their role as agents of the committee Chairman, often themselves become influential shapers of policy—to the extent that reports of staff members acting on their own initiative to slip quite significant amendments into legislation just before it is voted on in committee (so that none of the committee members actually are aware that the amendments are there) have at least been widely regarded as credible.

The state legislatures

Although the states are not themselves federal,[22] every state except Nebraska has a bicameral legislature. Nebraska is also unique among the states in that its legislature is not organized by party. Before the reapportionment revolution, the upper house (usually called the Senate) generally gave equal representation to the counties making up the state, while the lower house (Assembly, or House of Delegates, or House of Representatives) would represent towns or be allocated among towns in rough proportion to population (possibly as population was distributed decades before). Since then, legislative boundaries have been no respecters of subdivision boundaries. In 2001, the largest state senate was in Minnesota (67) and the smallest were in Delaware and Nevada (21); the largest lower house was the New Hampshire House of Representatives with 400! members, while the smallest was the House of Representatives of Alaska (40)—although the unicameral legislature of Nebraska with 49 members was the smallest in total. State senatorial terms most commonly are four years (although 12 states have two-year senatorial terms)[23]; the terms for members of the lower houses of all but five states (plus Nebraska) are two years.

As observed in Chapter 5, the state legislatures generally are weaker *vis-à-vis* their governors than is Congress *vis-à-vis* the president, although the relative strength of the two branches is highly variable among the states. The power position of legislative leaders is also highly variable. Some are little more than presiding officers, but others, such as the speakers of the New York or Maryland lower houses, hold virtual veto power over legislation.

Two further ways in which many of the state legislatures differ from Congress are term limits and limited session lengths, both of which tend to further the weakness of the legislature *vis-à-vis* the executive. Altogether, 21 states have enacted statutory limitations of between six and twelve years on the length of individual service in the legislature (either consecutively or in total; either calculated separately for the two chambers or in total), although one term-limits law was repealed and three more were overturned by state courts (on the ground that constitutionally set qualifications for office could not be augmented by statute). Except in Louisiana and Utah, these limits were all imposed through the process of popular initiative—and in Utah, the legislature enacted limits in order to pre-empt an initiative that would have been even more restrictive. One obvious effect has been to weaken both the leaders of the legislatures (because they are subject to term limits as members, and freshman members are unlikely to be elected to leadership, the tenure of a particular individual in leadership will be even shorter than the legislative term limit) and to reduce the incentives for members to take a long-term view, either with regard to developing their own expertise or with regard to their legislative agendas.

In contrast to the Congress, which is continuously in session except for recesses and adjournments upon which it decides itself, all but six of the states impose formal or informal (by cutting off pay and allowances for legislators) limits on the length of legislative sessions; in six states, in fact, the legislature only meets in the odd-numbered years, and in six more, the legislature is basically limited to considering matters of finance and emergency legislation in the even-numbered years. Short sessions and an inflexible date for adjournment profoundly alter the pattern of legislative work, with virtually all legislation coming up for final passage in the last few days of the session. Serious consideration of individual bills becomes impossible due to the time pressure, which increases the influence of the legislative leaders, both as a source of voting cues (or simply instructions) and as the gate-keepers to the floor.

Both terms limits and session limitations reflect in part a cultural hostility to professional politicians. This is also embodied in the legislative salary structures, which for the most part clearly envision that legislating will be a part-time job (although it is common, notwithstanding constitutionally limited sessions and low salaries, for candidates to promise the voters that they will be 'full-time legislators'). Although the legislative salary in California was $99,000, in New York $79,500, in Michigan $77,400, and in Pennsylvania $61,889 (not coincidentally, four of the six states without limits on legislative sessions), in 2001, only 16 states had legislative annual salaries of at least $40,000. (In contrast, the annual salary of a member of Congress is $162,100.) The intention, as with term limits, has been to keep the state legislatures from being taken over by profession politicians. To a great extent, this goal has been achieved, but at the same time it has largely limited legislative service to those with the kinds of jobs that can be combined with (or even enhanced by) service in the legislature—lawyers in private practice, insurance brokers, retired people, etc. The result can be a legislative process that is even more strongly influenced by 'special' interests than is Congress.

KEY TERMS

- authorizing committee
- budget committee
- budget resolution
- close rule
- committee of the whole
- conference committee
- continuing resolution
- earmarks
- filibuster
- joint committee
- majority/minority leader
- open rule
- pork barrel legislation
- Rules Committee
- select committee
- senatorial courtesy
- seniority system
- Speaker of the House
- standing committee
- whip

NOTES

1 In addition to the 435 regular members of the House, there are three delegates (from American Samoa, the District of Columbia, and the US Virgin Islands), who have no vote in the full House, but are voting members of committees.

2 This means that the Senate does not have to adopt its rules at the beginning of each session, but rather convenes with rules in place. As a result, a proposal to amend the Senate's rules must be debated under the rules in place from the previous Congress rather than under generic rules of parliamentary procedure. In particular, it means that a resolution to limit or eliminate the filibuster would itself be subject to being filibustered.

3 House Republicans divide committees into three classes: exclusive (Appropriations; Energy and Commerce; Rules; Ways and Means), non-exclusive, and exempt (House Administration; Select Committee on Intelligence; Standards of Official Conduct); without special waiver, a member of an exclusive committee cannot serve on any other standing committee, and no member may serve on more than two non-exclusive committees. For the House Democrats, the exclusive committees are Appropriations; Rules; Ways and Means; Energy and Commerce (for those first serving after the 103rd Congress), and Financial Services (for those first serving after the 108th Congress).

In contrast, each senator serves on at least two standing committees, with most on three or four. Both parties limit members to serving on one of the 'Big Four' committees (Appropriations; Armed Services; Finance; Foreign Relations). Republican rules and Democratic tradition bar both of a state's senators from serving on the same committee if they are from the same party.

Exceptions to these rules are common, and are made by resolution of the Senate on recommendation of the relevant party conference.

4 Formally, the organizations of Democrats in the House of Representatives and Senate are called 'caucuses', while the analogous organizations of the Republicans are called 'conferences'. In this chapter, the term caucus is used in its generic sense.

5 In all of these statistics, abstentions and absences are ignored.

6 The party unity score is the proportion of party unity votes on which the member voted with the majority of his or her own party. While the average party unity score cannot be below 50, an individual party unity score substantially below 50 is possible.

7 Leadership political action committees (PACs) are devices used by one member of Congress to raise funds for other members outside the contribution limits that apply to the 'leader's' own campaign funds.

8 According to the Parliamentarian of the House of Representatives, the official title of a female committee chair is Madame Chairman. Following that practice, the word 'chairman' should not be understood to imply anything about the gender of the incumbent.

9 The apparent strength of the leaders of a united party has led to the idea of 'conditional party government' (Rohde 1991; Aldrich and Rohde 2001). The virtual tautology that parties tend to be more united when their members are already in agreement leaves open to question any real room either for party as an autonomous actor or for leadership power as an intervening variable. In particular, if, as Weber suggested, power is the ability to get one's way against opposition, can one say that power increases simply because opposition decreases?

10 Exceptions include the Committees on Ethics, on which the two parties are represented equally, regardless of the partisan balance of the chamber, and the House Committees on Rules and House Administration, on which the majority party is given roughly a 2 : 1 margin, in the first case because of its control over the legislative agenda and in the second because of its control over internal patronage— parking spaces, offices, staff, etc. There is no Senate committee analogous to the House Rules Committee, and the folkways of the Senate preclude the use of the prerogatives of the Senate Rules and Administration Committee for political advantage.

11 In the 108th Congress, the House Republican Steering Committee had 28 members, with a total of 35 votes. Five votes were cast by the Speaker, and two more by the chairmen of the Rules and Administration Committees, whom the Speaker appoints. The Majority Leader had two votes.

12 The other difference in powers of the two chambers is that only the Senate is required to confirm appointments or ratify treaties.

13 The Senate Parliamentarian, who serves at the pleasure of the majority leader but is expected to be non-partisan, is the Senate's adviser concerning the interpretation of its rules and procedures. There is also a Parliamentarian in the House of Representatives.

14 Analogous to the ability of any senator to place a hold on action, although in this case limited to members of the president's party, is the tradition of 'senatorial courtesy', whereby the senators (of the president's party) exercise a veto power over presidential appointments within their state.

15 Before 1917, when the first cloture rule was adopted, debate in the Senate could only be ended by unanimous consent.

16 Although technically against the rules, these rules are not enforced.

17 For example, the 2005 Transportation Bill earmarked money for thousands of specifically identified projects, in a few cases even dictating that the resulting bridge or highway be named after the member of Congress at whose behest it was added to the bill. While many of these projects (for example, a bridge in Alaska to an island with only 50 residents) were attacked as pork barrel politics at its worst, they were not without some justification, demonstrating the truth of the American adage that 'one man's pork is another man's vital government project'.

18 Since the Constitution gives Congress the authority to borrow money on the credit of the United States, the national debt can only be increased within limits set by Congress. And since the debt is simply rolled over as it becomes due, and increased by succeeding annual budget deficits, this limit must periodically be increased.

19 These figures are from the fiscal year 2004 Agriculture, Rural Development, Food and Drug Administration, and Related Agencies appropriations bill, 108th Congress, HR 2673. In contrast, the 1998 British appropriation for the Ministry of Agriculture, Fisheries and Food consisted of only two items: £733,296,000 for 'Supply Grants' and £150,975,000 for 'Appropriations in Aid'. Two similar items provided for the expenses of the Common Agricultural Policy of the European Union.

20 These figures include an allowance for travel to and from the district or state represented. The range for members of the House is largely a function of different distances from Washington. The range for senators also reflects larger allowances for the senators from more populous states.

21 Lobbyists are also a major source of on-presidential information for Congress.

22 In the sense that substate governments (counties, towns, cities) are creatures of the states which control their powers, institutions, boundaries, and even their continued existence.

23 The entire Illinois senate is elected every ten years, but is divided into groups with terms of 4–4–2, 4–2–4, and 2–4–4 years.

....

GUIDE TO FURTHER READING

DAVIDSON, R. H. and W. J. OLESZEK (2006), *Congress and Its Members* (Washington, DC: Congressional Quarterly Press).

A general overview of Congress and of the people who serve in it.

DODD, L. C. and B. I. OPPENHEIMER (eds.) (2005), *Congress Reconsidered* (Washington, DC: Congressional Quarterly Press).

A collection of essays considering the evolution of congressional institutions and folkways in recent years.

FENNO, R. J. (1997), *Learning to Govern: an Institutional View of the 104th Congress* (Washington, DC: Brookings Institution).

How the Republicans coped with controlling Congress for the first time in forty years, and how that altered the character of congressional life.

MAYHEW, D. R. (1974), *Congress: the Electoral Connection* (New Haven, CT: Yale University Press).

An experiment to see how much about Congress can be explained by assuming that members are single-minded seekers of re-election.

SINCLAIR, B. (2000), *Unorthodox Lawmaking: New Legislative Processes in the US Congress* (Washington, DC: Congressional Quarterly Press).

An analysis of the multiple paths and strategies used to advance legislation, in contrast to the traditional 'textbook' treatment of how a bill becomes a law.

7

The Bureaucracy

Overview

This chapter focuses both on the bureaucracy of the executive departments, and on the independent semi-executive agencies such as the Federal Trade Commission, the Federal Reserve Board, etc. The themes are: the divided loyalties of the bureaucracy (among the president, the Congress, professional norms); the role of the bureaucracy in policy-making; and the connections between the bureaucracy and organized interests. An additional set of themes includes the use of the bureaucracy as a scapegoat by politicians, and the bureaucracy and independent regulatory agencies as a reflection of American ambivalence about partisanship and politics in general.

In popular myth and in some political theory, there is a neat distinction between policy-making, which is the province of politically accountable officials, and administration, which should be free of politics. In reality, the two are inseparable. Although political appointment reaches deeper into the American bureaucracy than is true in many other countries, and even including the rather blurry boundary between explicitly political appointments and the discretionary presidential appointment of civil servants from the senior executive service, 'non-political' bureaucrats inevitably are left discretion to adapt general policies to the circumstances of particular cases. They also provide much of the information and expertise required for policy-making (although private sector and partisan research institutes increasingly give nominal policy-makers alternative sources, with ideological biases that will more reliably match their own), and in doing so can shape the range of alternatives that are considered, even if they do not determine the final choice in detail. Although they generally become the subject of widespread public attention only when there has been a significant failure, the permanent bureaucracy has an important influence on virtually every aspect of the policy-making and governing processes.

Everyone loves to hate bureaucracy, and Americans are no exception. On the one hand, many Americans have an exaggerated view of the efficiency and rationality of the private sector, even as obvious inefficiencies and miscalculations drive major corporations into bankruptcy. On the other hand, they insist on standards of personal disinterest and disclosure, procedural regularity and neutrality, public consultation and accountability, that would never be tolerated in the private sector, and yet object to the 'red tape' and delays that are not just their inevitable consequence, but are in fact the means through which they are achieved—to the extent that they are achieved. And, of course, since much of the bureaucracy does not appear to make anything (except rules, which are only apparent when they prevent one from doing what one wants to do, or when they fail to prevent others from doing what one does not want done), there is always a strong temptation to economize by cutting the bureaucracy, followed by complaints that the agencies whose staffs were decimated and whose budgets were cut were not there quickly enough to respond to a crisis.

Attacks on the bureaucracy, and promises to reform it, come from both parties, whether in opposition or in the majority. Politicians often find it expedient to blame the bureaucracy for failures that ultimately are the fault of policy decisions that the politicians made themselves. Although, as observed in earlier chapters, the Republicans have positioned themselves in the public mind as the party of small government and opposition to 'red tape', the growth of the federal bureaucracy and of federal rule-making has been effectively uninterrupted regardless of which party was in power, and when in recent years there was a temporary retrenchment, it was during the Democratic administration of Bill Clinton, although whether that was a result of Clinton's own policy preferences or of divided control of the government, it is impossible to say.

In 2003, there were a bit over 2,659,000 civilian employees of the executive branch of the federal government. Of these, under 7 per cent worked in the District of Columbia (Washington), and indeed only about 17 per cent worked in the District or the two surrounding states (Maryland and

Virginia), both of which contain large numbers of federal employees who *cannot* be described as working in the Washington suburbs. The rest are scattered among the other states and abroad. In addition to these direct employees of the executive branch, there are several million more who work for the government indirectly, through contractors and suppliers. In some states, and in many localities, the federal government is one of the largest employers and vital to the local economy, which helps to explain why reduction of the federal workforce is far more popular in the abstract than it is when real cuts, and real job losses, are proposed. While the federal workforce is many times the size of that of the largest private sector employer, however, it represents only about 16 per cent of the total number of workers at all levels of government.

The civil service

Although a Civil Service Commission was authorized in 1871, the real spur to the establishment of a civil service based on merit selection rather than political patronage and a spoils system[1] was the 1881 assassination of President James Garfield by a disappointed office seeker. The resulting legislation (the Pendleton Act) created a bipartisan Civil Service Commission, under which about 10 per cent of federal jobs were filled based primarily on the results of competitive examinations. This share was gradually increased, so that now roughly 73 per cent of civilian employees are covered by the competitive system—a proportion that has been declining at least since 1988, when the figure was 81 per cent.

The Civil Service Commission combined two roles that on occasion came into conflict: support of management in the pursuit of its administrative *and political* goals, and defence of the merit system against political interference. The Commission was also charged with assuring equal employment opportunity, a role that a 1972 report of Ralph Nader's Public Interest Research Group charged it had failed adequately to perform. Bureaucratic reform was one of Jimmy Carter's campaign promises, and in 1978 the Civil Service Commission was abolished and these roles were separated. The objectives were to bring modern personnel management techniques to the federal service, make managers more accountable to the political leadership, and to give them incentives to be responsive.

The Carter reforms transferred the equal employment opportunity functions of the old Civil Service Commission to the Equal Employment Opportunity Commission (EEOC), which also enforces federal laws against employment discrimination in the private sector. A new Merit Systems Protection Board was created to hear appeals from federal employees regarding personnel actions, as was a Federal Labor Relations Authority. Finally, the reforms created the Office of Personnel Management to make the rules regulating the merit appointment system and to serve as the government's 'employment agency'.

The other major reform was to create the Senior Executive Service (SES), located above the top of the 'regular' civil service and below (and overlapping with) politically appointed officials. Unlike the regular service, in which rank (and therefore pay) is attached to the position, in the SES there are no ranks; although there are five pay levels, these are attached to the person rather than the position, allowing top managers to be moved within (or between) agencies as the need arises. SES positions are divided between 'career reserved' (merit appointment) and 'general' (which may be filled by career or non-career appointment), with the 'general' category limited to 25 per cent of the positions in any agency, and 10 per cent of the positions in the government as a whole. Overall, there are about 7,600 individuals in the SES.

Jobs in the SES were intended to carry higher status, higher rewards, but also somewhat less security, than jobs in the regular service. The bottom basic pay ($104,927 in 2005) is 120 per cent of the basic pay for the top category of the regular service (GS–15), and the maximum basic pay is $158,100, and in addition members of the SES can be awarded substantial performance bonuses. On the other hand, career members of the SES can be removed for less than fully successful performance. Such individuals have the right to placement in their agency at the GS–15 level without loss of pay, or to retire if their combined age and years of service are adequate. While this system responded to Carter's pledge to increase the individual accountability of senior bureaucrats, it risks aggravating the problem that at the upper levels of the civil service the distinction between non-partisanship and unsatisfactory performance may not be particularly clear.

Roughly 87 per cent of federal civilian workers hold full-time permanent jobs. The gender balance (56 per cent men, 44 per cent women) is about the same as in the overall civilian labour force. Over time, the proportion of women in the lowest pay grades has decreased and their proportion in the higher grades has increased, although it is still the case that over 60 per cent in the bottom pay grades (GS1–8, basic salaries of $15,625–$42,935) are women, in comparison to well under 40 per cent in the upper grades (GS13–15, basic salaries of $62,905–$113,674). Roughly 74 per cent of the SES is male. With regard to ethnicity, the federal workforce is significantly more Black (17.6 per cent versus 10.4 per cent) and less Hispanic (7.0 per cent versus 13.1 per cent) than the overall civilian labour force.

Executive departments and agencies

The core of the federal bureaucracy, both historically and in size, is organized in the 15 cabinet departments, each headed by a secretary and a number of deputy secretaries, under secretaries, and assistant secretaries (except the Department of Justice, which is headed by the Attorney General and a deputy and numerous assistant Attorneys General), all appointed (subject to Senate confirmation) and removable by the president. As shown in Table 7.1, these departments vary enormously in size and budget (and in status), but roughly 25 per cent of the federal civilian workforce is employed in just one of them—the Department of Defense.

In addition to the cabinet departments, there are a number of executive agencies (for example, the Environmental Protection Agency (EPA), the Small Business Administration, and NASA) that are not under the jurisdiction of a cabinet department but which would have effectively the same standing in a 'federal organization chart'. The heads of these agencies generally have lower status (and salaries) than cabinet secretaries and are not included in the cabinet, although some (for example, the Director of the Central Intelligence Agency) may be accorded 'cabinet rank' and included in the cabinet at the president's discretion. Often (but not always) the heads of these agencies will have more professional experience in the fields for which they are responsible than do cabinet secretaries, but they too are appointed and removable by the president. In principle, they are part of a unified hierarchically organized administration, taking their direction from the White House, and working to implement and enforce the policies and laws decided upon by the president and Congress, as interpreted by the courts.

TABLE 7.1	Outlays and employment by cabinet departments, fiscal year 2003	
Cabinet department	Outlays in millions of dollars	Employment in thousands
Agriculture	72,390	101.4
Commerce	5,676	34.5
Defense–Military	388,870	648.9
Education	57,400	4.5
Energy	19,385	15.6
Health and Human Services	505,345	60
Homeland Security	31,967	144.5
Housing and Urban Development	37,474	10.4
Interior	9,210	71
Justice	21,539	99.4
Labor	69,593	16.9
State	9,261	29.5
Transportation	50,807	59
Treasury	366,987	115.4
Veterans' Affairs	56,887	211.8

Source: Budget of the United States Government, Fiscal Year 2005, Table 23.1, Historical Table 4.1

This, however, only captures part of the reality. First, all of the executive agencies ultimately depend on Congress for their budgets and for any legislation they require/desire. All are subject to congressional oversight hearings, which are as often opportunities for Congress (and individual Representatives or senators) to give direction as for Congress simply to gather information. Second, executive agencies are in competition with one another for budget and responsibility; both for agency heads and for their division and bureau chiefs, increased staff and increased funds are not only opportunities to better achieve their objectives, but are also public recognition that their work is important and a measure of their professional success. Third, like all professionals, bureaucrats and technocrats have their own ideas about how things should be done and their own professional reference groups. They also tend to exaggerate the efficacy and underestimate the side-costs of 'their kind' of policy instruments, while doing the reverse for other kinds of solutions to problems. Particularly tenured civil servants tend to have much longer time horizons than politicians, for whom the election cycle is necessarily much more salient. For a president (particularly one nearing the end of his first term and therefore concerned about re-election) or a member of Congress (particularly members of the House of Representatives who effectively are always facing the imminent need to be re-elected), short-term amelioration may trump long-term solution—without amelioration now, they may not be in office to worry about the problems then. A career civil servant, however, not only must expect to deal with long-term consequences, but also may reasonably anticipate being blamed for them.

Being caught, and having their loyalties divided, between the president and his political appointees on the one hand and the Congress and its committees on the other, can make life difficult for the likes of bureau directors (generally about three or four steps down the organization chart from the Secretary),[2] but also can provide opportunities to play one off against the other. Not just cabinet departments, but many of the individual units within them, will have their own congressional liaison officers, responsible not only for satisfying congressional requests for information but also for maintaining friendly relations with both the members and staff of oversight and appropriations committees and for presenting the agency's perspective on issues before them. When agency preferences and White House policy diverge, congressional allies can be asked to insert language into legislation which, while apparently tying the agency's hands, in fact requires it to do what it wanted to do even if the White House wanted something else. Conversely, the agency may be able to enlist the political resources of the White House in order to further its agenda with a recalcitrant Congress.

Political considerations also provide an incentive for agencies to develop a positive relationship with their clientele groups, which can then be called upon as political allies in the agency's dealings with its political 'masters'. Some agencies, for example the Departments of Labor, Agriculture, or Commerce, were created in part for the purpose of representing particular interests within the government, but even when the original intention was regulation rather than representation, agencies often try to establish mutually supportive relationships with the groups that they are supposed to be regulating—the Bureau of Land Management and ranchers who lease public lands for cattle grazing at well-below-market rates; the FBI and local police departments; the Food and Drug Administration and drug companies that look at FDA approval not simply as a hurdle to be jumped but also as insurance against future liability. Particularly because the members and staff of congressional committees often develop the same kinds of close and durable relationship with the same interest groups, a triangular relationship, sometimes identified as an 'iron triangle', may develop among agency, committee and affected interest that allows them to pursue their own agenda independent of either the congressional leadership more generally or the White House. Conversely, failure to have a good relationship with those most directly affected by the agency's work can mean having a powerful enemy in Congress. To be effective either as an ally or as an enemy, however, requires organization at least as much as intensity of feeling, which may encourage bureaucrats to be more sympathetic to, and to define their objectives more with reference to, the concerns of organized interests instead of those who lack organization: lumber companies rather than hikers or nature lovers in the management of public forests; teachers rather than students in education policy; trucking companies rather than private automobile owners in the allocation of highway resources. And, of course, this in turn has stimulated organizations to represent the other side, such as the Sierra Club (which advocates for conservation) or the American Automobile Association (which claims to speak for private motorists, notwithstanding that most of its members joined to receive emergency road service and free road maps). Bureaucrats then may play a significant role as brokers (and shapers) of compromises among interest representatives that subsequently can be presented to Congress and the president as *faits accomplis*.

The resulting limitations and circumvention of presidential authority are rarely appreciated by the occupant of the White House, particularly if he wants to make a substantial change in policy—and in these terms, the cuts that conservatives claim to want count even more as substantial changes than the additions or simple redirections advanced by liberals. Over time, this has led to a series of reforms aimed at increasing the centralization of control, such as the increased authority of the Office of Management and Budget discussed in Chapter 5.

Both the desire to increase political control and the perhaps inevitable attempts of senior administrators to demonstrate their own importance by increasing the number and pretentiousness of titles of their subordinates (for example, by having a 'chief of staff') have led to what Paul Light (1995, 2004) has described as the 'thickening' of the top levels of the bureaucracy. In 1960, no cabinet secretary had a chief of staff, let alone a deputy chief of staff; in 2004, almost all had both. In 1960, there were roughly twice as many deputy or under-secretaries as there were cabinet secretaries; in 2004, there were more than five times as many. And in 1960, those deputy or under-secretaries averaged 0.57 assistants, associates, deputies, chiefs of staff or the like, while in 2004, the average was 2.3—roughly a quadrupling. In other words, there has not just been an increase in the range of governmental activities leading to an increase in operating staff, there has also been an increase in the number of layers of management that separate those who are actually executing the responsibilities of their departments from those nominally in charge—the cabinet secretary or head of an independent agency, and ultimately the president. By Light's count, even the 'flattest hierarchy' (the Department of State) has ten layers, followed by Housing and Urban Development at 15, and ultimately reaching the Defense Department with 30 distinct executive titles. Especially given the relatively short tenure of people in these upper management positions, rather than increasing accountability and control, the result is as often confusion and isolation—information sent up the chain of command and directions sent down that never reach their intended recipients, or only reach them in garbled form.

Unlike ministries in parliamentary (and some presidential) systems that depend on multiparty coalitions for legislative support, this proliferation of political positions at the top of the hierarchy is not intended to give coalition partners a foot-in-the-door of departments headed by a minister from another party, although there is often a pressure to give some representation in key agencies to diverse interests within the president's single-party coalition or to plant a presidential loyalist in an agency given to one of his less trustworthy or less ideologically compatible allies. Another important contrast is that, except for the top positions in the most important agencies, and often not even for them, these are not positions to which members of Congress typically aspire. Unlike junior ministerial appointments in many countries, they are not steps on a career ladder to higher office, but more likely to be consolation prizes for members of Congress or state officials who were not re-elected. Tenure also tends to be fairly short at the cabinet level, and even shorter (under two years) at the levels below that, making these positions way stations on diverse political career paths, including the path *to* Congress. The results are to encourage these upper-level executives to be attentive to reference groups outside the administration, lessening both their capacity and their incentives for coordinated control.

Independent regulatory commissions

Beginning in the late nineteenth century with the expansion of federal regulatory activity, Congress decided that the traditional governmental model—that Congress makes the rules, the president and bureaucrats acting as his agents administer and enforce the rules, the regular courts resolve conflicts, assess the culpability of, and impose penalties on, those who violate the rules—was not appropriate to some policy areas. On the one hand, they required the kind of technical expertise and continuous monitoring and adjustment in regulations that are beyond the capacity of Congress. On the other hand, they were too important to leave to the permanent clerks of the bureaucracy or to the unilateral discretion of the president, who would at any time be of the opposite party from many members of Congress.

The solution, adopted first with the Interstate Commerce Commission (ICC) in 1887, was to create a new kind of agency within, but not exactly of, the executive. These agencies are headed by boards that are appointed by the president and confirmed by the Senate for staggered terms, and with the restriction that no more than half of their members (rounded up) may come from a single political party. Unlike most other executive branch appointees of the president, the independent regulatory commissions do not report to the president, and once confirmed regulatory agency commissioners cannot be removed by him, although the president does retain the authority to designate which member of the commission will serve as chairman.[3] Although the original Interstate Commerce Act did not give the ICC effective enforcement powers, these were expanded over time, and the Supreme Court's interpretation of its powers became more expansive.

It became the model for other regulatory commissions, although in detail, each of the independent regulatory commissions has a unique organizational structure.

What the independent regulatory commissions have in common, aside from their collegial heads and their location outside the presidential chain of command, is that they combine legislative, executive, and judicial functions. Although many bureaucratic agencies are authorized by statute to make rules (in part because Congress can take the credit for establishing a regulatory framework to deal with a problem, and then take credit again for undoing rules that turn out to be unpopular with powerful constituencies—a tactic that Fiorina (1977: 48–9) has identified as part of 'the Washington system'), the grants of authority to the regulatory commissions are much broader, and subject to far less specific direction. For example, as a part of the 'Fairness Doctrine' (itself simply a commission policy), in 1967 the Federal Communications Commission (FCC) adopted a specific rule requiring that:

When, during the presentation of views on a controversial issue of public importance, an attack is made upon the honesty, character, integrity or like personal qualities of an identified person or group, the [broadcast] licensee shall, within a reasonable time and in no event later than 1 week after the attack, transmit to the person or group attacked (1) notification of the date, time and identification of the broadcast; (2) a script or tape (or an accurate summary if a script or tape is not available) of the attack; and (3) an offer of a reasonable opportunity to respond over the licensee's facilities. (47 Code of Federal Regulations 73.123)

The statutory authority for this rule, and indeed for the Fairness Doctrine as a whole, was merely that the Communications Act authorized the Commission to regulate broadcasting 'in the public interest, convenience and necessity'. In making rules of this sort, commissions are required to issue a 'Notice of Proposed Rule Making' in the Federal Register. They then act like legislative bodies deciding by majority vote, and their rules have the force of law.

The commissions also perform functions analogous to those of 'normal' executive agencies. They process applications, gather information to make legislative recommendations (although often for their own use rather than to be forwarded to the OMB and Congress), conduct inspections (for example, dam safety inspections performed by the Federal Energy

Regulatory Commission staff), and prepare cases against alleged rule violators. Finally, the commissions also have a judicial function, assessing penalties (generally fines, but also potential licence revocations or the like) for violations. Perhaps reflecting their quasi-judicial standing, appeals from commission decisions generally are heard in the Circuit Court of Appeals for the District of Columbia, rather than beginning in District Court, as would be the case for appeals from 'ordinary' administrative decisions.[4] In either case, the courts tend to show great deference to the fact-finding of the executive, and even when the court finds the factual record inadequate to support the decision, the usual response is to remand the case for more fact-finding by the agency itself.

As part of the movement towards deregulation (see below), a number of independent regulatory commissions, including the ICC, have been abolished, with some of their functions (particularly things like safety inspections) folded into regular executive agencies and others (such as the ICC's rate-setting authority) allowed to lapse. Among those independent regulatory agencies remaining, the most significant are:

- The Federal Trade Commission (FTC), with primary responsibility for limiting monopolistic or other anti-competitive practices, deceptive or false advertising or packaging, and the like;

- The Federal Communications Commission (FCC), which regulates the use of the electromagnetic spectrum for broadcasting and other radio transmission, including the licensing of broadcasters, and also regulates wired communication (telephone and telegraph) in interstate commerce;

- The Securities and Exchange Commission (SEC), which regulates stock exchanges and companies offering securities for sale (plus the Commodity Futures Trading Commission, which performs analogous functions with regard to the commodity markets);

- The Federal Energy Regulatory Commission (FERC), which regulates gas and oil pipelines and electric utilities engaged in interstate commerce;

- The Consumer Product Safety Commission, which was created to protect the public from unreasonable risks of injuries and deaths associated with some 15,000 types of consumer product.

Other independent regulatory commissions include the Federal Maritime Commission and the Federal Housing Finance Board.

It is in the nature of the independent regulatory commissions that they will develop a close relationship with the industry that they regulate. To the extent that technical expertise or experience is required either for commissioners or for members of the commission staff, it is often to be found primarily in that industry (or in the law firms that have represented major interests within the industry). Similarly, the most likely career possibilities for those leaving the commission is also in that industry, or in legal or lobbying firms representing it. Because commission decisions can have a profound impact on the conduct of business, it makes economic sense for those businesses to devote significant resources to cultivating a positive relationship with their regulators. All of this creates a significant danger of 'agency capture', as suggested in Chapter 5. Even when the result is not to allow the industry to avoid regulation altogether, it often means that the regulations are framed with as much or more attention to the interests of the industry to be regulated as to the interests of the public in whose interest the regulations are presumably to work. Indeed, although industries rarely want to be regulated in the first place (an exception might be the radio industry, which quickly recognized that lack of regulation of the broadcast spectrum would lead to chaos that would make broadcasting impossible), they often were able to turn regulation to their advantage—for example, effectively turning a regulatory regime intended to prevent predatory or extortionate pricing into a publicly maintained cartel, with guaranteed profits regardless of their own inefficiencies. And because this insulation of profits from costs extended to wages and benefits for workers, organized labour also benefited not only from health and safety requirements (which management would be less likely to oppose once they were assured that the costs could be passed on to consumers), but from easier contract negotiations as well. Thus, when Congress moved in 1978 to eliminate the fare-setting and route-allocating powers of the Civil Aeronautics Board, the effort was opposed both by the airlines and by their unions.

The problem of agency capture is by no means limited to the independent regulatory commissions. Analogous regulatory functions are performed by a large number of agencies either housed within cabinet departments (for example, the Food and Drug Administration in the Department of Health and Human Services; the Occupational Safety and Health Administration

(OSHA) in the Department of Labor) or as free-standing executive agencies (for example, the Environmental Protection Agency). In each case, there is frequently a trade-off between diffuse and anonymous public benefits and highly concentrated and easily identifiable corporate costs, complicated by potential conflicts of interest (like an FDA official coming from, or planning to return or retire to, a position in a pharmacy school that depends on research contracts from drug companies).

Public corporations and foundations

In addition to the formal executive agencies and the independent regulatory commissions, there are a large number of additional agencies that perform what would otherwise be governmental functions, and whose chief executives or governing boards are appointed by the president (generally subject to confirmation by the Senate), but which otherwise are structured as private corporations. In part, these reflect (or have been justified on the basis of) a feeling that some decisions should be removed from partisan politics altogether—a generalization of the idea often raised in local government that 'there is no Democratic or Republican way to build a road'. In part, they reflect a widely held prejudice that the private sector is automatically and necessarily more efficient than the public sector. In part they reflect an attempt by Congress and the president to externalize responsibility for unpopular but necessary decisions.

Among the public corporations, the largest is the United States Postal Service (USPS), which accounts for roughly 30 per cent of the federal civilian workforce. From colonial times until 1971, the post office was a government department (represented in the cabinet from 1829), and until 1969 it was a major source of executive patronage through the political appointment of postmasters and rural letter carriers. In 1971, the post office was converted from an executive department into an 'independent establishment of the Executive Branch', which operates as an independent corporation governed by an 11-member Board of Governors, nine members of which are appointed by the president and confirmed by the Senate and the other two of which (the Postmaster General and the Deputy Postmaster General) are selected by the Board itself. Postal rates are determined by what is, in effect, an independent regulatory agency, the Postal Rate Commission, which considers requests for increases from the Postal Service. The USPS was created in large measure to allow postal rates to be increased without politicians having to take responsibility[5] and to eliminate a large public subsidy, while reforming labour practices outside the civil service system.

A second major (albeit regional) public corporation is the Tennessee Valley Authority (TVA). Created in 1933 as one of the New Deal agencies designed in response to the Great Depression, the TVA was to be 'a corporation clothed with the power of government but possessed of the flexibility and initiative of a private enterprise'.[6] Since then, it has become the nation's largest public power company, and a major force in the economic development and environmental protection (or degradation, depending on one's perspective) of the seven-state area surrounding the Tennessee River. The TVA is governed by a three-member Board of Directors.

The National Railroad Passenger Corporation (Amtrak) was created in 1971 in the face of the impending (or actual) bankruptcy of the nation's railroads, which they attributed to their legal obligation to provide a passenger service. Amtrak is organized as a private, for-profit, corporation, although all of its preferred stock is held by the government (common stock is held by railroad companies, but has never paid a dividend) and the directors are appointed by the president. The result has been some improvement of passenger rail services in the corridor between Washington, DC and Boston, but the virtual (or literal) abandonment of a rail passenger service in much of the rest of the country, coupled with a continuing need for substantial public subsidy. Other public, or semi-public, corporations include the Federal Deposit Insurance Corporation (FDIC), which insures bank accounts; the Pension Benefit Guarantee Corporation, which protects workers in case of insolvency of their private employer based pension plans; the Corporation for Public Broadcasting, which serves as a conduit for public money into the public television and radio systems in a way that is supposed to insulate them from political influence; and Fannie Mae (the Federal National Mortgage Association), Ginnie Mae (the Government National Mortgage Association), and Freddie Mac (the Federal Home Loan Mortgage Corporation), all of which support the availability of home loans.

The federal government also maintains a number of agencies that are patterned after private charitable foundations. The most prominent of these are the National Endowment for the Arts (NEA), the National Endowment for the Humanities (NEH), and the National Science Foundation (NSF). Their primary function is to make grants to private entities (and in some cases to public entities, as when they make grants to public television stations to support the production of programming), and their structure is supposed to combine insulation from political pressure with 'expert' or 'peer-reviewed' allocation decisions. In each case, the chief executive is a presidential appointee, but grant decisions are largely determined by panels of experts.

The Federal Reserve system

One additional agency that is in many ways structured as a private corporation is the Federal Reserve system ('the Fed'), which is the central bank of the United States. Established by the Federal Reserve Act in 1913, the Fed, like the independent regulatory agencies, is independent in the sense that its decisions do not need the approval of, and cannot be blocked by, the president or other executive branch officials. It is also particularly independent given the unusually long terms (14 years, non-renewable in the case of Governors who have served a full term) of the seven members of its Board of Governors, which means that it would take two full presidential terms to replace a majority of the Board's members. On the other hand, like all of the independent agencies, the Fed remains subject to congressional oversight, and its policies, and indeed its authority to make policies, can be altered by statute.

In addition to the Board of Governors, the Fed includes 12 regional Federal Reserve Banks.[7] Each of these is headed by a board of nine directors (three representing the commercial banks that are members of the Federal Reserve system, three representing the public but elected by the commercial banks, and three representing the public elected by the Board of Governors). The directors nominate a president and first vice-president, subject to the approval of the Board of Governors. The Reserve Banks serve as banker to the US Treasury and provide a range of services to the banking industry, as well as supervising and regulating member banks and bank holding companies.

Beyond its regulatory functions, the Fed has primary responsibility for American monetary policy—indeed 'to furnish an elastic currency' was one of the principal reasons for its creation. The Fed influences the money supply through three primary means. First, it sets the reserve requirements and contractual clearing balances (the share of deposits that banks must hold in cash or in an account at a Reserve Bank, and therefore do not have available for loans). Second, it determines the discount rate (the interest rate at which the Fed lends money to banks), thereby influencing interest rates throughout the economy. Third, it buys and sells securities (primarily US Treasury securities) on the open market, thus either expanding (when it buys) or contracting (when it sells) the amount of currency in circulation.

Of these, the principal tool is the Fed's 'open market operations', which, in addition to the buying and selling of domestic securities, include the Fed's interventions in foreign exchange markets. By statute, these are overseen by the Federal Open Market Committee, which consists of the seven Governors, the president of the Federal Reserve Bank of New York, and four other Federal Reserve Bank presidents who serve one-year terms on a rotating basis.

Unlike the European Central Bank, the Fed is not obliged by its statute to give primacy to controlling inflation, but rather it is expected to balance price stability, high levels of employment, and reasonable, long term interest rates. In general, the Fed tries to 'lean against the prevailing economic wind', but given the professional biases that Fed Governors are likely to bring to the job as well as the general replacement of Keynsianism by neo-liberalism as the dominant ideology, the Fed in recent decades has tended to give priority to inflation. Especially when the president or Congress has wanted to pursue policies that might be expected to be inflationary, in particular dramatic tax cuts without corresponding cuts in spending, this has sometimes led to conflict between the Fed and the White House, which given the independence of the Fed with regard to monetary policy has tended to play out in congressional debate over fiscal (taxing and spending) policy.

Political control of the bureaucracy

The political position of the bureaucracy, and of the independent agencies, corporations, and foundations is somewhat paradoxical. On the one hand, civil service reform, with merit appointment and security of tenure, laws (for example, the Hatch Act) limiting the political activities in which federal employees may engage,[8] and the separation of the independent agencies from direct White House control all are meant to remove them from partisan politics, if not from politics altogether, predicated on the idea that neutrality is both possible and desirable. On the other hand, the decisions made by these agencies are of great importance to many politically relevant interests. Moreover, the information at the disposal of bureaucrats, and the timing and manner of its release or suppression, can profoundly affect both public opinion and the deliberations of the more overtly political agencies of government. To expect Congress and the president to treat these actions as beyond their legitimate scope of intervention and simply stand back and accept them is unrealistic, particularly given that authority ultimately rests with the political arms of government.

Given that all of the executive agencies are created by legislation, or by executive order authorized by legislation, the ultimate instrument of control is simply to change the law. Policies made by executive agencies, including the so-called independent agencies, can be abrogated or modified by statute, and the credible threat to do so will often be enough to get the agency to rethink its decision without overt action. Ultimately, the agency could have its authority to make decisions in certain areas reduced, or the agency might simply be abolished. On the other hand, because legislation requires the concurrence of both houses of Congress and the president (or a sufficient congressional majority to override a presidential veto), and moreover runs the political risk of being perceived as 'politically motivated' meddling, this is generally reserved either for 'big' questions, or for circumstances in which the agencies have become seriously out of step both with the political branches of government and with public opinion.

More commonly, either the president or Congress can reward or punish bureaucratic agencies through their budgets, either by increasing or decreasing them or by inserting narrowly drawn restrictions on how the money appropriated may or may not be spent. And again, the agencies' anticipation of the reactions of those who control the purse strings often makes overt action unnecessary. Budgetary control is an instrument that is more often used with regard to the normal executive agencies than the independent commissions or corporations, some of which—like the Federal Reserve—are funded largely outside the appropriations process. But even there Congress and the president can, for example, determine how much emphasis should be placed on safety inspections by determining how much money is appropriated to pay inspectors.

Notwithstanding the protections afforded by the civil service system, and laws that purport to protect 'whistleblowers', particularly at the upper reaches of the executive service, the president and his appointees have sufficient discretion to make the threat of demotion or other job-related retaliation (for example, transfer to an undesirable location, loss of authority or staff) significant. For example, the chief actuary for Medicare and Medicaid Services in the Department of Health and Human Services declared in 2004 that he had been threatened with dismissal for insubordination if he had given Congress his assessment of the likely cost of the administration's prescription drug plan.[9] Similarly, in 2005 the director of the Bureau of Justice Statistics (BJS) reportedly was ordered to resign (which he avoided doing only by exercising his civil service right to be demoted to a job outside BJS where he could do the remaining six months' service that he required to retire with a full pension) in retaliation for objecting to an order to downplay a report that appeared to show racial disparity in the way police handled traffic stops.[10] Finally, the woman who had been the Army Corps of Engineers' top procurement official since 1997 was abruptly demoted for poor job performance after she objected to the volume of no-bid contracts for Iraq that had been awarded to Halliburton, the company formerly headed by Vice-President Cheney.[11]

That these may be isolated cases does not lessen, and indeed may indicate, the effectiveness of these devices. Once a threat is recognized as credible, it need not often be repeated, let alone carried out, in order for the law of anticipated reactions to make it effective. As the investigation into intelligence failures before the Iraq War showed, it may only be necessary for supervisors repeatedly to send reports back for revision 'until they get it right' for staff members to learn and do what is expected of them.

Deregulation

Beginning in the 1970s, the mood in Washington shifted away from government regulation of business and towards letting the market determine outcomes. In part, this move was fuelled by complaints from businesses that excessive regulation was undercutting their competitiveness and thus

costing jobs, which was a powerful argument in a period of high unemployment—in the early 1980s, unemployment was roughly triple what it had
been in the late 1960s. In part, the stagflation of the 1970s undermined faith
in Keynsianism among economists, whose disciplinary 'centre of gravity'
had already moved in the direction of monetarism and neo-liberalism. In
part, it was driven by recognition of agency capture—and the perception
that in many cases regulation was serving the interests of the regulated
rather than the public.

Federal regulatory agencies that set, or severely constrained, the ability
of firms to set prices and determine services, or otherwise straightforwardly
respond to market forces, were among the first targets. Between 1978 and
1985, the Civil Aeronautics Board, which regulated airline routes and fares,
was phased out, with the results of markedly lower (and more complicated)
fare structures, loss of service to many small markets, the rise of low-cost,
no-frills carriers, and a spate of bankruptcies among the major carriers,
accompanied by dramatic wage and benefit cuts for airline employees. In
1980, legislation substantially reduced the regulation of the trucking and
railroad industries, and in 1995 the Interstate Commerce Commission went
out of existence. Also in 1980, the authority to regulate interest rates paid
to depositors was taken from the Federal Reserve Board, the Federal Home
Loan Bank Board, and the National Credit Union Administration Board
and given to a Deregulation Committee that was directed 'to provide for
the orderly phase-out and the ultimate elimination of the limitations on the
maximum rates of interest and dividends which may be paid on deposits
and accounts as rapidly as economic conditions warrant'.[12]

Even when there was no statutory change, by the end of the 1980s the
deregulatory ideology of the Reagan administration, and of the economics
profession, had spread to many of the surviving regulatory agencies. After
Reagan appointed the first economist on the Federal Trade Commission
(FTC), and the first non-lawyer in over thirty years, to be chairman of
the Commission (which gives unusually wide administrative discretion
to its chairman), the FTC's consumer protection activism was noticeably
decreased. For example, in 1983 the Commission narrowed its definition
of deceptive advertising, and adopted rules making it harder for the staff
to prove deception. It also tried to extend its authority—in the name of
deregulation—by bringing an action against the cities of New Orleans and
Minneapolis, charging that agreements to fix fares and limit the number

of taxicabs violated the antitrust laws. More generally, both procedures and staff were changed to favour a case-by-case approach to regulation that predicated enforcement on widespread material harm to 'reasonable' consumers, with the result that deceptive practices would only be penalized if they were 'expensive' enough.

The Federal Communications Commission also moved to reduce regulation. Most notably, in 1987 the Commission abandoned the Fairness Doctrine as an unconstitutional abridgement of broadcasters' freedom of speech, notwithstanding that in 1969 the Supreme Court had specifically ruled that the Fairness Doctrine was constitutional. While the statutory provisions requiring equal access for legally qualified political candidates remained in place,[13] broadcasters were relieved of any affirmative obligation to cover controversial issues of public importance, or to be balanced in their treatment of those that they do cover. In the late 1990s and early 2000s, the Commission also began to weaken its cross-ownership rules, which limit concentration of ownership of media outlets within a single market (and, in part as a result of legislation, to weaken rules regarding concentration of ownership nationally as well).

Under Republican Presidents Nixon, Ford, and Reagan, but also under the intervening Democratic administration of President Carter, and continuing under Republican George H. W. Bush and Democrat Clinton, the move to reduce the regulatory burden on business was even more pronounced. This was brought about partially by executive order, and partially by legislation. In general terms, there were two major changes in the regulatory process. First, agencies were required to prepare a Regulatory Impact Analysis (RIA) of the costs and benefits of a proposed regulation. While they were to take account of effects that cannot readily be monetarized, this requirement greatly increased the weight given to economics (and to the standing of economists, with the ideological orientation implied) in the regulatory process. Second, agencies were required to submit proposed regulations and their RIAs to the Office of Information and Regulatory Affairs in the Office of Management and Budget, and to refrain from final publication (and therefore effectiveness) of the regulation until they had responded to the OMB Director's views. The result was a significant number of proposed regulations that never went into effect.

On the other hand, deregulation did not necessarily extend to ordinary people or to fields other than economics. On questions like abortion, and under George W. Bush on education, the deregulatory Republicans have been happy to enforce ever more regulations. Moreover, on questions of health, safety, and the environment, the 1970s and 1980s saw increases in the authority of agencies like the EPA, EEOC, and OSHA. And although Congress did in the 1990s manage to weaken the Clean Water Act and the Endangered Species Act, public demand for regulations to ensure worker and consumer safety have led to stricter standards in some fields. In fact, in large measure, the question never was whether or not to regulate. It was what to regulate, and in whose interest.

Reinventing government

By the 1990s, the perception that the public was disenchanted with bureaucracy was widespread among politicians of both parties. Although the Democrats supported some aspects of deregulation, the ideas that regulation was suspect *per se*, and that reducing the size and scope of government was a valuable end in itself, were supported primarily by the conservative (and dominant) wing of the Republican Party. The Democratic response to public discontent was to propose reforming government rather than simply shrinking it. Emblematically, in his October 1991 speech formally announcing his presidential candidacy, Bill Clinton said:

I want to reinvent government to make it more efficient and more effective. I want to give citizens more choices in the services they get, and empower them to make those choices. . . . [I]n Arkansas . . . [w]e've balanced the budget every year and improved services. We've treated taxpayers like our customers and our bosses, because they are.

This statement has two aspects. On the one hand, given the belief that their electoral defeats were in significant measure rooted in the perception of the Democrats as the party of 'tax and spend', it is hardly surprising that Clinton would promise balanced budgets and efficient administration. In this respect, 'reinventing government' could be understood as a way of 'downsizing government' without reducing its functions. On the other hand, the emphasis on cost–benefit analysis, and its implicit privileging of economic impact over other criteria for the evaluation of government actions, which were central to the deregulatory movement, had implications not only for *what* the government should regulate, but also for *how* the government should conduct its business and how the relationship between bureaucracy and citizens should be understood. And this, too, is evident in the idea of reinventing government, with its focus on taxpayers (as opposed to citizens) and its analogizing of them to customers. Similarly, the emphasis on services and on [consumer] choice suggests that government is more like a firm producing private goods or services for the market than it is a democratic institution 'producing' public goods, prominent among which is regulation of the market.

Although rooted in very different circumstances than the 'New Public Management', which was advanced for parliamentary democracies with highly centralized control, the reinvention of government shared with it the idea that management tools that were successful in the private sector could be directly translated to the public sector. Among these were a flattening of hierarchies, empowering of staff to adapt to customer demand, reduction of staff by outsourcing of tasks, and increasing the efficiency of the remaining staff. Perhaps most significantly, both involve evaluative standards based on results, whereas bureaucracies (and democracies) traditionally had been evaluated primarily on the basis of process.

The success of the Clinton administration in actually reinventing government was quite limited (see Kettl 1998 for a fuller evaluation). Although Clinton's claim in his 1996 State of the Union address that 'the era of big government is over' was matched by significant reductions-in-force during the rest of his time in office, these were not well matched to reductions-in-mission, but largely attempted to get more work out of fewer people. Some of the emphasis on entrepreneurial management was already embodied in the Senior Executive Service well before Clinton took office. As observed above, the flattening of administrative hierarchies has not occurred. Outsourcing produced some real savings, but sometimes at the expense of the workers who were paid less in the private sector, and at the expense of reliability. Moreover, even if efficiency was increased, in some views, this was not just an increase in efficiency, which is hard to define in the public sphere, where simple profit is not available as a single quantifiable measure of success, but which is also very hard to oppose, but an increase in efficiency at the expense of democratic accountability.

Although the creation of the Department of Homeland Security represented a reversal of some of these trends in its incorporation of previously independent agencies like the Federal Emergency Management Agency (FEMA) into a new and more elaborate hierarchy, many of the failures of the trends to downsize, deregulate, and reinvent became apparent in the second term of the George W. Bush administration (as, indeed, they had become apparent in the private sector as well). Flexibility and accountability to the political executive were shown to have a real danger of being translated into cronyism. Efficiency sometimes translated into inadequate resources, demoralized staff, and unpreparedness.

FEMA's failures in responding to the devastating hurricanes of 2005 (Katrina and Rita) are emblematic of many of the problems of American public administration. Although public opinion naturally tends to blame the administration in office for the failures of government that occur 'on its watch' (and public approval of the Bush administration plummeted in the wake of the hurricane-related failures), and although many of the failures during the Bush administration were at least made more serious by the administration's deliberate choices, much of the blame is more systemic. The appointment of Michael Brown to head FEMA clearly was based more on political loyalty than on managerial competence, let alone technical expertise in emergency management, but it was not Bush's decision that jobs like Director of FEMA should be filled by political appointments rather than from a career service—although he did choose to appoint Brown rather than someone with greater experience in the field. While Bush was instrumental in the decisions to include FEMA as a division of the Department of Homeland Security and then to reduce its budget in favour of the 'anti-terrorist' divisions of the Department, he only supported the creation of the Department in the first place once it became clear that Congress was going to force his hand, and then acquiesced in the diversion of funds to activities that were (depending on one's priorities and either foresight or hindsight) either more important or politically more expedient. The questions of who was in charge and who had the authority to do what—FEMA, the state governors, local mayors—were particularly troublesome because of the time pressure involved in responding to a disaster, but they pervade the American system. The restrictions on the use of the military to enforce, or even to assist in, evacuation orders (dating from the Posse Comitatus Act of 1878, originally passed as part of the ending of post-Civil War Reconstruction in the South) may have made an effective federal response more difficult, but even if these restrictions were interpreted too narrowly, neither the restrictions themselves nor ambiguity in their interpretation are unique to the Bush administration or to problems of disaster relief. Rather, the imprecise definition of lines of responsibility and authority—among the various levels of government, between Congress and the executive, and within the executive branch itself—and the fact that powers are overlapping, shared, and contested rather than neatly divided and separated, which are among the central features of American government, simply became more obvious in a crisis.

KEY TERMS

- Federal Reserve system
- Hatch Act
- independent regulatory commission
- iron triangle
- Regulatory Impact Analysis
- senior executive service
- spoils system
- whistleblower

NOTES

1 'To the victors belong the spoils', as Andrew Jackson is reputed to have said.

2 For example, the Bureau of Land Management, which administers 261 million acres of public lands, is headed by a Director. The Director of the BLM reports to the Assistant Secretary for Land and Minerals, who reports to the Deputy Secretary, who reports to the Secretary of the Interior.

3 The Federal Election Commission, with a rotating chairmanship, is an exception to the practice of presidential nomination of commission chairmen. The FEC is also exceptional in having an even number of commissioners (6), and requiring the votes of four commissioners (a two-thirds majority) to make decisions. As with other independent regulatory commissions, no more than half (in this case without rounding) may be of the same political party.

4 The most common appeals from ordinary agencies concern the rejection of claims for social security benefits.

5 First-class postage rates were more than quadrupled between 1971 and 2001, a rate of increase that roughly equalled (and tracked) the increase in the consumer price index (CPI), in contrast to an increase of only 33 per cent between 1932 and 1958, during which time the CPI had more than doubled. The first-class postage rate then unpopularly doubled between 1958 and 1971, a rate of increase that far exceeded inflation during that period, but that brought the total increase from 1932 back into line with inflation over the same longer period.

6 From Franklin Roosevelt's message to Congress suggesting the creation of the TVA, 10 April 1933.

7 The Federal Reserve Banks are located in Boston, New York, Philadelphia, Cleveland, Richmond, Atlanta, Chicago, St Louis, Minneapolis, Kansas City, Dallas, and San Francisco. There are also 25 branch Reserve banks.

8 According to the US Office of Special Counsel, covered employees may not: use official authority or influence to interfere with an election; solicit or discourage political activity of anyone with business before their agency; solicit or receive political contributions (may be done in certain limited situations by federal labour or other employee organizations); be candidates for public office in partisan elections; engage in political activity while on duty, in a government office, wearing an official uniform, using a government vehicle; wear partisan political buttons on duty (http://www.osc.gov/ha_fed.htm).

9 For example, see http://www.cnn.com/2004/ALLPOLITICS/03/17/medicare.investigation/.

10 'Democrats Want Official To Be Reinstated over Report on Profiling', *New York Times*, 26 August 2005, p. 11.

11 'Army Contract Official Critical of Halliburton Pact Is Demoted', *New York Times*, 29 August 2005, p. 9.

12 Depository Institutions Deregulation Act of 1980, section 204.

13 The so-called Zapple Rule, that extends the equal access requirement to use of a broadcast station by the supporters of a candidate as well as the candidate him- or herself also remains in force.

....

GUIDE TO FURTHER READING

MEIER, K. J. (1993), *Politics and the Bureaucracy: Policymaking in the Fourth Branch of Government* (New York: Harcourt Brace).

An overview of the federal bureaucracy and its role in making policy.

OSBORNE, D. and P. PLATRIK (1998), *Banishing Bureaucracy: the Five Strategies for Reinventing Government* (New York: Penguin).

A follow-up to the 1992 book *Reinventing Government*, the authors advocate reforms to make government more efficient.

SHULL, B. (2005), *The Fourth Branch: the Federal Reserve's Unlikely Rise to Power and Influence* (Westport, CT: Praeger).

Traces how the Federal Reserve system, despite being a significant contributor to a series of economic crises, has managed to emerge from each of them more powerful than it was before.

WILDAVSKY, A. and N. CAIDEN (2003), *The New Politics of the Budgetary Process* (5th edn) (New York: Longman).

An updated and revised version of the classic analysis of the American budgetary process.

8

The Judiciary

Overview

This chapter describes the structures of the federal and state court systems, and introduces the ongoing debate about how the courts should interpret both the Constitution and statutory or regulatory decisions. The courts have played a central role in American politics, particularly through the use of their power to declare actions of the other branches of government to be in violation of the Constitution and therefore void. This has made judicial appointments extremely important, and the subject of intense political contestation. The chapter also reviews the major questions currently before the courts. Finally, it gives an overview of the state court systems.

The American judiciary consists of 51 separate court systems, one federal and 50 independent state systems, administering 51 separate bodies of law. They intersect in those cases in which federal law supersedes state law or that the federal constitution limits the powers of the states, but beyond that they are independent. For example, the federal Supreme Court and a state supreme court may decide that the same words have different meaning when they appear in the federal constitution (where the federal courts have the final say) than they do when they appear in a state constitution (where the courts of that state have the final say). Decisions of state courts can be appealed to the federal courts, and ultimately to the Supreme Court of the United States, only in cases that present a federal question, and even then the Supreme Court of the United States is bound by the highest state court's interpretation of state law.

The federal courts

The Constitution established only the Supreme Court of the United States, leaving it to Congress to establish such inferior courts as it deemed necessary. Ultimately, Congress created a three-tiered system of general courts. At the middle of 2005, the base of this system consisted of 89 federal district courts, at least one in each state plus courts in the District of Columbia, Puerto Rico, the US Virgin Islands, Guam, and the Marianas. Each district court had a maximum authorized (by statute) bench of between one and 28 active judges, making a total of 667 federal district judges. Above these are the 13 federal courts of appeals, authorized to have between six and 28 judges each, making a total of 179 federal appeals court judges. Twelve of these courts serve particular areas, while the thirteenth, the Court of Appeals for the Federal Circuit, has national jurisdiction over a defined range of subjects. At the top is the Supreme Court, with eight associate justices plus the Chief Justice of the United States. Judges of all of these courts are appointed by the president with the 'Advice and Consent' of the Senate, and serve 'during good Behaviour'—that is, for life or until they choose to retire (or are impeached and convicted). As shown in Table 8.1, although the size of the Supreme Court has not varied since 1869, the number of judgeships for the courts of appeals and district courts has increased with the growth of the country and of the role of the federal government, and in particular has nearly doubled since 1977.

In addition to this hierarchy of regular courts, Congress has also created a number of specialized courts for areas where highly technical expertise is required: the Court of Federal Claims, the Tax Court, the Court of International Trade, the Court of Appeals for the Armed Forces, the Court of Appeals for Veterans' Claims. The judges of these courts are also appointed by the president and confirmed by the Senate, but except for the judges of the Court of International Trade, they are appointed for terms of 15 years.[1]

Finally, the Foreign Intelligence Surveillance Act (FISA) of 1978 created a special court, the Foreign Intelligence Surveillance Court, consisting of 11 district court judges (increased from seven by the USA Patriot Act in 2001), named by the Chief Justice. The purpose of the FISA Court is to approve warrants for surveillance involving suspected espionage or terrorism. There is also an Intelligence Surveillance Court of Review made up of

TABLE 8.1	Authorized federal judgeships		
	Supreme Court	Courts of Appeals	District courts
1789–1806	6		13–18
1806–1836	7		18–29
1837–1863	9		29–45
1864–1868	10		46–47
1869–1890	9	9–10	47–64
1891–1921	9	19–32	64–91
1922–1935	9	33–46	118–147
1936–1953	9	47–65	163–212
1954–1960	9	68	238–241
1961–1965	9	78	301
1966–1969	9	88–97	337
1970–1977	9	97	394
1978–1983	9	132–144	510
1984–1989	9	168	563
1990–2004	9	179	632–667

district or court of appeals judges, also named by the Chief Justice, to which the government may appeal the (extremely rare—in fact, the Surveillance Court of Review did not meet until 2002) denial of a warrant. Members of the FISA Court sit individually—in a special room in the Justice Department Building rather than in a court house—while members of the Court of Review sit in three-judge panels. Both courts meet in secret, and only the government is represented. Records of their proceedings are kept, but only redacted versions are ever made public. The basic structure of the federal court system is shown in Figure 8.1.

Federal district and appeals court judges who are at least 65 years of age and whose age plus years of service total at least 80 have the option of retiring to 'senior' status. Senior judges can continue to sit, essentially on a volunteer basis and with a radically reduced work load. Finally, there are a number of federal magistrates, selected for eight year terms by majority

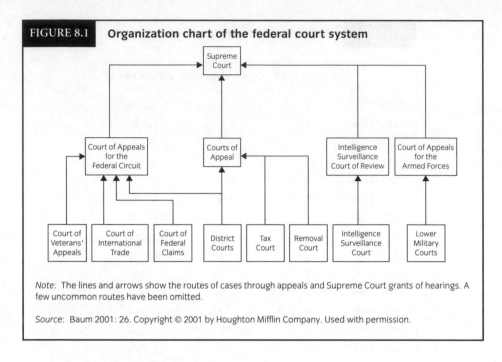

FIGURE 8.1 **Organization chart of the federal court system**

Note: The lines and arrows show the routes of cases through appeals and Supreme Court grants of hearings. A few uncommon routes have been omitted.

Source: Baum 2001: 26. Copyright © 2001 by Houghton Mifflin Company. Used with permission.

vote of the active judges of a district court, and bankruptcy judges, selected for 14-year terms by vote of the active judges of a court of appeals. Federal magistrates and bankruptcy judges exercise judicial authority defined by statute or delegated to them by the relevant district court or court of appeals.

In contrast to many countries in which separate court systems deal with administrative law, the American federal courts, with the exceptions just noted, are all courts of general jurisdiction, dealing with both law and equity, civil and criminal cases, etc. There is no separate body of administrative law such as is administered by the French Conseil d'Etat; complaints of government abuse are heard in the same courts as disputes between private parties. There also is no separate constitutional court; although most constitutional rulings are made by appellate courts, any court in the United States may rule (subject, of course, to appeal) that a statute is void because it violates the higher ('supreme') law of the Constitution.

Courts and politics

One of the central problems confronting any democratic system is to establish the proper balance between the judiciary and the 'political' branches of government—given that the judicial function is necessarily political. This problem has had three important foci in the United States. The first was basically settled in the case of *Marbury v. Madison* (1 Cr 137, 1803), which established the power of the Supreme Court (judicial review), and by extension all American courts, to declare an Act of Congress, and by extension any Act of any federal or state official, including the president, to be null and void if it exceeded the authority granted by the Constitution.[2] Particularly after the ratification of the Fourteenth Amendment clearly (or as clearly as anything ever is in American constitutional law) extended the protections against federal actions embodied in the Bill of Rights to apply against state actions as well, this power of the federal courts to nullify laws or other government actions as being in violation of the federal constitution has also applied to the states. More generally, *Marbury v. Madison* established the courts as the ultimate arbiters of the meaning of the Constitution. The effect is to make decisions of the Supreme Court the real 'supreme law of the land', subject to change only by constitutional amendment or by convincing a subsequent Supreme Court to overrule itself.[3] While it is rare for the Supreme Court to overrule a prior judgment of the Court, it is even rarer for this to happen without a prior change in the composition of the Court. This makes the appointment of Supreme Court justices (and indeed all federal judges) with life tenure supremely political. If the Supreme Court were infallible, the attempt to insulate the courts from partisan politics might not be problematic, although it still would be anti-democratic. But as Justice Robert H. Jackson once famously remarked concerning the Supreme Court: 'We are not final because we are infallible, but we are infallible only because we are final.' In the medium term, however, the anti-democraticness of life tenure may be less serious than it appears, since as Finley Peter Dunne's fictional Chicago bartender Mr Dooley observed, 'th' Supreme Court follows th' iliction returns', whether as a result of replacement or as a result of the belief of the judges themselves that they should not be too far out of step with public opinion.

The second problem remains unsettled, and by its nature is bound to remain so. How pervasive is the courts' power to be? Are there important questions that are 'not justiciable'? How narrowly or expansively crafted should the courts' decisions be? How radical should the remedies ordered be? How deferential should the courts be to the judgments of other branches of government (and perhaps also to public opinion)? In sum, to use the word generally applied by those who do not like their decisions, how 'activist' should judges be?

The third problem also is necessarily unsettled. This is the question of how a judge properly decides the meaning of the law. In contemporary American politics, this has involved two related disputes. Principally at the level of constitutional jurisprudence, there has been a dispute between, on the one hand, those who believe that the original meaning or original intent of the Constitution must govern the courts' interpretations (unless, of course, there has been an amendment, in which case, presumably, the intent of the amenders must prevail) and, on the other hand, those who believe that the Constitution must be interpreted as a living document, the meaning of which evolves along with the development of society. A somewhat older framing of essentially the same dispute juxtaposed strict constructionists and those who believe in greater flexibility (and creativity) in interpretation. Particularly with regard to statutory or regulatory interpretation (but not limited to those), the dispute has been between the 'textualists', who believe that only the plain, or dictionary, meaning of the words of the statute or regulation at the time of enactment are relevant, and those who might be called 'contextualists', who believe that the context in which the law or regulation was drafted, including for example its legislative history, are also relevant to understanding the intent of those who made it.[4]

These questions have been particularly important in the United States because American courts have at times played an unusually central role in resolving, in blocking the resolution, or even in creating some of the most vexing social and political problems confronting the country. Most of the complaints from those on the losing side have been directed at the Supreme Court, both because its decisions have the widest impact and because it is the court of last resort, but they have not been limited to the Supreme Court, or to the federal courts as a whole.

The Supreme Court

With very few exceptions, hearings before the Supreme Court are granted at the Court's discretion through a writ of *certiorari*. In one of the few examples of submajority rule, the writ is granted whenever four of the nine justices vote to hear a case.[5] *Certiorari* is likely to be granted only for the most important and controversial cases, particularly when there is conflict between decisions reached on similar cases in different circuits. On the other hand, extreme controversy has sometimes been a reason for declining to hear a case (or, after a hearing, for the Court to change its mind about the wisdom of having granted *certiorari*) on the ground that the issue is not yet ready for decision. Overall, the Court now receives over 6,000 petitions for *certiorari* every year (roughly twice as many as it received thirty years before), and grants only about 100 of them.[6]

The Supreme Court also has original jurisdiction in a limited range of cases. Most often, which is not often at all, this involves disputes between states (for example, a 1999 case between Kansas and Nebraska over use of water from the Republican River or a 2005 border dispute between New Jersey and Delaware). In these cases, the Court generally appoints a Special Master who actually conducts the fact-finding portion of the trial, and then hears arguments, reads briefs, and then the Court itself decides the case in a manner analogous to that used for appeals. Unlike the constitutional courts of some other countries, the Supreme Court (and the other federal courts) do not issue advisory opinions; they only act in 'cases and controversies', for which there are real opposing parties with real interests at stake.

The Supreme Court normally sits from the first Monday in October until June. Unlike the federal courts of appeals, which usually hear and decide cases in three-judge panels (with discretionary appeal to the whole court *en banc*), the Supreme Court makes all of its final judgments *en banc*. The primary input to the justices' decisions are the record of the courts below and briefs filed by the parties to the case as well as *amicus curiae* (literally, friend of the court) briefs from other concerned parties (frequently including the Department of Justice).[7] Attorneys for the parties also are given time (generally 30 minutes per side) for oral argument before the Court. Much of that time, however, is usually spent responding to questions from the bench.

The Court meets in conference on Wednesday afternoons and Friday mornings to discuss and vote on cases and to decide whether to grant petitions for *certiorari*. These meetings are completely private, with not even the justices' law clerks admitted. Once the Court has reached a provisional decision on a case, the Chief Justice (if in the majority, otherwise the senior justice in the majority) assigns one justice to draft the Opinion of the Court. Because different justices may emphasize different lines of reasoning, or interpret the case more broadly or narrowly, this can be a significant decision. Once written, the draft opinion is circulated among the justices, as are draft dissenting and concurring opinions. In some cases, these drafts may change votes (possibly even changing the outcome of the case), but in all cases one objective is to reach a consensus among at least five or six justices to form a majority not only with regard to outcome, but also with regard to the reasons for the outcome.

Although the Supreme Court has the final legal say in any particular case that it hears, its real power stems from the legal precedents that those decisions set. And the power of Supreme Court precedents stems not only from the fact that they are binding on all other courts—although a creative lawyer or judge may sometimes find a way of 'distinguishing' the case in hand from the existing body of precedents—but particularly in the case of constitutional jurisprudence, from the reverence with which Americans generally regard the Constitution. Perhaps because of the importance of constitutional decisions, the Supreme Court generally tries to avoid making them, preferring whenever possible to decide cases on narrower or more procedural grounds.[8]

Other things being equal, the strength of a precedent increases with the size of the majority, at least in the sense that more judges would have either to be replaced or to change their decisions before the precedent could be overturned. The real necessity for precedent, however, is a majority of at least five justices who subscribe not only to the outcome of the case, but also to the opinion justifying it, and once that majority is obtained, the power of the precedent rests primarily on the clarity and breadth of the opinion. Given that the compromises necessary to build and increase the size of a majority may require softening the language or narrowing the scope of the opinion, these two criteria may work at cross-purposes.

Although the objective generally is to have one opinion that speaks for the Court's majority, justices sometimes issue concurring opinions. Most often, these express overall agreement with the majority, but suggest that the concurring justice would not go quite as far, or would go a bit farther, on some point. Sometimes, however, the concurring justice will agree only with regard to the outcome, but disagree significantly with the reasoning underlying what was to be the 'majority opinion'; while there may then be a majority decision of the case itself, there is no majority opinion, and the result has substantially less value as a precedent to be applied in later cases.[9] Justices who are in the minority often issue dissenting opinions, either individually or as a group. While these have no direct legal weight, they allow the dissenters to argue forcefully (perhaps more forcefully than the author of the majority opinion, who must always be concerned to hold the majority together) for the other side. This underlines the potential legitimacy of the alternative point of view, suggests arguments to lawyers and judges in courts below, and invites the bringing of actions that might be used to restrict, weaken, or ultimately to overturn the majority's decision.

The Supreme Court's final judgments are all made collectively. Each justice, however, also has responsibility for one or more of the federal circuits. Originally, this involved actually hearing cases in the circuit, a practice that was dropped in 1891. Today, this responsibility primarily involves deciding on emergency appeals for stays of judgments of the circuit court to allow time for the Supreme Court as a whole to decide whether it will hear the case. The most highly publicized of these cases involve the issuing of emergency stays of execution, which, because warrants for executions generally are valid only for a limited time, can have the effect of staying an execution for a considerable period of time even if the justice's temporary stay is dissolved by the full Court.

Appointment and confirmation

On average, Supreme Court justices serve for more than 25 years before death or retirement removes them from the Court. At the beginning of 2005, the average tenure of the current justices was just under 20 years, and the most junior justice had served since 1994. Given both the desire to appoint judges who share their political philosophy and will continue to influence policy in that direction for decades to come (and the long-term consequences of inaccurately predicting what a nominee will do on the Court),[10] and the political embarrassment of appointing someone later found to have a personal or professional skeleton in the closet, presidents now go to extraordinary lengths to investigate the backgrounds and philosophies of possible nominees for all federal judgeships, but especially for the Supreme Court.

From the first Chief Justice, John Jay, to the confirmation of John Roberts as the seventeenth Chief Justice[11] in 2005, 107 men and two women had served as justices of the Supreme Court. In addition, there had been 42 nominations that failed, including seven who declined to serve,[12] one triple and two double failures (the same individual nominated multiple times without ever being confirmed), five nominations that were postponed and later confirmed, and two failed attempts to elevate a sitting justice to be Chief Justice. Roughly half of the failed nominations came between 1844 and 1874. There were two nominees rejected in 1893–94, one in 1930, and not another until Lyndon Johnson tried to promote Justice Abe Fortas to be Chief Justice in 1968. Since then, there have been six more failed nominations: one more from Johnson; two from Nixon; one from Reagan (plus one whose nomination was announced but never formally submitted to the Senate); and one from George W. Bush. Of the six failed nominations since 1964, three were rejected by votes in the Senate and the other three were either withdrawn or died through Senate inaction. The three rejected nominations were all proposed by Republican presidents to Democratic Senates; the other three were proposed by presidents to Senates controlled by their own party (two Democrat and one Republican).

There has been debate concerning the criteria appropriate for Senate confirmation decisions, in particular whether the Senate should consider only the abstract 'competence' of the nominee or whether political philosophy and policy preferences are valid considerations as well, since the first Senate rejection of a nomination, that of sitting Justice John Rutledge to be Chief Justice in 1795.[13] Particularly beginning with President Nixon's nominations of Clement Haynsworth and G. Harold Carswell (both rejected), Republican presidents have quite overtly attempted to reshape the Supreme Court, and the federal judiciary more generally, by purposefully appointing conservative judges. While they have claimed not to have applied specific litmus tests, they have been quite open (if sometimes using slightly coded language) about their desire to see a string of developments concerning civil liberties, criminal justice, and most recently abortion, stopped or preferably reversed. They have also become quite open about preferring younger nominees, with the intention of leaving a longer-lasting mark on the judiciary even if the Democrats were to regain the White House.

In 2001, George Bush ended the practice that had begun under President Eisenhower of asking the American Bar Association's Committee on the Federal Judiciary to evaluate the professional qualifications of nominees before their names were submitted to the Senate. According to Bush, it was inappropriate to 'grant a preferential, quasi-official role in the judicial selection process to a politically active group'.[14] Although the vast majority of nominees judged to be 'not qualified' by the American Bar Association (ABA) had been named by Democrats, the dissent of four members of the Committee from the 'well qualified' evaluation given to Robert Bork was seen by conservatives as significantly to have contributed to the rejection of his nomination in 1987 and to indicate a 'liberal bias' on the part of the ABA. From the other side, this move was seen as an attempt to avoid having the 'judicial temperament' of doctrinaire conservatives challenged. While the ABA still reports its evaluations of actual nominees to the Senate Judiciary Committee, it now has the same standing as any other group, including right-wing think tanks.

William Rehnquist in 1971 was the last person with no judicial experience to be successfully appointed to the Supreme Court (Harriet Miers in 2005 is the most recent unsuccessful nominee), but over one-third of all Supreme Court justices (and nearly one-third of those appointed since 1960) had no experience as a judge when they were appointed. In recent years, the path to the Supreme Court has clearly run through the federal circuit courts; Sandra Day O'Connor in 1981 was both the first woman and the last person without federal appellate court experience (she had been an Arizona state legislator and state judge) to go on to the Court.

Once a nomination is made to the Senate, it is considered by the Judiciary Committee. Committee members (in reality, the staff of the Committee and of the individual senators) will pore over the nominee's record, including especially opinions he or she will have written as a judge on other courts, memoranda written in previous jobs in government, types of client represented as an attorney, and so forth. The nominee also will meet privately with individual members of the Committee as well as other leading senators, and will be questioned in public hearings before the Committee. Although the obvious objective of this scrutiny is to predict how the nominee will decide cases on the Supreme Court, it is considered inappropriate to ask, and certainly for the nominee to answer, direct questions about matters that might come before the Court. Thus, although the possibility that a new justice might vote to overturn *Roe v. Wade* (410 US 113), the decision that legalized abortion, has clearly been paramount in the politics of Supreme Court nominations for more than two decades, presidents have denied asking prospective nominees whether they would vote to overturn the decision, and, even if asked by members of the Judiciary Committee, nominees have refused to answer.

Although the debate about a nomination often is phrased in terms of technical qualifications or judicial temperament, these concerns generally are raised only by those who are opposed to the nominee on ideological grounds. Phrases like 'a judicial philosophy that is outside the mainstream' are used to characterize a nominee that opponents think is too conservative, while in the past the label 'judicial activist' was applied to nominees thought to be too liberal. In deciding how vigorously to oppose a nomination, senators have to balance a number of considerations. One is the public belief (however detached from reality) that the judiciary should be above partisan politics. A second is the undoubted fact that the appointment of judges is a presidential prerogative, although tempered by the requirement of senatorial advice and consent. Both of these raise the possibility of political fallout from being seen as 'obstructionist' or to have 'injected politics into the judiciary'. Against these is the reality that once confirmed a judge will be on the bench long after the president who appointed him or her has left office. Moreover, there is the danger that should they defeat a nominee, opponents will be confronted with a new nominee whom they consider to be even worse.

Given the general presumption that the president has the right to name whomever he wishes, and especially if the president's party is in the majority in the Senate, it is unlikely that opponents of a nomination will be able to defeat it in a straight vote. The rules and informal practices of the Senate, however, allow a substantial minority—and in the case of inferior court nominations, sometimes even a single senator (particularly if from the state or states where the judge would sit)—to prevent a nomination from ever coming to a vote. Whether this is an example of a salutary pressure to assure that lifetime appointments are broadly acceptable rather than narrowly partisan, or alternatively an example of the danger of minority partisanship and obstructionism, has clearly depended on whose ox is being gored. As an example of the former, when Bill Clinton had the occasion to appoint Supreme Court justices, he reportedly gave a list of potential nominees to the (majority) Republican leadership in the Senate, and then chose from among those that the Republicans indicated would be acceptable to them. The results were moderate liberal justices who were confirmed easily. Recent Republican presidents, however, have often nominated more doctrinaire individuals without attempting to reach a prior consensus and then to take their chances with the Senate, or even to deliberately provoke the Democrats to oppose the nominee. In some cases they have been successful and in others not, but even when the nominee has not been confirmed, the president has been able to use the fight to energize his political base.

The lower federal courts

The vast majority of the business of the federal courts concerns civil litigation. In 2004, there were 281,338 civil cases and 71,022 criminal cases filed in federal district courts. In the same year, the 12 regional courts of appeal disposed of 27,438 appeals on the merits, roughly two-thirds solely on the basis of the briefs filed, but 8,645 (31 per cent) after oral hearing. One obvious consequence of the small number of cases decided by the Supreme Court is that for the vast majority of cases the decision of the court of appeals is final. While conflicting decisions by different circuit courts greatly increases the likelihood that the Supreme Court will choose to hear a case, the sheer disparity in numbers assures that many inconsistencies will remain.

Particularly with the smaller circuits, differences may simply reflect the fact that the majority of judges on different circuits have been appointed by presidents with different ideological predilections—whether because of different partisanship or simply because the relevant issues change over time. More generally, because circuit court judges almost always are chosen from among lawyers and judges in the region where the court sits, and because there are significant cultural differences among American regions, there are often significant differences in the jurisprudence of different circuits. Even though they theoretically administer the same law, circuit courts for the south (the 4th, 5th, and 11th circuits) generally are regarded to be less sympathetic to criminal defendants than circuits (1st and 2nd) in the northeast; the 9th circuit (covering nine states stretching from Arizona to Alaska and Hawaii) has developed a strong pro-environment reputation.[15] The 9th circuit is also sometimes identified as the 'circuit court for Hollywood', which has meant that it has been called upon to decide a far higher than random proportion of the kinds of cases likely to inflame social conservatives.

Both criminal and civil federal trials begin in the district courts. In both types of case, the Constitution guarantees a jury trial, although this right can be waived by a criminal defendant or by agreement of the parties in a civil suit. Federal criminal juries must consist of 12 members, while federal civil juries generally have six members. In both cases, the jury's verdict is supposed to be unanimous, but the parties to a civil action may agree to accept a less-than-unanimous verdict. Criminal acquittals may not be appealed, but all other verdicts may be appealed. The district courts are the only courts to hear evidence and establish the factual record. While appeals may claim that the evidence is inadequate to support the verdict reached in the district court, more often they concern matters of procedure and legal interpretation rather than facts.

The federal courts only hear cases in which there is a federal question involved; notwithstanding the American colloquialism about 'making a federal case' of something, it is not the intrinsic importance of the case but rather its nature *vis-à-vis* federalism that matters. For criminal cases, this means either that the defendant is alleged to have broken a federal law (which generally means either that the offence was committed on federal property, involved the crossing of state lines, or is, however tendentiously, related to interstate commerce or national security) or alleges that a state violated the defendant's *federally protected* rights. (Technically, the last of these is a civil case, even though the underlying issue is criminal. Often these begin with a *writ of habeas corpus*—an order requiring those holding a person to justify his or her detention.) For civil cases, the federal courts have jurisdiction based either on the nature (federal or state) of the law invoked or on the diversity of citizenship of the parties —subject to the limitation that the federal courts will not hear cases involving less than $75,000.[16] Moreover, cases can only be brought by parties with 'standing'—that is, who have a personal and direct interest in the outcome.

In principle, not just the law to be enforced but the jurisdiction of the federal courts is decided by Congress. Most notoriously, in 1868 Congress repealed the right of the Supreme Court to hear appeals regarding denial of *habeas corpus* (fearing that the Court would overturn the Reconstruction Laws) while a case actually was before it (*ex parte McCardle* 74 US 506 (Wall.)). The Court obediently ruled that it no longer had jurisdiction. Attempts to restrict federal jurisdiction have periodically been made by those who do not like the courts' decisions: regarding forced school bussing to achieve racial integration; appeals from administrative hearings regarding immigration; death penalty review. Whether attempts to short-circuit constitutional review, even if those attempts are apparently sanctioned by the Constitution, are consistent with constitutional government in a broader sense, remains an open question.

Contemporary issues before the courts

The substance of the central questions confronting the federal courts naturally has changed over time. In the opening decade of the twenty-first century, however, there appear to be several classes of issue that are, have been for some time, and are likely to remain, among the most important and contentious.

Before 1962, the courts avoided what Justice Frankfurter identified as the 'political thicket' of legislative apportionment, ruling these to be non-justiciable political questions. Beginning with *Baker v. Carr* (369 US 186), however, the courts imposed ever more stringent and far-reaching requirements of population equality. As one politician put it, in doing so the courts 'just made gerrymandering easier',[17] and this, in conjunction with the Voting Rights Act (which, among other things, requires pre-clearance by the Justice Department or the federal courts of changes in electoral laws that might adversely affect the representation of minorities), raised a series of further questions. Through the 1990s, the most prominent among these concerned race: Did the victims of an alleged racial gerrymander have to prove intent or merely effect? To what extent could legislatures take race into account in drawing district lines if the intent was to promote rather than inhibit minority representation? More recently, the question has shifted to the permissibility of partisan gerrymanders, focusing especially on the midterm redrawing of congressional districts by the Republican state legislature of Texas. The contested 2000 presidential election, and subsequent 'corrective' legislation (especially the Help America Vote Act) has led to federal court involvement in many other aspects of election administration as well. The continuing dilemma of how to reconcile regulation of political finance with freedom of speech has also contributed to the explosion of court involvement in the conduct of elections.

The Warren Court dramatically extended the federally protected rights of criminal defendants[18] as well as the free speech and privacy rights of dissidents. In the view of many self-described conservatives, these rulings went too far, with the result that obviously guilty criminals were released on 'technicalities' and protesters were allowed to profane cherished national symbols, and the police and prosecutors were unduly restricted in their efforts to catch and convict criminals and to protect the public. Those on the other side point to convictions of individuals later proven to be innocent as evidence of the importance of procedural protections to a fair trial (especially given the disparity of resources between often poor defendants and the state) and accept that a certain amount of offensive behaviour is the price one pays for free debate. While the Burger and Rehnquist Courts have restricted some of these rights, both the rights themselves and the use of the federal courts to enforce them (particularly in what death penalty advocates tend to see as groundless ploys to delay executions) remain highly contentious.

Both questions of election administration and criminal rights have often raised the perennial American problem of race. (Are gerrymanders that are constructed to promote or inhibit minority representation permissible? Are African Americans disproportionately likely to be sentenced to death?) The broader question, however, concerns the meaning of 'equal protection of the laws' as guaranteed by the Fourteenth Amendment, and the limits of governmental power to enforce non-discriminatory treatment (for example, in employment or public accommodation) under the commerce clause of Article I. These issues returned to the judicial forefront with the Warren Court's ruling in *Brown v. Board of Education* (347 US 483, 1954) that racially segregated public schools were inherently unequal and therefore unconstitutional under the Fourteenth Amendment, thus overturning the legal basis for the American version of apartheid—'separate but equal'—that had been sanctioned in the 1896 case of *Plessy v. Ferguson* (163 US 537). The most recent flashpoint has been 'affirmative action', and the question has been whether these programmes are necessary and proper measures to redress past injustices, or cases of unfair discrimination that, counter to the objective of a 'colour blind society', give unmerited advantages to members of some groups supposedly in compensation for wrongs they did not themselves suffer. While race and gender are the most prominent foci, the limits of allowable discrimination (for or against) based on physical or mental disability, sexual orientation or religion also continue to be defined in the courts.

A fourth complex of questions in large measure revolves around the role of religion in public life. While separation of church and state issues such as the propriety of public support for church-related schools, officially sanctioned prayers at state-sponsored events and in public schools, and displays of religious symbols on public property (most often in Christmas displays, but more recently displays of the Ten Commandments in courts) continue to arise, much of the emphasis has shifted to cases in which conservative Christians see the government as advancing teachings (evolutionary biology) or allowing behaviours (abortion, same-sex unions) that they see as offensive to their religious beliefs.[19] Ironically, many of these cases involve conservatives simultaneously trying to justify their position with the historically dubious claim that the Framers intended to establish a 'Christian nation' and that their position is not based on religion at all—that nativity scenes are merely secular symbols of the secular Christmas season or that creationism and more recently 'intelligent design' are merely alternative scientific theories.

The balance between federal and state authority remains an open question. In the 1990s and 2000s, this has been manifested most significantly in two areas. The first concerns the right of the federal government to pre-empt state law, or in other ways to intrude into fields that traditionally were regarded as preserves of the states. Particular questions have involved the legalization of marijuana for medicinal purposes and the legalization of physician-assisted suicide, both of which have been approved by popular referendum in one or more states, but which the Bush Justice

Department has attempted to prevent by invoking federal drug laws. The second concerns the reach of federal power to regulate the behaviour of the states themselves, particularly with regard to their employment practices.

A relatively new, but potentially extremely significant, question concerns the extent of the Fifth Amendment's protection against the taking of 'private property . . . for public use without just compensation'. While the right of the government (at whatever level) to force the sale of private property for such public purposes as the building of roads or schools is not in doubt, several jurisdictions have used this power of eminent domain to purchase property that is then turned over to private developers for commercial exploitation—the 'public use' being the cleaning up of blighted neighbourhoods, economic development, and increasing the local tax base. In a 5–4 decision, in 2005 the Supreme Court ruled that this was permissible (*Kelo et al. v. City of New London et al.* 125 S. Ct. 2655). A second aspect of this question that has come to the fore concerns the meaning of the word 'take'. Here the question is when land use regulations (for example, prohibiting the draining of wetlands, restrictions on building in certain areas) become so onerous as to amount to the taking of the property.[20] Although the Supreme Court ruled in 1926 (*Village of Euclid v. Ambler Realty Company* 272 US 365) that zoning regulations were a legitimate use of the government's police power and did not constitute a 'taking', the boundary between legitimate exercise of police powers and the illegitimate shifting of the costs of public projects, no matter how laudable, on to a few property owners remains unclear. As the ideological balance of the Supreme Court has shifted, however, the possibility that a far broader range of regulations will be found to require financial compensation has increased.

From Abraham Lincoln's suspension of the writ of habeas corpus and the Emancipation Proclamation during the Civil War to the Reagan administration's apparently illegal transfer of weapons to Iran (part of the 'Iran-contra'affair), the question of the limits, if any, on the so-called implied powers of the presidency with regard to national defence has surfaced periodically. After the attacks of 11 September 2001, the announcement of the 'war on terrorism', and the invasion of Afghanistan, the question arose again. Initially, Congress and the courts appeared ready to acquiesce to the Bush administration's claims that the exigencies of 'war' allowed it to take actions—including the designation of individuals as 'enemy combatants' (a status that they claimed affords neither the protections of criminal law nor of the Geneva Conventions) and the indefinite detention of American citizens so classified at the sole discretion of the executive and without access to the courts—that in ordinary times would be blatantly unconstitutional. As the crisis faded in memory, and as the extent of the executive claims, and their disregard for apparently settled law, became more apparent, however, the courts began to step in, ruling against the administration with some frequency. When the need to renew some provisions of the USA Patriot Act[21] (passed with virtually no debate or dissent less than five weeks after the 11 September attacks) coincided with revelations that the administration had authorized the interception of foreign communications of American citizens without judicial warrants—and the apparent collapse of public confidence in the Bush administration's handling of the war on terror and the war in Iraq—Congress appeared more willing to challenge the executive's claim of blanket authority as well (by the end of 2005, some members of the administration were claiming that there were literally no legal or constitutional limits to the president's authority with regard to national defence). While the administration appeared anxious to avoid a judicial showdown if possible,[22] at the beginning of 2006 the issue showed no signs of going away quickly.

State courts and state law

The vast majority of judicial business in the United States both originates and ends in the state courts. In 2000, there were more than 20 million civil cases and more than 14 million criminal cases filed in state trial courts, and nearly 300,000 cases filed in state appellate courts. Each state defines its own court system and no two are exactly alike. In general, they have four tiers:

1. Minor trial courts that handle petty crimes and civil cases where the amount at issue is highly limited, often using relatively informal rules of procedure and no jury.

2. Major trial courts that handle serious crimes and larger civil cases, and may also hear appeals from the minor trial courts (most often in the form of a right by the loser in the minor trial court to have

the case retried *de novo* under more formal rules of procedure and with a jury trial).

3. One or more intermediate courts of appeal (not all states have such a court or courts).

4. A single supreme court.[23]

At one extreme, the court system of California (Figure 8.2) consists simply of a Supreme Court (7 justices), six Courts of Appeal (105 justices), and 58 Superior Courts (one for each county; 1,498 judges plus 417 commissioners

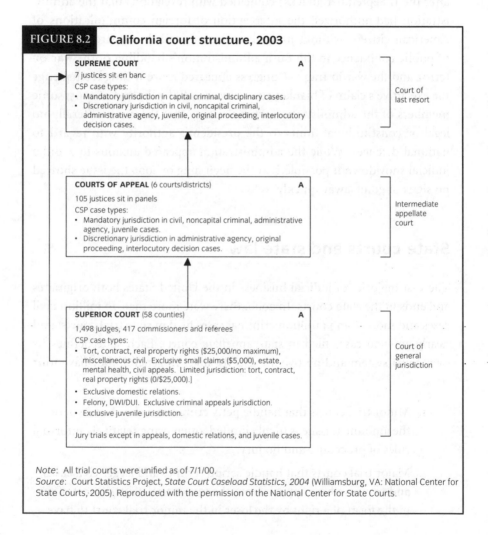

FIGURE 8.2 California court structure, 2003

SUPREME COURT   A
7 justices sit en banc
CSP case types:
- Mandatory jurisdiction in capital criminal, disciplinary cases.
- Discretionary jurisdiction in civil, noncapital criminal, administrative agency, juvenile, original proceeding, interlocutory decision cases.

Court of last resort

COURTS OF APPEAL (6 courts/districts)   A
105 justices sit in panels
CSP case types:
- Mandatory jurisdiction in civil, noncapital criminal, administrative agency, juvenile cases.
- Discretionary jurisdiction in administrative agency, original proceeding, interlocutory decision cases.

Intermediate appellate court

SUPERIOR COURT (58 counties)   A
1,498 judges, 417 commissioners and referees
CSP case types:
- Tort, contract, real property rights ($25,000/no maximum), miscellaneous civil. Exclusive small claims ($5,000), estate, mental health, civil appeals. Limited jurisdiction: tort, contract, real property rights (0/$25,000).]
- Exclusive domestic relations.
- Felony, DWI/DUI. Exclusive criminal appeals jurisdiction.
- Exclusive juvenile jurisdiction.

Jury trials except in appeals, domestic relations, and juvenile cases.

Court of general jurisdiction

Note: All trial courts were unified as of 7/1/00.
Source: Court Statistics Project, *State Court Caseload Statistics, 2004* (Williamsburg, VA: National Center for State Courts, 2005). Reproduced with the permission of the National Center for State Courts.

and referees). At the other extreme, New York (Figure 8.3) has a Court of Appeals (7 judges), the Appellate Division of the Supreme Court (56 justices in four courts) *and* the Appellate Terms of the Supreme Court (15 justices), the Supreme Court (12 districts, 346 judges) and County Courts (57 counties outside of New York City; 128 judges), as well as a Court of Claims, 62 Surrogates' Courts (for estates and adoptions), 62 Family Courts, 79 City Courts, District Courts in Nassau and Suffolk counties, separate civil and criminal courts for New York City, and 1,487 town and village justice courts.

As shown in Table 8.2, the states also differ with regard to the method of selection for judges. Only Maine, New Hampshire, and New Jersey mirror the federal practice of straightforward executive appointment, and only Rhode Island mirrors the federal practice of granting judges tenure for life. Even judges who are appointed through so-called merit selection procedures often are required to face the voters in judicial retention elections. In some cases, these are simple yes or no votes, but in others sitting judges can be challenged by aspirants who can thereby by-pass the merit selection procedure. Unlike federal judges, for whom appointment and confirmation is the only qualification legally required, almost all states require judges to be lawyers licensed in that state, in many cases with at least five years' (or more) experience in practice. Some states also mandate pre-bench and/or continuing judicial education.

Of even greater significance than their differences in judicial structure and recruitment, are differences among the states with regard to the content of their laws. The most systematic (although not in every case the most substantively significant) difference is between Louisiana's civil law system, derived from its pre-1803 experience as a French colony, and the common law system of the rest of the country.[24] For example, based on this tradition, Louisiana is the only state to allow appellate review of the facts in a civil case.[25] In contrast to the 'lemon laws' in other states (which allow the purchaser of an automobile to demand a refund if the manufacturer cannot fix significant defects within a reasonable time) or the implied warranty of merchantability of the Uniform Commercial Code, Louisiana retains the far more general and consumer-friendly civil law action in redhibition.

While some states have adopted constitutional amendments explicitly directing their courts to interpret their state constitution in conformity with the US Supreme Court's interpretation of the federal constitution

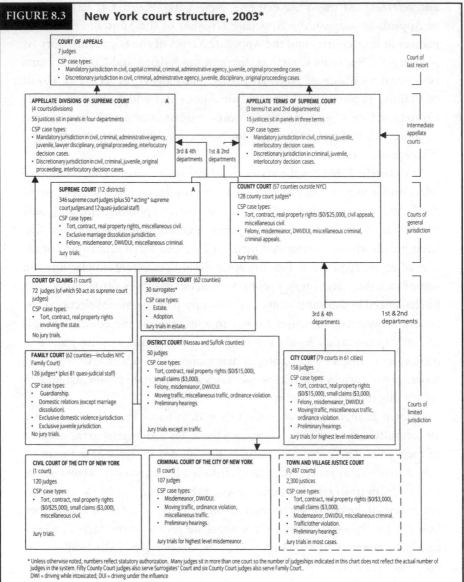

FIGURE 8.3   New York court structure, 2003*

COURT OF APPEALS
7 judges
CSP case types:
- Mandatory jurisdiction in civil, capital criminal, criminal, administrative agency, juvenile, original proceeding cases.
- Discretionary jurisdiction in civil, criminal, administrative agency, juvenile, disciplinary, original proceeding cases.

Court of last resort

APPELLATE DIVISIONS OF SUPREME COURT   A
(4 courts/divisions)
56 justices sit in panels in four departments
CSP case types:
- Mandatory jurisdiction in civil, criminal, administrative agency, juvenile, lawyer disciplinary, original proceeding, interlocutory decision cases.
- Discretionary jurisdiction in civil, criminal, juvenile, original proceeding, interlocutory decision cases.

3rd & 4th departments | 1st & 2nd departments

APPELLATE TERMS OF SUPREME COURT
(3 terms/1st and 2nd departments)
15 justices sit in panels in three terms
CSP case types:
- Mandatory jurisdiction in civil, criminal, juvenile, interlocutory decision cases.
- Discretionary jurisdiction in criminal, juvenile, interlocutory decision cases.

Intermediate appellate courts

SUPREME COURT (12 districts)   A
346 supreme court judges (plus 50 "acting" supreme court judges and 12 quasi-judicial staff)
CSP case types:
- Tort, contract, real property rights, miscellaneous civil.
- Exclusive marriage dissolution jurisdiction.
- Felony, misdemeanor, DWI/DUI, miscellaneous criminal.
Jury trials.

COUNTY COURT (57 counties outside NYC)
128 county court judges*
CSP case types:
- Tort, contract, real property rights ($0/$25,000), civil appeals, miscellaneous civil.
- Felony, misdemeanor, DWI/DUI, miscellaneous criminal, criminal appeals.
Jury trials.

Courts of general jurisdiction

COURT OF CLAIMS (1 court)
72 judges (of which 50 act as supreme court judges)
CSP case types:
- Tort, contract, real property rights involving the state.
No jury trials.

SURROGATES' COURT (62 counties)
30 surrogates*
CSP case types:
- Estate.
- Adoption.
Jury trials in estate.

3rd & 4th departments | 1st & 2nd departments

DISTRICT COURT (Nassau and Suffolk counties)
50 judges
CSP case types:
- Tort, contract, real property rights ($0/$15,000), small claims ($3,000).
- Felony, misdemeanor, DWI/DUI.
- Moving traffic, miscellaneous traffic, ordinance violation.
- Preliminary hearings.
Jury trials except in traffic.

FAMILY COURT (62 counties—includes NYC Family Court)
126 judges* (plus 81 quasi-judicial staff)
CSP case types:
- Guardianship.
- Domestic relations (except marriage dissolution).
- Exclusive domestic violence jurisdiction.
- Exclusive juvenile jurisdiction.
No jury trials.

CITY COURT (79 courts in 61 cities)
158 judges
CSP case types:
- Tort, contract, real property rights ($0/$15,000), small claims ($3,000).
- Felony, misdemeanor, DWI/DUI.
- Moving traffic, miscellaneous traffic, ordinance violation.
- Preliminary hearings.
Jury trials for highest level misdemeanor.

Courts of limited jurisdiction

CIVIL COURT OF THE CITY OF NEW YORK
(1 court)
120 judges
CSP case types:
- Tort, contract, real property rights ($0/$25,000), small claims ($3,000), miscellaneous civil.
Jury trials.

CRIMINAL COURT OF THE CITY OF NEW YORK
(1 court)
107 judges
CSP case types:
- Misdemeanor, DWI/DUI.
- Moving traffic, ordinance violation, miscellaneous traffic.
- Preliminary hearings.
Jury trials for highest level misdemeanor.

TOWN AND VILLAGE JUSTICE COURT
(1,487 courts)
2,300 justices
CSP case types:
- Tort, contract, real property rights ($0/$3,000), small claims ($3,000).
- Misdemeanor, DWI/DUI, miscellaneous criminal.
- Traffic/other violation.
- Preliminary hearings.
Jury trials in most cases.

* Unless otherwise noted, numbers reflect statutory authorization. Many judges sit in more than one court so the number of judgeships indicated in this chart does not reflect the actual number of judges in the system. Fifty County Court judges also serve Surrogates' Court and six County Court judges also serve Family Court..
DWI = driving while intoxicated; DUI = driving under the influence

Source: Court Statistics Project, *State Court Caseload Statistics, 2004* (Williamsburg, VA: National Center for State Courts, 2005). Reproduced with the permission of the National Center for State Courts.

TABLE 8.2	Methods of selection of judges to full terms on state courts	
	Major Trial Courts	Supreme Courts
Partisan election	Alabama, Arkansas, Illinois, Indiana, New Mexico, New York, Pennsylvania, Tennessee, Texas, West Virginia	Alabama, Arkansas, Illinois, New Mexico, North Carolina, Pennsylvania, Texas, West Virginia
Non-partisan election	Arizona, California, Florida, Georgia, Idaho, Kentucky, Louisiana, Michigan, Minnesota, Mississippi, Montana, Nevada, North Carlina, North Dakota, Ohio, Oklahoma, Oregon, South Dakota, Washington, Wisconsin	Georgia, Idaho, Kentucky, Louisiana, Michigan, Minnesota, Mississippi, Montana, Nevada, North Dakota, Ohio, Oregon, Washington, Wisconsin
Merit selection[1]	Alaska, Colorado, Delaware, Hawaii, Iowa, Kansas, Maryland, Massachusetts, Missouri, Nebraska, Utah, Vermont, Wyoming	Alaska, Arizona, California, Colorado, Delaware, Florida, Hawaii, Indiana, Iowa, Kansas, Maryland, Massachusetts, Missouri, Nebraska, New York, Oklahoma, Rhode Island, South Dakota, Tennessee, Utah, Vermont, Wyoming
Appointment by governor	Maine, New Hampshire, New Jersey, Rhode Island	Maine, New Hampshire, New Jersey
Appointment by legislature	Connecticut, South Carolina, Virginia	Connecticut, South Carolina, Virginia

[1] In some cases, 'merit appointment' means that the governor appoints judges, but is required to select from a merit-based list submitted by a judicial nominating committee.
Source: Based on Rottman et al., 'Judicial Selection and Service', State Court Organization, 1998 (Williamsburg, VA: National Center for State Courts, 1999).

or have had their own courts explicitly rule that some state and federal constitutional provisions 'are, in all material aspects, the same',[26] because each state's highest court is the final arbiter of the meaning of that state's constitution, it is possible for the same phrase to mean different things in state and in federal law, or between the law of one state and another. For example, although the federal Supreme Court has ruled that the execution of minors or of those with severe mental handicaps would constitute 'cruel and unusual punishment' in violation of the Eighth Amendment of the

US Constitution, the Court has never found the death penalty *per se* to be unconstitutional. Relying on the bar to 'cruel or unusual punishment' in Article 26 of the Declaration of Rights of that state's constitution, however, the Supreme Judicial Court of Massachusetts made precisely that ruling (*District Attorney for Suffolk Dist. v. Watson* 381 Mass 648, 1980), making the state's use of the death penalty unconstitutional—until it was specifically authorized in 1982 by a constitutional amendment.[27]

Even among the 49 'purely' common law states, there are significant differences in the states' openness to certain kinds of suit, in their rules of evidence, and in the penalties likely to be imposed, both in criminal and in civil cases. In those cases in which a choice of state in which to bring a suit is possible, the outcome of a case may be significantly affected by that choice (and even when there is no choice, the results of similar cases may be quite different depending on the state[28]). In particular, conservative Republicans have tried to rein in what they see as the resulting 'forum shopping', especially with regard to class action suits against major corporations. On the other hand, they have not been above venue shopping themselves, as for example when the federal government seized control of serial snipers John Muhammad and Lee Malvo and turned them over to Virginia for trial even though most of the murders with which they were charged had been in Maryland and they had been arrested in Maryland. This was apparently because Virginia law would allow the execution of Malvo, who was a minor, whereas Maryland law would not[29] (*USA Today*, 25 November 2003).

One consequence of the increased reliance of state courts on their own constitutional guarantees (sometimes identified as 'the new judicial federalism') has been to limit the ability of the more conservative Burger and Rehnquist Courts to reverse the Warren Court's expansion of civil and criminal rights—since most of the laws and most of the trials involved are state rather than federal. A second has been to put state courts in the role of 'activist judges' (a term of opprobrium previously directed by the right at federal judges whose rulings they did not like). For example, rulings requiring states to grant gay couples at least the substantial rights of marriage in the form of 'civil unions' (Vermont) or full marriage itself (Massachusetts) were issued by state courts interpreting state constitutions. As with state referenda on medical use of marijuana and physician-assisted suicide, conservatives (because they are in power in Washington) have been confronted with a dilemma. On the one hand, they have for decades claimed to be committed to states' rights, but on the other hand they find some states using their autonomy to pursue policies that the conservatives find abhorrent. If nothing else, their attempts to square this circle have demonstrated that it is impossible to separate law from politics.

KEY TERMS

- *amicus curiae*
- civil law
- common law
- federal question
- Foreign Intelligence Surveillance Act
- judicial activism

- judicial review
- *Marbury v. Madison*
- original jurisdiction
- standing
- writ of *certiorari*
- writ of habeas corpus

NOTES

1 The distinction between the courts with life tenure and those with 15-year terms is that the former ('Article III courts') were created pursuant to Article III of the Constitution whereas the latter ('legislative courts') were created pursuant of the powers granted to Congress by Article I.

2 While in principle even the lowest court can declare an act to be unconstitutional, lower courts generally leave this to appellate courts. Moreover, each court's decisions are effective only within that court's jurisdiction, so that unless and until the conflict is resolved by the Supreme Court, a law that has been ruled to be unconstitutional in one part of the country may still be effective in another.

3 Although *Marbury v. Madison* might have been interpreted as a usurpation of power

on the part of the Supreme Court, it was widely accepted as a legitimate exercise of judicial power, and ironically the law that was declared unconstitutional was one granting power to the Court.

4 One indicator of the growing importance of textualism is that the Supreme Court has cited dictionary definitions in its opinions more often since 1990 than it did in its previous 200 years. It is worth noting that the leading textualists on the Supreme Court (especially Justices Scalia and Thomas) have not always been consistent regarding their choice of dictionary, choosing broader or narrower definitions as seems to justify their preferred outcome.

Ironically, given his praise for the textualists, President Bush has frequently issued 'signing statements' when he has signed legislation into law to dispute the plain language meaning of the laws he is signing—especially as they might apply to the executive branch. Presumably, these are meant to be interpreted by the courts as indicating what he meant when he signed the bill, in the same way that the legislative history of a bill might be construed to indicate what Congress meant by any ambiguous language in the bill. But this is precisely what the textualists argue courts should not take into account.

5 While this is an example of minority rule, it is limited by the fact that it still requires a majority of the Court to decide the case. A minority of four that would be adequate to put a case on the Court's docket may choose to deny *certiorari* rather than risk having the case decided adversely to their view, and thus setting a national precedent.

6 In the year ending 30 September 2004, the Court received 6,391 new petitions and of these (plus the 3,267 petitions that were pending at the beginning of the year) granted 104 and denied or dismissed 6,230, leaving 3,324 pending for consideration in the next year. Of the 104 granted, 16 concerned criminal cases, 28 concerned US civil proceedings, 54 concerned private civil proceedings, and six were administrative appeals.

7 The Solicitor General, who is the chief litigator for the federal government (organizationally, subordinate to the Attorney General and the Deputy Attorney General), has a statutory right to file an *amicus* brief; others require the permission of the opposing party or of the Court itself (which is almost always granted).

8 An example would be the challenge to inclusion of the words 'under God' in the Pledge of Allegiance as a violation of the First Amendment's bar to the 'establishment of religion'. Although the case (*Elk Grove Unified School District v. Newdow* 542 US 1) generated extensive and emotional

constitutional debate, the Supreme Court ultimately decided the case on purely procedural grounds, ruling that the plaintiff (the non-custodial father of a public school student) did not have the standing to have brought the suit in the first place.

9 In *Vieth v. Jubelirer*, which challenged a partisan Republican gerrymander in Pennsylvania, the Court dismissed the Democrat's appeal. The plurality opinion by four justices argued that there was no 'judicially enforceable limit on the political considerations that the states and Congress may take into account when districting'. The deciding Justice, Anthony Kennedy, voted with the plurality to reject the Democrat's appeal, but 'would not foreclose all possibility of judicial relief . . .'. The lack of a clear precedent barring a judicial remedy for partisan gerrymanders allowed a series of challenges to the midterm gerrymander of Texas's Congressional Districts to go forward.

10 The best example of a president 'getting it wrong' is probably Eisenhower's appointment of the presumably moderate Republican Earl Warren to be Chief Justice. Although from the liberal perspective, this was a first-rate appointment, the Warren Court, with its landmark decisions on civil and criminal rights, became the symbol of everything that the conservatives found wrong about 'judicial activism'. Eisenhower is said to have called the appointment 'the biggest damn-fool mistake I ever made.' (Joseph W. Bishop, Jr., 'The Warren Court Is Not Likely to be Overruled', *New York Times Magazine*, 7 September 1969, p. 31.

11 This count includes John Rutledge, who received a recess appointment as Chief Justice and served for five months before his nomination was rejected by the Senate.

12 The last person nominated to the Supreme Court who declined to serve was Roscoe Conkling in 1882, who declined after his nomination had been approved in the

Senate 39–12. This count excludes the nomination of John Roberts to be Associate Justice, which was withdrawn and replaced by his nomination as Chief Justice following the death of Chief Justice Rehnquist.

13 Rutledge came out in opposition to Jay's Treaty, a position that was unpopular with the Senate, and was also interpreted by some as evidence of advancing mental illness.

14 Letter from Alberto Gonzales (then Counsel to the President) to Martha Barnett (president of the American Bar Association), 22 March 2001, http://www.whitehouse.gov/news/releases/2001/03/20010322–5.html.

15 Although sometimes justified on the basis of the size and workload of the nation's largest circuit, proposals from the late 1990s to split the 9th circuit as much reflect the desire of more conservative areas, and areas more economically dependent on mining and forestry, to get out from under the dominance of a circuit dominated by California.

16 Although the Constitution apparently gives the federal courts jurisdiction in all law suits between citizens of different states, from the beginning of the federal court system, Congress has limited that jurisdiction to suits in which a significant amount is in question: $500 in the Judiciary Act of 1789, gradually increased to $75,000 in 1996. Whether this is a significant limitation depends in part on the plaintiff's ability to add intangible (for example, psychological) damages to reach the threshold. Some cases, such as civil rights violations, patent or copyright claims, cases concerning naturalization, or admiralty law, will be heard by the federal courts regardless of the amount at issue.

17 The assistant counsel to the New York Senate majority leader after the decision in *Wells v. Rockefeller* 394 US 542 (1969), quoted in *New York Times*, 22 January 1970.

18 For example, the affirmative right to counsel (*Gideon v. Wainwright* 372 US 335) and the right to be informed of one's rights before being questioned by the police (the so-called Miranda warnings, *Miranda v. Arizona* 384 US 436).

19 It should be remembered that, at least into the 1960s, many people who supported racial segregation also cited biblical authority, while advocates of gay rights often draw an analogy between their cause and the struggle for racial equality.

20 It has long been recognized that restrictions that are so onerous as to bar any economic use of the land in question ('inverse condemnation') require compensation.

21 Although generally identified simply as the Patriot Act, the full name is an acronym for 'Uniting and Strengthening America by Providing Appropriate Tools Required to Intercept and Obstruct Terrorism (USA PATRIOT ACT) Act of 2001'. As part of the effort to speed passage without extensive scrutiny or debate, several provisions that would prove to be quite controversial, were set to expire at the end of December 2005.

22 For example, after more than three years in the custody of the Defense Department after he was arrested in Chicago, the administration tried to transfer 'enemy combatant' Jose Padilla to the regular criminal courts in what the Court of Appeals for the 4th circuit identified as a ploy to render moot the pending judicial review of the government's right to have held him in the first place. At the end of December 2005, the Court barred the transfer and refused to vacate its original order authorizing Padilla's detention, saying that the administration's request left 'an appearance that the government may be attempting to avoid consideration of our decision by the Supreme Court'. In the end, however, the Supreme Court allowed the transfer of custody.

23 Two states, Oklahoma and Texas, have separate supreme courts for criminal and civil cases. Not only the structure of the court systems, but the names of the courts, also vary among the states. The majority of states call their highest court the Supreme Court, but in New York the Supreme Court is the major trial court, while the highest appellate court is called the Court of Appeals. In Massachusetts, the highest court is called the Supreme Judicial Court, presumably to distinguish it from the General Court, which is the state legislature.

24 One should note that the phrase 'civil law' has two distinct meanings in American legal parlance. Most commonly, it refers to the distinction between criminal law and other legal disputes, sometimes between two private parties but often involving the state as one of the parties. Less often, but particularly relevant in the case of Louisiana, it refers to the distinction between the legal system ultimately derived from Roman law and more immediately from the Napoleonic Code, and the legal system derived from the English Common Law.

25 While appellate courts in other states may find that the factual record does not support the trial court's judgment, they are expected to remand the case for further fact-finding, rather than substituting, as in permissible in Louisiana, their own judgment of the facts for that of the trial judge or jury.

26 *Brown v. State* 657 S.W.2d 797 (Texas Court of Criminal Appeals, 1983).

27 The death penalty statute enacted after the constitutional amendment required a jury trial before a sentence of death could be imposed. Because a defendant could avoid the possibility of a death sentence by pleading guilty, the Supreme Judicial Court ruled that this statute violated the defendant's right against self-incrimination and to have a jury trial guaranteed by Article 12 of the Declaration of Rights, and was therefore void. At the end of 2005, Massachusetts had no death penalty statute.

28 For example, see Ralph Blumenthal, 'A Family Feud Sheds Light on Differences in Probate Practices From State to State', *New York Times*, 28 December 2005, p. A12.

29 The US Supreme Court subsequently ruled the execution of minors to be unconstitutional under the federal constitution.

....

GUIDE TO FURTHER READING

ABRAHAM, H. J. (1998), *The Judicial Process: an Introductory Analysis of the Courts of the United States, England, and France* (6th edn) (New York: Oxford University Press).

An introductory and comparative study of the judicial process at federal, state, and local levels.

BAUM, L. (2001), *American Courts: Process and Policy* (5th edn) (Boston, MA: Houghton Mifflin).

A thorough treatment of judicial process in America. What courts and their officers do, and how they relate to the rest of the political system.

CARP, R. A., R. STIDHAM, and
K. L. MANNING (2004), *Judicial
Process in America* (Washington,
DC: Congressional Quarterly
Press).

Both the history and politics of judicial
decision-making at federal and state levels.

MURPHY, W. F., C. H. PRITCHETT, and
L. EPSTEIN (2002), *Courts, Judges, &
Politics: an Introduction to the Judicial
Process* (Boston, MA: McGraw-Hill).

An updated classic study of the American
legal system and of judicial power and
decision-making.

9

The American Secret

Overview

Is the success of the United States due to the 'efficiency' of its political system, or due to being rich enough to afford the inefficiency? What are the challenges facing American government as it enters the twenty-first century with what remains essentially an eighteenth-century constitution? Can the United States continue to afford this level of 'veto group liberalism' in confronting its responsibilities as the only remaining super-power, or in addressing such pressing issues as climate change and economic globalization?

The United States is, and at least since 1945 has been, both the richest and most powerful nation on earth. It has avoided the interruptions of democratic government, whether through invasion or internal collapse, that have afflicted the vast majority of democracies. Although one who listened only to domestic alarmists might doubt it, there has never been a significant internal subversive movement: neither fascism nor socialism (let alone communism) reached the levels of support or extra-legal action found in many European countries over the course of the last century. Notwithstanding the 1993 attack on the World Trade Center in New York, and then the horror of the attacks on New York and Washington on 11 September 2001, the United States has had relatively little experience with terrorism within its borders, and notwithstanding the 1995 bombing of the Alfred P. Murrah Federal Building in Oklahoma City, and occasional experience with snipers and serial murders more properly identified as 'normal' crime, the United States has had even less experience with domestic terrorism.

It has been tempting for Americans to cite these obvious successes as evidence that they have somehow found the secret of good and effective government. Americans have a long tradition of seeing their country as 'a city upon a hill' (a phrase from a 1630 sermon by John Winthrop before the Pilgrims embarked to found the Massachusetts Bay Colony, and repeated, *inter alia*, by Ronald Reagan in his farewell address in 1989) and 'chosen by God and commissioned by history to be a model to the world' (George W. Bush in a campaign speech to B'nai B'rith, 28 August 2000). When the Spanish colonies of South and Central America became independent, many of them closely followed the model of the United States in drafting their own constitutions. Even though the twentieth-century European models of parliamentary democracy are now available as alternatives for newly democratizing countries, such American practices as an independently elected president, separation of powers, and judicial review still are widely emulated.

At the same time, even if one rejects the idea that the United States was somehow anointed by God, there can be no doubt that the United States was blessed by nature with an abundance of resources. When Europeans arrived in America, they found seemingly endless forests and enormous tracts of fertile land that were untouched by the plough. As they pushed west, they found even more of these, plus vast mineral wealth: iron and coal; gold, silver and copper; oil. For most of its history, the United States benefited from an apparently inexhaustible supply of cheap and relatively malleable immigrant labour, not to mention immigrant entrepreneurship and scientific and artistic genius; even many of the Framers of the Constitution were themselves immigrants, and they both foresaw and wanted to encourage immigration. Although Americans proved extremely capable of killing one another in the Civil War (with a death toll estimated to be between 600,000 and 700,000, roughly 214,000 in battle, out of a population of about 33 million), and fought 'wars' with Mexico (1846–48, roughly 1,750 US battle deaths), Spain (1898–1902, 385 US battle deaths), and the aboriginal population (roughly 1,000 US battle deaths between 1817 and 1898), the Atlantic and Pacific Oceans largely protected the United States from the upheavals and destruction of European and Asian wars. Between military and civilian deaths, the United States lost roughly 0.25 per cent of its population in the Second World War. In contrast, Germany lost roughly 7 per cent; Finland, China, and Japan lost between 2.3 and 2.9 per cent; Italy lost 0.91 per cent; the UK

0.96 per cent; France 1.24 per cent; Canada, Australia, and New Zealand between 0.38 and 0.50 per cent; Norway 0.50 per cent; Belgium 1.4 per cent; the Netherlands 2.93 per cent; and Denmark, which had the 'good fortune' to be conquered quickly and not to be a major battlefield later in the war, lost only 0.08 per cent; and all these are dwarfed by Soviet losses of over 14 per cent. Moreover, while the European and Asian industrial infrastructures were being destroyed, American industry—the 'arsenal of democracy'—was booming.

On the political side, the Constitution adopted in 1787 has survived for over 200 years with only a handful of amendments, none of which have fundamentally altered the overall structure of government.[1] On the other hand, there were the Civil War, the extra-constitutional resolution of the disputed 1872 presidential election, and at least one local 'coup d'état' (the 1898 overthrow of the elected government of Wilmington, North Carolina, by white supremacists). In contrast to the rhetoric of freedom and equality, there is not only the history of slavery, but also of racial segregation and Jim Crow,[2] leading to the civil rights movement of the 1950s and 1960s, a series of race riots that destroyed the centres of several cities, and finally to legal reforms that have ameliorated, but hardly eliminated, the stain of racial bias. The United States has a recurring history of 'witch hunts', beginning with the literal witch hunt of Salem Massachusetts in 1692, and continuing through the anti-foreigner (especially anti-Catholic foreigner) Know Nothing movement of the 1850s, the anarchist scares of the 1920s, the anti-communist hysteria of the McCarthy era, through perhaps to the hunt for Al Qaeda sympathizers and terrorists in the post 9–11 era.[3] Despite the virtues often claimed for electoral competition, much of the United States is uncompetitive. In 2004, only 24 of the 435 members of the House of Representatives were elected with less than 55 per cent of the vote (and therefore 421 had a margin of at least 10 per cent over their nearest competitor); of the 49 state Senates elected in partisan elections, 21 were controlled continuously by the same party (24 if one not does not count ties as breaking the string) from 1984 to 2004; for the lower houses of state legislatures, the corresponding figure was 22 (23 with the one tied election).[4] American newspapers regularly report a variety of events and practices—recurring episodes of unpunished police violence and abuse, prosecutorial misconduct, overtly partisan judges and election administrators, claims of sweeping and extra-legal if not flatly illegal executive authority in the name of national security—that Americans find troubling in other countries, but to which they regularly turn a blind eye, or even defend as necessary and proper, when practised at home. And looking abroad to South America, Liberia, the Philippines, the success of 'transplanted' American governments in institutionalizing stable liberal democracy has certainly been less than spectacular.

Taken together, the tremendous economic and geographic advantages with which the United States began, the somewhat spotty record of democracy in the United States, and the frequent failures of attempts to copy American institutions, raise the question of whether the United States has achieved its current status in the world because of its political institutions, or despite them. Has the United States found an 'efficient secret', or has it merely benefited from such comparative advantages of abundant natural and human resources that it has been able to thrive despite its inefficiencies?

And this then leads to a second question. The Constitution of the United States, notwithstanding both formal amendments and informal evolution in interpretation, remains a visionary document, but the vision is very much one of the eighteenth century. In contrast to some more recent constitutions (including those of some states of the United States) that enumerate affirmative rights (such as a right to a public education) or rights attributable to groups, the federal constitution's conception of rights is virtually exclusively individual and negative (the right not to have something done to one).[5] While extraordinarily democratic by eighteenth- and even early twentieth-century standards, particularly in its mode of ratification by conventions often elected with a broader franchise than granted in the same states for ordinary elections (Amar 2005: 6–18), the Constitution still reflects the liberal/contractarian bias in favour of the *status quo* typical of eighteenth-century elite revolutionaries. Although the Constitution formed an irrevocable union in place of the dissoluble Articles of Confederation (Amar 2005: 25–33), it reflected a fear of central authority (even while recognizing the strategic and economic necessity of union), and still left the states with a central role in the new federation. Simply, the federal government was not designed to be efficient or to respond quickly: to paraphrase one of humorist Will Roger's comments on the presidency of Calvin Coolidge, the federal government often doesn't do nothin', but that was what the Founders wanted done. We no longer live in an eighteenth-, or even in a twentieth-century world. Can the United States continue to afford this level of 'veto group liberalism' in confronting its responsibilities as the only remaining super-power, or in addressing such pressing issues as climate change, economic globalization, and so forth? And projecting current (2006) trends into the future, what are the prospects and dangers for American democracy?

Successful in spite of itself?

American power was built largely on a combination of immigration and expansion. In the 89 years between 1832 and 1914, there were only 14 years in which annual immigration was not at least 0.4 per cent of the total resident population; even in 2004 the figure was over 0.3 per cent. In contrast, throughout the nineteenth century, most European countries experienced net emigration, and even in the twenty-first century rates of immigration into the United States are significantly higher than those experienced by the countries of the European Union, even counting migration entirely within the EU. Between 1800 and 1960, the population of the United States increased by a factor of more than 50, whereas the populations of European countries generally increased by factors of between two and five. But at the same time, the land area of the United States more than quadrupled. Even at its starting point, it included vast tracts of essentially empty territory to which immigrants could come and be productive without straining existing resources or overly crowding the existing population. The combination virtually assured dramatically higher growth in aggregate national wealth, regardless of relative efficiency at the individual (per capita) level.

Of course, both population growth and territorial expansion were at least in part consequences of government policy. Despite numerous attempts at exclusionism, the United States was more welcoming more early in its history of more diverse immigrants than other European 'settler' countries, like Canada, New Zealand, or Australia. Only 14 years after George Washington took the oath of office as the first president of the United States, the third president, Thomas Jefferson, nearly doubled the area of the country by purchasing the Louisiana territory from France. The federal government also took a direct role in facilitating the development of the west, for example by building a road (opened in 1811) across the Allegheny Mountains from

Cumberland, Maryland, to Wheeling, (now West) Virginia. Building on the Northwest Ordinance of 1787 (one of the real achievements of the Congress of the Confederation), which organized the territories that would become the states of Ohio, Indiana, Illinois, Michigan and Wisconsin, for the most part the government facilitated expansion by providing minimal security against the native peoples who were being displaced by the settlers, some structure of laws and governance, and land for those who were willing to take their chances in the wilderness (for example, through the Homestead Act of 1862, which in exchange for a filing fee of $18 gave 160 acres of public land—in aggregate, roughly 8–10 per cent of the land area of the United States by the time the policy was abandoned in 1986—to any 21-year-old head of household who would build a house and live on the land for at least five years).

At least if one ignores its consequences for the native peoples, whose treaty rights were unilaterally abrogated with great regularity, today the Homestead Act would probably be regarded as enlightened public policy. Other programmes would more likely be identified as 'crony capitalism'. For example, the building of a transcontinental railroad was advanced through the Pacific Railroad Act of 1862, which gave railroad companies a 400 foot (roughly 122 metres) right-of-way, plus 10 square miles of land for every mile of track built (that is, half of the land within 10 miles of the railroad). Not surprisingly, this massive give-away was accompanied by various scandals, most notably the Crédit Mobilier (a company formed by major shareholders of the Union Pacific Railroad) scandal. Other scandals involved the leasing of mineral rights on federal lands at rates completely unrelated to their value in exchange for pay-offs (for example, the Teapot Dome scandal), but even when the graft was 'honest'[6] much of government development policy entailed the conversion of public resources into private fortunes, and was effective primarily because the pool of public resources available for conversion was so great that the skimming of rents (in the sense in which the term is used in economic theory) was easily supportable.

Particularly after civil service reform reduced the ability of party organizations to fund politics through 'taxes' on the salaries of patronage appointees and elected officials, and compounded by the spread of the direct primary, which forced politicians to be increasingly concerned with individual fund-raising efforts, and the increasing importance of capital-intensive campaign techniques (paid television advertising, polling, telephone banks, etc.), a second stream of rents grew in significance: payments in the form of campaign contributions (rather than personal bribes—to the extent that the distinction can be maintained) from the largely corporate beneficiaries of public policies to the politicians who made or will make those policies. Looking at these contributions as investments, the donors naturally expect the result to be public policy that generates higher marginal profits than would have occurred without their contributions. While not all of these expectations will be realized, they still represent an additional overhead cost to the corporations, which they build into the prices charged to both government and private consumers.

The decline of patronage jobs did not mean a decline in the importance of governmental resources to the maintenance of personal and party political organizations. Rather, it simply highlighted the importance of directing, and being seen to direct, the flow of government spending to particular groups, industries, or places. The notorious complexity of the American tax code is in significant measure attributable to the insertion of special 'incentives' or 'reliefs' for activities or industries centred in the district of a particular member of Congress or that is responsible for a particularly significant political contribution. On a perhaps more positive note, the majority of American government support for art and culture (and religion) also takes the form of an 'incentive'—the deduction of most cultural or charitable contributions from taxable income. Congressmen from farm states have successfully defended, and even increased, a massive programme of farm subsidies, supported in the name of 'family farmers' and obviously popular with them, notwithstanding that most of the money actually goes to agribusinesses, which not coincidentally are significant campaign contributors. Although pork barrel spending is never a total waste (as critics sometimes imply), neither does it represent the most efficient use of resources. Likewise, the building of coalitions for particular pieces of legislation through log-rolling and the mutual accommodation of provisions advanced by particular representatives is another source of inefficiency. In both cases, there are targeted benefits for which individual politicians can claim credit, while the costs are diffused and there is no one who is forced to take the collective blame. And in large measure they answer Richard F. Fenno's question (in Ornstein 1975): 'If As Ralph Nader Says, Congress Is 'The Broken Branch,' How Come We Love Our Congressmen So Much?'

Contemporary examples of the consequences of these inefficiencies readily abound. Beyond the more than 6,000 earmarked projects (totalling over $24 billion) in the 2005 Transportation Bill,[7] to which reference was made in Chapter 6, many programmes mandate a pattern of federal spending based more on distributive justice than on actual need. Thus, over $200,000 of a programme that was generally supposed to be funding preparedness for possible terrorist attacks went to Madison County, Idaho (population 30,700), which used about half of it to equip a mobile emergency command centre, and Saratoga County in upstate New York spent even more Homeland Security money for a similar recreational vehicle/mobile command centre. Many other rural areas used similar grants to update their fire-fighting equipment. While these certainly are legitimate public purposes, and Madison County's claim that the equipment used to deal with a terrorist attack is essentially the same as that needed in a natural disaster may be valid, these expenditures also represent money not spent in areas that are far more likely terrorist targets, and often also spending beyond real local needs more broadly conceived, simply because the federal money was made available.

Public support of medical coverage also illustrates these points. As was observed in Chapter 1, the United States spends more for medical care, and gets inferior aggregate results, than nearly all other industrialized countries. In part this is because of the high overheads for the marketing, administration, and (ironically) cost-containment efforts of private insurance companies, and in part it is the consequence of extremely high profits in the pharmaceutical industry.[8] Yet when Congress introduced a prescription drug benefit into the Medicare programme, they channelled it through private insurance companies and barred the government from using its purchasing power to negotiate lowered drug costs. The result was to make the programme as much, if not more, a subsidy for the insurance and pharmaceutical industries, as a subsidy for the elderly. While a 'fundamentalist' conviction that the private sector is always and necessarily preferable to the public sector undoubtedly contributed to these decisions, so too did the extensive lobbying networks and campaign largess of the industries involved.

The policies of allowing public exploitation of public resources at well below market rates has also continued, although without the justification of 'settling the wilderness'. In addition to mineral rights, examples include cattle grazing rights and the harvesting of timber in publicly owned forests.

While these inefficiencies may be marginally contained by reforms such as those proposed by both parties in the wake of the 2005 Jack Abramoff lobbying scandal (for example, tightening limits on what lawmakers can receive from lobbyists), they are fundamentally inevitable given the structure of American government.[9] They are not so much waste, as they are the essential lubricants for a political system that was designed to be sticky. At least into the beginning of the twenty-first century, however, they have been costs that the United States has been rich enough to bear.

Beyond these economic inefficiencies, the American system, again by design, tends to be very slow to respond to problems—and for much the same reason. Most policy changes involve losers as well as winners, and by designing a system with multiple veto points (to use the jargon of modern political science), the Framers made it relatively easy for those losers to block change. Perhaps the most significant examples from the twentieth century are the ability of rural state legislators to prevent any substantial reapportionment of legislative seats to reflect the dramatic growth of cities, and the ability of segregationists, particularly but by no means exclusively in the south, to prevent the real emancipation and equality of African Americans. Significantly, both of these log-jams were broken by the courts, but only after decades of struggle in which the courts had been complicit in maintaining the log-jam.

In other cases, rather than relying on the courts, reformers have in effect been forced to compensate the losers, even when the reform is to prevent those losers from continuing to impose costs on others. The most obvious examples of this type concern pollution abatement, in which particularly large scale industrial polluters have been able to block regulations unless the taxpayers cover a substantial portion of the clean-up costs.

Challenges of the twenty-first century

Moving into the twenty-first century, American democracy faces a number of challenges, some of which are common to all post-industrial democratic societies, but some of which appear to be especially, if not uniquely, American, stemming either from the American socio-cultural experience or from the peculiarities of American political institutions. Moreover, even those problems that are common to post-industrial societies tend to take a somewhat different form in the United States. While any selection of such challenges is necessarily arbitrary, three of them—one economic, one partisan-political, and one institutional/constitutional—may be taken as exemplary.

Economic challenges

All post-industrial societies are faced with challenges arising from the conjunction of economic globalization and demographic change, putting institutions providing economic security for members of the working and middle classes under severe strain. In contrast to most of the rest of the post-industrial world, where two main elements of this package—medical care and retirement pensions—have been largely in the public sector, in the United States both have been more commonly provided directly by employers, especially for the middle class.[10] This has meant that, in addition to the strain on public social security systems occasioned by the reduction in the proportion of the population that is economically active resulting from longer post-retirement life expectancies and longer pre-employment periods of education and training, American workers have faced the growing threat of severe curtailment, dramatically increased cost, or even outright termination, of benefit packages on which they have relied. Moreover, this problem has been compounded by two related problems: the 'legacy' costs faced by older firms with commitments to large numbers of retired workers; and the tendency of firms both to underfund their retirement programmes, and to regard those programmes as a cheap source of 'internally generated' finance.

Not only medical and retirement benefits, but employment itself has become less secure as firms merge and downsize, outsource production to lower cost (that is, lower wage and benefit) suppliers, or simply move their facilities to countries where workers are satisfied with a lower standard of living. While the greater 'labour market flexibility' of the United States in comparison to western Europe may be beneficial for firms, it is not necessarily beneficial for most citizens; and while free trade and easy mobility of capital may improve aggregate economic performance, this is of small comfort to those who are unemployed or underemployed. Simply, with free trade and the emergence of the multinational conglomerate, General Motors President Charles Wilson's claim at his 1953 confirmation hearing for a position in President Eisenhower's cabinet that 'What's good for the United States is good for General Motors, and vice versa' no longer has even the element of truth that it had then.

While the squeezing of the middle class, manifested both in growing income inequality[11] and in growing economic insecurity, is not a uniquely American problem, the United States has had a particularly difficult time addressing it. Although the Employment Retirement Income Security Act (ERISA) of 1974 was intended to correct the problems of underfunding pension plans, by the time the regulations were promulgated, lobbying by business had weakened the programme significantly. Indeed, ERISA may in some cases have had an effect opposite to that intended by creating a moral hazard problem in the form of an (also underfunded) federal guarantee. Although there is no serious disagreement about the long-term unsupportability of the Social Security and Medicare systems without some combination of increased taxes, transfers from general revenue, increased retirement age, or reduced benefits, in ignoring the transition costs, the Bush administration's proposals partially to privatize the system did not actually address the problem of solvency and had the potential to aggravate the problem of insecurity, while the administration's opponents in large measure have argued for deferring action, implicitly because it is not a crisis *yet*.[12]

In part, support for the privatization of Social Security, like support for the Bush administration's tax cuts that primarily benefited those with the very greatest wealth and incomes, can be explained by unrealistic self-assessment by citizens of their place in the current and future income distributions[13] — in other words, a denial of the problems, at least at the personal level. To the extent that citizens hold these views, and therefore vote for politicians who likewise ignore the problems, the failure of the American government to address them might in part be described as a shortcoming of democracy in general, but not of the United States in particular. At the same time, however, the American system itself encourages, and gives political leaders incentives to encourage, these misperceptions in the first place. More generally, the failure to address the long-term problems of Social Security and the squeezing of the middle class reflects three fundamental problems of American government. The first is the fragmentation of power and responsibility, which means that it is more politically advantageous in the short run—and if, as is often said, 'a week is a long time in politics', there may be nothing but the short run—to take positions and play to prejudices than it is to try to solve problems. Given the impossibility of claiming credit for solving structural problems and the ease of deflecting the blame for having failed to solve them, it is rarely in the interest of politicians even to be the messengers who bring the bad news that there are structural problems. Second, the atomization of politics and the absence of strong party organizations encourage short-term thinking and coalition-building based on private advantage rather than public interest. Third, given the absence of strong parties, and the fragmentation of politics, the American system, more than most democracies, makes it relatively easy for those who would have to bear the costs to block any serious action—and indeed often to block any serious consideration. Ultimately, however, unless something is done, Herbert Stein's law, 'If something can't go on forever, it will stop', will catch up with the United States: the Social Security and Medicare trust funds will run dry; the collapse of private retirement and health care plans will create tremendous pressure on public welfare systems; foreign governments will stop funding an ever-growing current account deficit. The question is whether the American system will be able to deal with these problems effectively before they truly become crises.

The challenges of social and cultural politics

In the partisan-political sphere, the problem is the politicization of social issues and the rise of political fundamentalism. Three issue clusters have either spurred this development, or been exploited by politicians seeking to use them as wedge issues to mobilize potential supporters. The first of these issues was racial desegregation, gradually expanding into the issue of civil rights more generally. Aside from becoming, as Lyndon Johnson predicted it would when he decided to make civil rights a priority of his presidency, the wedge issue that allowed Richard Nixon's 'southern strategy' to make the Republicans the dominant party in the south, this moral crusade served as a catalyst to bring churches directly into politics, as exemplified by the prominence of ministers in the civil rights movement and by Martin Luther King's Southern Christian Leadership Conference.

The second cluster involved the women's movement in general, and the question of abortion in particular. Although the Civil Rights Act of 1964 included sex as a protected category,[14] this came to particular prominence in the early 1970s, with the passage by Congress of a proposed Equal Rights

Amendment (introduced annually from 1923, but not approved by both Houses of Congress until 1972);[15] the enactment in 1972 of Title IX of the Education Act, which bars discrimination, exclusion, or denial of benefits on the basis of sex in any educational programme receiving federal funds, but became particularly controversial with regard to athletic programmes; and then in 1973 with the Supreme Court's decision in *Roe v. Wade* (410 US 113, 1954) that the Constitution contains an implicit right to privacy, which in turn means that during the first trimester the government (at either state or federal level) must leave the decision to terminate a pregnancy entirely to the woman and her physician, although in the second trimester the state can regulate abortions in the interest of the mother's health, and in the third trimester may seek to preserve foetal life, going so far as to ban abortions except in cases when an abortion is necessary to preserve the life or health of the mother.

These issues, especially the question of abortion, galvanized many social and religious conservatives, who were already upset by Supreme Court decisions barring officially sanctioned Bible reading and prayers from the public schools, and by what they saw as a general moral decay. Casting the issue as a confrontation between 'radical feminism' and 'family values', opponents of the Equal Rights Amendment (ERA), led among others by Phyllis Schlafly, who in 1972 founded the Eagle Forum, argued that it would, among other things:

take away the traditional benefits in the law for wives, widows and mothers. ERA would make unconstitutional the laws ... that impose on a husband the obligation to support his wife ... give Congress the power to legislate on all those areas of law which include traditional differences of treatment on account of sex: marriage, property laws, divorce and alimony, child custody, adoptions, abortion, homosexual laws, sex crimes, private and public schools, prison regulations, and insurance ... would mean the end of single-sex colleges. ERA would force the sex integration of fraternities, sororities, Boy Scouts, Girl Scouts, YMCA, YWCA, Boys State and Girls State conducted by the American Legion, and mother–daughter and father–son school events ... put abortion rights into the U.S. Constitution, and make abortion funding a new constitutional right.[16]

Other prominent leaders of the opposition to what they ultimately branded as the 'radical feminist agenda' included Rev. Jerry Falwell, whose Moral Majority (founded in 1979 and dissolved in 1989) even more directly sought to bring conservative religious organizations into the political process, and to identify their opponents as not merely misguided, but as positively 'evil'.[17] Supporters of what they (the supporters) identified as 'women's rights' were sometimes equally harsh in their characterization of the religious right.

The third cluster of issues, homosexual rights, was already relevant in the 1970s (as indicated in the quotation from Phyllis Schlafly). One question concerns the outlawing of consensual and private homosexual sodomy. Although the Supreme Court in 1986 had ruled that such laws were permissible (*Bowers v. Hardwick* 478 US 186), some states (for example, Delaware in 1972) had already repealed their bans on private and consensual sodomy and others did so, either through statutory repeal or (state) constitutional invalidation, through to 2003 when, in *Lawrence et al. v. Texas* (539 US 558), the Supreme Court struck down the remaining state bans on private sodomy among consenting adults.

While these legal actions certainly were decried by the religious and social conservatives—as were sympathetic portrayals of homosexuals on television or in the cinema—they did not have the mobilizing power that the second major question, same-sex marriage or its functional equivalent demonstrated, beginning in 1993 when the state supreme court of Hawaii ruled that the equal protection clause of the state constitution meant that the state could bar same-sex marriage only for the kind of compelling reasons required in cases of 'strict scrutiny' (*Baehr v. Lewin* 74 Haw 530).[18] In 1996, in accordance with that decision, a trial court ruled the ban to be unconstitutional (*Baehr v. Miike* 910 P.2d 112). In response, Hawaii amended its constitution to bar same-sex marriage, and President Clinton supported the rapid passage of the federal Defense of Marriage Act, which explicitly defined marriage in federal law to mean 'only a legal union between one man and one woman as husband and wife' and provided that:

No State, territory, or possession of the United States, or Indian tribe, shall be required to give effect to any public act, record, or judicial proceeding of any other State, territory, possession, or tribe respecting a relationship between persons of the same sex that is treated as a marriage under the laws of such other State, territory, possession, or tribe, or a right or claim arising from such relationship.

Alaska's marriage statute was overturned by a state court as discriminatory in 1998, only to be reinstated after a state constitutional amendment.

In 1999, the Vermont Supreme Court ruled that that state's marriage law unconstitutionally discriminates against homosexual couples by denying them the many legal rights and privileges afforded by marriage, and ordered the state legislature to remedy the problem. They did so in 2000 by authorizing 'civil unions', which, while not marriage in name, conveyed the same benefits, protections, and responsibilities under Vermont law. In 2003, the Supreme Judicial Court of Massachusetts similarly ruled that that state's marriage law was unconstitutional, but supplemented that ruling in early 2004 with an advisory opinion that civil unions would not be an adequate remedy.[19] Later in 2004, Massachusetts became the only state to allow gay marriage as such. Also in 2004, local officials in San Francisco and in New Paltz, New York, decided on their own initiative to issue marriage licences to gay couples, although both ultimately were stopped from doing so. In 2005 New York's marriage law was found unconstitutional by a judge of the Supreme Court of New York (the state's *lowest* court of general jurisdiction), and in 2006 a Maryland circuit court judge made a similar ruling; the New York ruling was reversed by the Appellate Division of the Supreme Court of New York at the end of 2005 (a reversal that was upheld by the state's highest court in 2006), while the Maryland decision was being appealed at the time of writing.

Whether based on sincere belief, or in a cynical effort to exploit the issue to mobilize electoral support, well-connected opponents of homosexual rights suggested that gay marriage would challenge the very foundations of society, and might 'greatly accelerate ... pressures to marginalize the nation's religious communities' and lead to students being 'instructed that marriage, like slavery before it, is a vestige of America's discriminatory past ... '.[20] Building on their successes in Hawaii and Alaska, in 2004 opponents of gay marriage put state constitutional amendments that would define marriage as only the union of one man and one woman (and in most cases, would explicitly ban any equivalent status, such as civil union), and deny recognition of same-sex marriages (or unions) performed in other states or foreign countries, on to the ballots of 13 states (11 at the general elections, and two earlier in the year). All were approved by wide margins, and appear to have had the additional effect of increasing turnout among conservative voters. While recent scholarly analyses have questioned the assertion that these referenda, or the issue in general, played a major role in the election (Hillygus and Shields 2005; Lewis 2005), it is clear from the behaviour of both Democrats and Republicans that many politicians think it was significant—and that it threatens (or promises) to be greatly to their disadvantage (or advantage) to have the issue appear on their state's ballot in the future. More generally, issues such as gay rights and abortion, in implicating what for many people are deeply held religious convictions, over time have undermined the Democratic Party's hold on Catholics and poor whites (to the extent that they were not already lost by the civil rights issue). They even appear to threaten the Democratic Party's near monopoly of African American support, particularly as some Black ministers attempt to influence their communities based on social and religious conservatism rather than political and economic liberalism. And this, of course, gives the Republicans a strong incentive to keep the issues at the forefront of voters' attention.

Potentially more significant, however, is that these issues tend to activate a 'scorched earth' style of politics that is not open to compromise or discussion (as illustrated by the unwillingness of many pro-life advocates to allow abortion even when required to protect the health of the pregnant woman and of many pro-choicers to accept even the level of regulation that would be imposed on any other medical procedure, and by the unwillingness of many activists on both sides of the gay marriage issue to countenance the idea of civil unions as a compromise position). Liberal democracy, particularly in its American form, requires a spirit of compromise that is incompatible with fundamentalism and litmus tests. In the past (with the obvious exception of the Civil War), even if the citizenry was deeply polarized with regard to some issue, party loyalty would generally override particular issues in determining elections, and party elites could be counted upon to act with reasonable moderation and responsibility. With the substantial dealignment of the electorate, however, politicians increasingly are finding themselves captives of vocal and well-funded minorities, who are able to prevent moderate compromises, even if the politicians themselves would like to make them. Ironically, rather than leading to a kind of mushy centrism, dealignment has had the effect of facilitating the polarizing of national politics and has been accompanied by the emptying of the congressional centre, and gradual disappearance of moderates in either party.

Institutional/constitutional challenges

The institutional/constitutional question concerns the scope of the president's powers as commander-in-chief, and has been particularly activated by the debates concerning the detaining of prisoners at the Guantanamo

Bay naval base in Cuba, renewal of the USA Patriot Act and the reve-
lation that President Bush had authorized electronic eavesdropping by
the National Security Agency without judicial warrants. When challenged,
particularly on the last, and notwithstanding the existence of the special
court established by the Foreign Intelligence Surveillance Act to deal with
the need of the government to move quickly and in secret to counter
foreign threats (see Chapter 8), the president, the Attorney General, and
others, claimed variously that the congressional resolution authorizing the
use of force in Afghanistan after the 9/11 attacks implicitly authorized the
president to do anything he thought expedient to protect the country,
or that his role as commander-in-chief similarly exempted him from any
constitutional or legal restraint with regard to national defence in time of
war. Opponents referred to 'King George', and pointed to the presidential
oath to 'preserve, protect, and defend *the Constitution* of the United States'
(emphasis added).

This was hardly the first time that a president had claimed extraordinary
powers in time of war, and Bush's supporters pointed to Lincoln's Civil
War suspension of the writ of habeas corpus, Franklin Roosevelt's order
for the internment of American citizens of Japanese descent during the
Second World War, and Harry Truman's attempted seizure of the steel
mills during the Korean War. All of these, however, were done in the
context of a traditional war, with a recognizable state as the enemy, and
a clear terminus that would be reached when that enemy surrendered.
Moreover, the first and third were ruled unconstitutional (the suspension
of the writ of habeas corpus without congressional authorization in 1861
in *Ex parte Merryman* 17 Fed. Cases 144, although the military refused to
obey the circuit court's writ, and again in 1866 in *Ex parte Milligan* 71 US
2; the seizure of the steel mills in *Youngstown Sheet & Tube Co. v. Sawyer*
343 US 579), and while the second was ruled to have been constitutional
(*Korematsu v. United States* 319 US 432), the ruling is generally regarded
as an embarrassing product of wartime hysteria that says more about the
limits of the willingness of courts to protect fundamental rights than it
says about the proper limits of those rights (see, for example, *Korematsu v.
United States* 584 F. Supp. 1406).

The so-called War on Terrorism, on the other hand, has no enemy who
could surrender, and suggests no obvious point at which the emergency
would be over and presidential power would revert to its 'normal' level. As

a result, it puts the efficacy of checks and balances as a way of restraining abuses of power under unusually severe strain, raising in the minds of some opponents the spectre of a permanent state of emergency akin to George Orwell's *1984*. This is especially so given the temptation presented to the president to foster and exploit the public's perception of threat in order to distract attention from other problems and to enhance his general approval ratings, and the reluctance of Congress and the courts to challenge the president on questions of national security.

Despite what might be taken as the alarmist tone of this section, none of these problems is without precedent. They are aggravated by a reduced margin for economic waste and political inefficiency brought about by a rate of consumption of natural resources (most obviously petroleum, but not only petroleum) that has outstripped domestic production; by growing problems of pollution and global climate change; by globalization and competition both for resources and for markets from the rest of the world; by demographic change; by the increased pace of transportation, communication, and indeed of life in general. Nonetheless, American democracy has proven remarkably resilient, and it is far too early to write its epitaph.

The United States in the world

In one respect, however, the situation at the beginning of the twenty-first century is without precedent. Notwithstanding the potential challenge from China at some point in the future, since the collapse of the Soviet Union the United States has been the world's only super-power. This is a situation to which neither the American public nor the American political system has really adjusted. Americans remain remarkably ignorant of the rest of the world: there is little foreign news in most American newspapers or television reports, and except for people living very near the Canadian or Mexican borders, most Americans cannot tune in to foreign broadcasts even on cable or satellite systems; relatively few Americans travel abroad, and if they do it is likely to be to a resort or as part of a tour that leaves them isolated from the culture and politics of the place they are visiting; American schools generally teach little about the history and cultures of Europe, and less about the rest of the world. Moreover, although different in specifics, this ignorance is not limited to the general population: in 2003, for example, Deputy Secretary of Defense Paul Wolfowitz gave an interview that suggested he was unaware that there were significant Islamic holy sites in Iraq (Cole 2003: 543), and yet he was one of the architects of American policy in Iraq.[21]

This ignorance reflects a history in which most of the rest of the world was safely well across the seas. There were plenty of challenges and opportunities at home, and foreign affairs appeared to be either a diversion or a trap. Although sometimes ignored, from the earliest days of the Republic one of the basic pillars of American foreign policy was to stand apart from the alliances and wars of Europe.

While isolationism was in many ways beneficial for the United States, it left both the norms of politics and the institutions of government ill-prepared for global responsibilities. Ironically, although support for or opposition to a war may play a large role in determining electoral results (with support often based on unthinking patriotism and opposition on equally unthinking unwillingness to accept casualties), foreign policy more generally is likely to be the by-product of domestic politics. Although Americans recognize foreign policy to be important in the abstract, it is also very distant. The news they receive tends to be highly oversimplified, and to portray the world in stark tones of black and white, friends and enemies, good guys and bad guys, and this kind of thinking apparently reaches to the highest levels of government. Particularly for members of Congress, most of whom have little individual influence on foreign policy anyway, and for presidential candidates, this both justifies and encourages posturing over serious analysis, and leads to a real danger that subtlety will be exploited by political opponents as a sign of weakness. Even for the president himself, once a line of policy has been started, American presidents frequently become captives or victims of their own domestic rhetoric (including their campaign rhetoric)—unable to accept reasonable compromise solutions to international problems for fear of appearing at home to have been weak.

As in the field of domestic politics, the American system is structured to give strong influence to vocal minorities in foreign policy. Thus Jews have had a disproportionately strong influence on American policy with regard to the Middle East; Cuban exiles with regard to Cuba; the children and grandchildren of Irish immigrants with regard to Northern Ireland. The preferences of these groups are not necessarily in the national interest of the United States, but opposing them is rarely in the political interest of

American politicians: offending an intense minority can be costly in terms of campaign support directed to a primary or general election opponent, whereas pleasing even a very large majority that is also inattentive and basically indifferent has few benefits.

On the one hand, this means that many members of Congress and even the president, come to office committed to simplistic positions that they took for electoral reasons, often because they feared offending a group of expatriates. On the other hand, because ultimately the political credit or blame for foreign affairs will primarily accrue to the president, from the perspective of Congress, foreign policy may become one more arena for partisan or inter-institutional battles. For example, the decision to grant or withhold 'fast-track' negotiating powers with respect to trade (see Chapter 5) has been driven as often by partisan interests in aiding or hindering the president for reasons of domestic politics as for its impact on foreign relations. Members of the president's party may support even obviously failed policies for fear that lower public support for the president will translate into lower electoral support for themselves, while members of the other party may do just the opposite. Of course, except for the problems of inter-institutional politics, this kind of partisan closing-of-ranks is not different from what one would expect in any democratic country.

One difference, however, is that when the United States acts in the international arena, the stakes for the rest of the world are higher. Although the Soviet Union may have been 'an evil empire', its power at least had the effect of forcing some element of realism and restraint on American foreign policy. With its collapse, however, the danger that foreign policy professionals will be further marginalized in favour of policy-makers driven by domestic politics and domestic ideology has been increased, and the immediately apparent costs of posturing or pandering to public prejudices have been reduced.

This book has concluded with a few paragraphs on foreign policy because if there is any field in which someone—the President of the United States—is unambiguously 'in charge', it is foreign and military affairs. Yet even in these fields, the basic themes of divided power and, as a result, a politics of individual position-taking rather than clearly accountable policy-making is apparent. And as in other fields, the resulting inefficiencies and irrationalities have been tolerable because the United States has been so rich and so powerful that they were acceptable to the American people. Whether they will continue to be acceptable and, if they do not, what adaptations will be made, are questions for the future.

··

NOTES

1 Although the same federal constitution has been in effect since 1787, the same cannot be said for all of the state constitutions. Although the difference between drafting a new constitution and significantly amending the old one can be exaggerated, one can observe, for example, that the current constitution of Delaware only dates from 1897, that of New Jersey from 1947, Connecticut from 1965. Georgia has had ten constitutions since 1777, the most recent dating from 1983.

2 Jim Crow is a colloquial expression used to refer to the pattern of laws and practices of discrimination against African Americans in the South. 'Jim Crow' was a character (played by a white actor with a blackened face) in minstrel shows.

3 It is not that these perceived threats were groundless (except for the Salem witches), but that the reactions, both the official reactions and the unchecked less formal societal reactions, quickly got out of hand and largely became indifferent to the actual guilt or innocence of the people targeted.

4 Probably reflecting the personalism of American politics, manifested in part in the likelihood that a sitting governor will be blamed for whatever problems arise, plus the existence of term limits that minimize the advantage of incumbency, only one state (South Dakota) had governors of a single party over the period from 1984 to 2004.

5 For example, with very limited exceptions in the case of broadcasting (justified by the fact that broadcasters are licensed by the government), freedom of the press is freedom from prior censorship and freedom from punishment for what one publishes. It is not an affirmative right to have one's views published by someone else, be it the state or a private publisher. In other words, the only people who are guaranteed 'freedom of the press' are those who have a press in the first place.

6 'Honest graft' is a phrase made famous by William L. Riodon's *Plunkitt of Tammany Hall: A Series of Very Plain Talks on Very Practical Politics, Delivered by ex-Senator George Washington Plunkitt, the Tammany Philosopher, From his Rostrum — The New York County Court House Bootblack Stand* (New York: E. P. Dutton & Co., 1963 [1905]). According to Plunkitt, honest graft can be summed up as 'I seen my opportunities and I took 'em' (p. 3).

7 See: http://www.taxpayer.net/ Transportation/safetealu/states.htm.

8 Factors that affect the general health of the population, such as diet, drug use, the availability of preventative education and care, of course also contribute to cross-national differences in costs and outcomes.

9 Abramoff was a lobbyist with close ties to the Republican Party, including former House Majority Leader Tom DeLay. In early 2006, Abramoff entered a guilty plea to charges of fraud, tax evasion, and conspiracy to bribe a public official. In exchange for his guilty plea and agreement to cooperate with prosecutors in the investigation of several members of Congress, he received a reduced jail sentence. Abramoff was well known in

Washington for providing luxurious trips, campaign contributions, free meals at his Washington restaurant, jobs for spouses, etc. for members of Congress and members of their staff. In at least some cases it was alleged that these were direct *quid pro quo* payments for influencing legislation, but in any case the appearance of impropriety led some politicians quickly to move into 'damage control' mode, including the public advocacy of reform measures.

10 Although many American retirees depend entirely on their public social security benefits, and although these have been increased enough to dramatically reduce the number of elderly people living in poverty, the American social security system was designed primarily as a safety net rather than as the primary source of income replacement in retirement.

11 Although family income inequality was reduced between 1947 and 1968, this trend was reversed between 1968 and 1998, to such an extent that there was greater inequality in 1998 than in 1947; between 1979 and 2002 after-tax incomes in the bottom fifth of the income distribution rose by 5 per cent, in the top fifth by 48 per cent, but in the top 1 per cent by 111 per cent. (US Census Bureau, 'Income Inequality (1947–1998)', www.census.gov/hhes/incineq/p60204txt.html; Congressional Budget Office, *Historical Effective Federal Tax Rates: 1979 to 2002* (March 2005).

12 Roughly the same things could be said about American dependency on oil in general, and imported oil in particular. Politicians of both parties have recognized this to be a serious and growing threat, but have been unwilling to propose significant actions, which would impose costs in the short run, for which they fear they would be blamed, in order to achieve benefits in the future, for which they could not claim credit.

13 Although the often cited statistic that 19 per cent of Americans think they are in the top 1 per cent of the income distribution is based on journalistic distortion of the data (the underlying survey question included Al Gore's campaign claim that the beneficiaries of the tax cuts proposed by Bush in the 2000 campaign would be primarily in the top 1 per cent of the income distribution, but actually asked only whether the respondent thought he or she would benefit from them), there is more solid evidence that Americans, and particularly young American males, vastly overestimate the likelihood that they will become rich.

14 Sex was not included in the original bill, but was added by southern Democrats in an unsuccessful attempt to kill the bill by holding it up to ridicule.

15 'Equality of rights under the law shall not be denied or abridged by the United States or by any state on account of sex.'

16 See: http://www.eagleforum.org/psr/1986/sept86/psrsep86.html.

17 For example, identifying supporters of abortion rights as 'baby killers'.

18 'Strict scrutiny' is a legal term of art applied to laws or regulations that have a real and appreciable impact on a fundamental right. In order for such rules to survive judicial review, they must be narrowly drawn and serve compelling state interests. Of course, neither 'fundamental right' nor 'compelling state interest' have meanings that are beyond dispute.

19 Although federal courts, under the 'cases and controversies' clause of the Constitution, do not issue advisory judgments, some state courts, as in Massachusetts, do so.

20 Matthew Spalding, 'A Defining Moment: Marriage, the Courts, and the Constitution'. Published by The Heritage Foundation, www.heritage.org/research/legalissues/bg1759.cfm.

21 In fact, Najaf, reputed to be the site of the tomb of Imam Ali, is the third most visited site of Muslim pilgrimage (after Mecca and Medina), followed closely in importance to Shi'a Muslims by Karbala.

GUIDE TO FURTHER READING

CRENSON, M. A. and B. GINSBERG (2002), *Downsizing Democracy: How America Sidelined its Citizens and Privatized its Public* (Baltimore, MD: Johns Hopkins University Press).

Shows how institutional changes from the elite, rather than moral failings from the citizens, have led to a weakening of democracy.

APPENDIX: THE CONSTITUTION OF THE UNITED STATES[1]

We the People of the United States, in Order to form a more perfect Union, establish Justice, insure domestic Tranquility, provide for the common defense, promote the general Welfare, and secure the Blessings of Liberty to ourselves and our Posterity, do ordain and establish this Constitution for the United States of America.

Article. I.

Section. 1.

All legislative Powers herein granted shall be vested in a Congress of the United States, which shall consist of a Senate and House of Representatives.

Section. 2.

The House of Representatives shall be composed of Members chosen every second Year by the People of the several States, and the Electors in each State shall have the Qualifications requisite for Electors of the most numerous Branch of the State Legislature.

No Person shall be a Representative who shall not have attained to the Age of twenty five Years, and been seven Years a Citizen of the United States, and who shall not, when elected, be an Inhabitant of that State in which he shall be chosen.

Representatives and direct Taxes shall be apportioned among the several States which may be included within this Union, according to their respective Numbers, which shall be determined by adding to the whole Number of free Persons, including those bound to Service for a Term of Years, and excluding Indians not taxed, three fifths of all other Persons. The actual Enumeration shall be made within three Years after the first Meeting of the Congress of the United States, and within every subsequent Term of ten Years, in such Manner as they shall by Law direct. The Number of Representatives shall not exceed one for every thirty Thousand, but each

State shall have at Least one Representative; and until such enumeration shall be made, the State of New Hampshire shall be entitled to chuse three, Massachusetts eight, Rhode-Island and Providence Plantations one, Connecticut five, New-York six, New Jersey four, Pennsylvania eight, Delaware one, Maryland six, Virginia ten, North Carolina five, South Carolina five, and Georgia three.

When Vacancies happen in the Representation from any State, the Executive Authority thereof shall issue Writs of Election to fill such Vacancies.

The House of Representatives shall chuse their Speaker and other Officers; and shall have the sole Power of Impeachment.

Section. 3.

The Senate of the United States shall be composed of two Senators from each State, chosen *by the Legislature thereof* for six Years; and each Senator shall have one Vote.

Immediately after they shall be assembled in Consequence of the first Election, they shall be divided as equally as may be into three Classes. The Seats of the Senators of the first Class shall be vacated at the Expiration of the second Year, of the second Class at the Expiration of the fourth Year, and of the third Class at the Expiration of the sixth Year, so that one third may be chosen every second Year; *and if Vacancies happen by Resignation, or otherwise, during the Recess of the Legislature of any State, the Executive thereof may make temporary Appointments until the next Meeting of the Legislature, which shall then fill such Vacancies.*

No Person shall be a Senator who shall not have attained to the Age of thirty Years, and been nine Years a Citizen of the United States, and who shall not, when elected, be an Inhabitant of that State for which he shall be chosen.

The Vice President of the United States shall be President of the Senate, but shall have no Vote, unless they be equally divided.

The Senate shall chuse their other Officers, and also a President pro tempore, in the Absence of the Vice President, or when he shall exercise the Office of President of the United States.

The Senate shall have the sole Power to try all Impeachments. When sitting for that Purpose, they shall be on Oath or Affirmation. When the

President of the United States is tried, the Chief Justice shall preside: And no Person shall be convicted without the Concurrence of two thirds of the Members present.

Judgment in Cases of Impeachment shall not extend further than to removal from Office, and disqualification to hold and enjoy any Office of honor, Trust or Profit under the United States: but the Party convicted shall nevertheless be liable and subject to Indictment, Trial, Judgment and Punishment, according to Law.

Section. 4.

The Times, Places and Manner of holding Elections for Senators and Representatives, shall be prescribed in each State by the Legislature thereof; but the Congress may at any time by Law make or alter such Regulations, except as to the Places of chusing Senators.

The Congress shall assemble at least once in every Year, *and such Meeting shall be on the first Monday in December,* unless they shall by Law appoint a different Day.

Section. 5.

Each House shall be the Judge of the Elections, Returns and Qualifications of its own Members, and a Majority of each shall constitute a Quorum to do Business; but a smaller Number may adjourn from day to day, and may be authorized to compel the Attendance of absent Members, in such Manner, and under such Penalties as each House may provide.

Each House may determine the Rules of its Proceedings, punish its Members for disorderly Behaviour, and, with the Concurrence of two thirds, expel a Member.

Each House shall keep a Journal of its Proceedings, and from time to time publish the same, excepting such Parts as may in their Judgment require Secrecy; and the Yeas and Nays of the Members of either House on any question shall, at the Desire of one fifth of those Present, be entered on the Journal.

Neither House, during the Session of Congress, shall, without the Consent of the other, adjourn for more than three days, nor to any other Place than that in which the two Houses shall be sitting.

Section. 6.

The Senators and Representatives shall receive a Compensation for their Services, to be ascertained by Law, and paid out of the Treasury of the United States. They shall in all Cases, except Treason, Felony and Breach of the Peace, be privileged from Arrest during their Attendance at the Session of their respective Houses, and in going to and returning from the same; and for any Speech or Debate in either House, they shall not be questioned in any other Place.

No Senator or Representative shall, during the Time for which he was elected, be appointed to any civil Office under the Authority of the United States, which shall have been created, or the Emoluments whereof shall have been increased during such time; and no Person holding any Office under the United States, shall be a Member of either House during his Continuance in Office.

Section. 7.

All Bills for raising Revenue shall originate in the House of Representatives; but the Senate may propose or concur with Amendments as on other Bills.

Every Bill which shall have passed the House of Representatives and the Senate, shall, before it become a Law, be presented to the President of the United States: If he approve he shall sign it, but if not he shall return it, with his Objections to that House in which it shall have originated, who shall enter the Objections at large on their Journal, and proceed to reconsider it. If after such Reconsideration two thirds of that House shall agree to pass the Bill, it shall be sent, together with the Objections, to the other House, by which it shall likewise be reconsidered, and if approved by two thirds of that House, it shall become a Law. But in all such Cases the Votes of both Houses shall be determined by Yeas and Nays, and the Names of the Persons voting for and against the Bill shall be entered on the Journal of each House respectively. If any Bill shall not be returned by the President within ten Days (Sundays excepted) after it shall have been presented to him, the Same shall be a Law, in like Manner as if he had signed it, unless the Congress by their Adjournment prevent its Return, in which Case it shall not be a Law.

Every Order, Resolution, or Vote to which the Concurrence of the Senate and House of Representatives may be necessary (except on a question of Adjournment) shall be presented to the President of the United States; and before the Same shall take Effect, shall be approved by him, or being disapproved by him, shall be repassed by two thirds of the Senate and House of Representatives, according to the Rules and Limitations prescribed in the Case of a Bill.

Section. 8.

The Congress shall have Power To lay and collect Taxes, Duties, Imposts and Excises, to pay the Debts and provide for the common Defence and general Welfare of the United States; but all Duties, Imposts and Excises shall be uniform throughout the United States;

To borrow Money on the credit of the United States;

To regulate Commerce with foreign Nations, and among the several States, and with the Indian Tribes;

To establish an uniform Rule of Naturalization, and uniform Laws on the subject of Bankruptcies throughout the United States;

To coin Money, regulate the Value thereof, and of foreign Coin, and fix the Standard of Weights and Measures;

To provide for the Punishment of counterfeiting the Securities and current Coin of the United States;

To establish Post Offices and Post Roads;

To promote the Progress of Science and useful Arts, by securing for limited Times to Authors and Inventors the exclusive Right to their respective Writings and Discoveries;

To constitute Tribunals inferior to the supreme Court;

To define and punish Piracies and Felonies committed on the high Seas, and Offences against the Law of Nations;

To declare War, grant Letters of Marque and Reprisal, and make Rules concerning Captures on Land and Water;

To raise and support Armies, but no Appropriation of Money to that Use shall be for a longer Term than two Years;

To provide and maintain a Navy;

To make Rules for the Government and Regulation of the land and naval Forces;

To provide for calling forth the Militia to execute the Laws of the Union, suppress Insurrections and repel Invasions;

To provide for organizing, arming, and disciplining, the Militia, and for governing such Part of them as may be employed in the Service of the United States, reserving to the States respectively, the Appointment of the Officers, and the Authority of training the Militia according to the discipline prescribed by Congress;

To exercise exclusive Legislation in all Cases whatsoever, over such District (not exceeding ten Miles square) as may, by Cession of particular States, and the Acceptance of Congress, become the Seat of the Government of the United States, and to exercise like Authority over all Places purchased by the Consent of the Legislature of the State in which the Same shall be, for the Erection of Forts, Magazines, Arsenals, dock-Yards, and other needful Buildings;–And

To make all Laws which shall be necessary and proper for carrying into Execution the foregoing Powers, and all other Powers vested by this Constitution in the Government of the United States, or in any Department or Officer thereof.

Section. 9.

The Migration or Importation of such Persons as any of the States now existing shall think proper to admit, shall not be prohibited by the Congress prior to the Year one thousand eight hundred and eight, but a Tax or duty may be imposed on such Importation, not exceeding ten dollars for each Person.

The Privilege of the Writ of Habeas Corpus shall not be suspended, unless when in Cases of Rebellion or Invasion the public Safety may require it.

No Bill of Attainder or ex post facto Law shall be passed.

No Capitation, or other direct, Tax shall be laid, unless in Proportion to the Census or enumeration herein before directed to be taken.

No Tax or Duty shall be laid on Articles exported from any State.

No Preference shall be given by any Regulation of Commerce or Revenue to the Ports of one State over those of another; nor shall Vessels bound to, or from, one State, be obliged to enter, clear, or pay Duties in another.

No Money shall be drawn from the Treasury, but in Consequence of Appropriations made by Law; and a regular Statement and Account of the Receipts and Expenditures of all public Money shall be published from time to time.

No Title of Nobility shall be granted by the United States: And no Person holding any Office of Profit or Trust under them, shall, without the Consent of the Congress, accept of any present, Emolument, Office, or Title, of any kind whatever, from any King, Prince, or foreign State.

Section. 10.

No State shall enter into any Treaty, Alliance, or Confederation; grant Letters of Marque and Reprisal; coin Money; emit Bills of Credit; make any Thing but gold and silver Coin a Tender in Payment of Debts; pass any Bill of Attainder, ex post facto Law, or Law impairing the Obligation of Contracts, or grant any Title of Nobility.

No State shall, without the Consent of the Congress, lay any Imposts or Duties on Imports or Exports, except what may be absolutely necessary for executing its inspection Laws: and the net Produce of all Duties and Imposts, laid by any State on Imports or Exports, shall be for the Use of the Treasury of the United States; and all such Laws shall be subject to the Revision and Control of the Congress.

No State shall, without the Consent of Congress, lay any Duty of Tonnage, keep Troops, or Ships of War in time of Peace, enter into any Agreement or Compact with another State, or with a foreign Power, or engage in War, unless actually invaded, or in such imminent Danger as will not admit of delay.

Article. II.

Section. 1.

The executive Power shall be vested in a President of the United States of America. He shall hold his Office during the Term of four Years, and, together with the Vice President, chosen for the same Term, be elected, as follows:

Each State shall appoint, in such Manner as the Legislature thereof may direct, a Number of Electors, equal to the whole Number of Senators and

Representatives to which the State may be entitled in the Congress: but no Senator or Representative, or Person holding an Office of Trust or Profit under the United States, shall be appointed an Elector.

The Electors shall meet in their respective States, and vote by Ballot for two Persons, of whom one at least shall not be an Inhabitant of the same State with themselves. And they shall make a List of all the Persons voted for, and of the Number of Votes for each; which List they shall sign and certify, and transmit sealed to the Seat of the Government of the United States, directed to the President of the Senate. The President of the Senate shall, in the Presence of the Senate and House of Representatives, open all the Certificates, and the Votes shall then be counted. The Person having the greatest Number of Votes shall be the President, if such Number be a Majority of the whole Number of Electors appointed; and if there be more than one who have such Majority, and have an equal Number of Votes, then the House of Representatives shall immediately chuse by Ballot one of them for President; and if no Person have a Majority, then from the five highest on the List the said House shall in like Manner chuse the President. But in chusing the President, the Votes shall be taken by States, the Representation from each State having one Vote; A quorum for this purpose shall consist of a Member or Members from two thirds of the States, and a Majority of all the States shall be necessary to a Choice. In every Case, after the Choice of the President, the Person having the greatest Number of Votes of the Electors shall be the Vice President. But if there should remain two or more who have equal Votes, the Senate shall chuse from them by Ballot the Vice President.

The Congress may determine the Time of chusing the Electors, and the Day on which they shall give their Votes; which Day shall be the same throughout the United States.

No Person except a natural born Citizen, or a Citizen of the United States, at the time of the Adoption of this Constitution, shall be eligible to the Office of President; neither shall any Person be eligible to that Office who shall not have attained to the Age of thirty five Years, and been fourteen Years a Resident within the United States.

In Case of the Removal of the President from Office, or of his Death, Resignation, or Inability to discharge the Powers and Duties of the said Office, the Same shall devolve on the Vice President, and the Congress may by Law provide for the Case of Removal, Death, Resignation or Inability, both of the President and Vice President, declaring what Officer shall then act as President, and such Officer shall act accordingly, until the Disability be removed, or a President shall be elected.

The President shall, at stated Times, receive for his Services, a Compensation, which shall neither be increased nor diminished during the Period for which he shall have been elected, and he shall not receive within that Period any other Emolument from the United States, or any of them.

Before he enter on the Execution of his Office, he shall take the following Oath or Affirmation: – 'I do solemnly swear (or affirm) that I will faithfully execute the Office of President of the United States, and will to the best of my Ability, preserve, protect and defend the Constitution of the United States.'

Section. 2.

The President shall be Commander in Chief of the Army and Navy of the United States, and of the Militia of the several States, when called into the actual Service of the United States; he may require the Opinion, in writing, of the principal Officer in each of the executive Departments, upon any Subject relating to the Duties of their respective Offices, and he shall have Power to grant Reprieves and Pardons for Offences against the United States, except in Cases of Impeachment.

He shall have Power, by and with the Advice and Consent of the Senate, to make Treaties, provided two thirds of the Senators present concur; and he shall nominate, and by and with the Advice and Consent of the Senate, shall appoint Ambassadors, other public Ministers and Consuls, Judges of the supreme Court, and all other Officers of the United States, whose Appointments are not herein otherwise provided for, and which shall be established by Law: but the Congress may by Law vest the Appointment of such inferior Officers, as they think proper, in the President alone, in the Courts of Law, or in the Heads of Departments.

The President shall have Power to fill up all Vacancies that may happen during the Recess of the Senate, by granting Commissions which shall expire at the End of their next Session.

Section. 3.

He shall from time to time give to the Congress Information of the State of the Union, and recommend to their Consideration such Measures as he shall judge necessary and expedient; he may, on extraordinary Occasions, convene both Houses, or either of them, and in Case of Disagreement between them, with Respect to the Time of Adjournment, he may adjourn them to such Time as he shall think proper; he shall receive Ambassadors and other public Ministers; he shall take Care that the Laws be faithfully executed, and shall Commission all the Officers of the United States.

Section. 4.

The President, Vice President and all civil Officers of the United States, shall be removed from Office on Impeachment for, and Conviction of, Treason, Bribery, or other high Crimes and Misdemeanors.

Article. III.

Section. 1.

The judicial Power of the United States shall be vested in one supreme Court, and in such inferior Courts as the Congress may from time to time ordain and establish. The Judges, both of the supreme and inferior Courts, shall hold their Offices during good Behaviour, and shall, at stated Times, receive for their Services a Compensation, which shall not be diminished during their Continuance in Office.

Section. 2.

The judicial Power shall extend to all Cases, in Law and Equity, arising under this Constitution, the Laws of the United States, and Treaties made, or which shall be made, under their Authority;–to all Cases affecting Ambassadors, other public Ministers and Consuls;–to all Cases of admiralty and maritime Jurisdiction;–to Controversies to which the United States shall be a Party;–to Controversies between two or more States;–*between a State and Citizens of another State*;–between Citizens of different States;–between Citizens of the same State claiming Lands under Grants of different States, and between a State, or the Citizens thereof, and foreign States, Citizens or Subjects.

In all Cases affecting Ambassadors, other public Ministers and Consuls, and those in which a State shall be Party, the supreme Court shall have original Jurisdiction. In all the other Cases before mentioned, the supreme Court shall have appellate Jurisdiction, both as to Law and Fact, with such Exceptions, and under such Regulations as the Congress shall make.

The Trial of all Crimes, except in Cases of Impeachment, shall be by Jury; and such Trial shall be held in the State where the said Crimes shall have been committed; but when not committed within any State, the Trial shall be at such Place or Places as the Congress may by Law have directed.

Section. 3.

Treason against the United States, shall consist only in levying War against them, or in adhering to their Enemies, giving them Aid and Comfort. No Person shall be convicted of Treason unless on the Testimony of two Witnesses to the same overt Act, or on Confession in open Court.

The Congress shall have Power to declare the Punishment of Treason, but no Attainder of Treason shall work Corruption of Blood, or Forfeiture except during the Life of the Person attainted.

Article. IV.

Section. 1.

Full Faith and Credit shall be given in each State to the public Acts, Records, and judicial Proceedings of every other State. And the Congress may by general Laws prescribe the Manner in which such Acts, Records and Proceedings shall be proved, and the Effect thereof.

Section. 2.

The Citizens of each State shall be entitled to all Privileges and Immunities of Citizens in the several States.

A Person charged in any State with Treason, Felony, or other Crime, who shall flee from Justice, and be found in another State, shall on Demand of the executive Authority of the State from which he fled, be delivered up, to be removed to the State having Jurisdiction of the Crime.

No Person held to Service or Labour in one State, under the Laws thereof, escaping into another, shall, in Consequence of any Law or Regulation therein, be discharged from such Service or Labour, but shall be delivered up on Claim of the Party to whom such Service or Labour may be due.

Section. 3.

New States may be admitted by the Congress into this Union; but no new State shall be formed or erected within the Jurisdiction of any other State; nor any State be formed by the Junction of two or more States, or Parts of States, without the Consent of the Legislatures of the States concerned as well as of the Congress.

The Congress shall have Power to dispose of and make all needful Rules and Regulations respecting the Territory or other Property belonging to the United States; and nothing in this Constitution shall be so construed as to Prejudice any Claims of the United States, or of any particular State.

Section. 4.

The United States shall guarantee to every State in this Union a Republican Form of Government, and shall protect each of them against Invasion; and on Application of the Legislature, or of the Executive (when the Legislature cannot be convened), against domestic Violence.

Article. V.

The Congress, whenever two thirds of both Houses shall deem it necessary, shall propose Amendments to this Constitution, or, on the Application of the Legislatures of two thirds of the several States, shall call a Convention for proposing Amendments, which, in either Case, shall be valid to all Intents and Purposes, as Part of this Constitution, when ratified by the Legislatures of three fourths of the several States, or by Conventions in three fourths thereof, as the one or the other Mode of Ratification may be proposed by the Congress; Provided that no Amendment which may be made prior to the Year One thousand eight hundred and eight shall in any Manner affect the first and fourth Clauses in the Ninth Section of the first Article; and that no State, without its Consent, shall be deprived of its equal Suffrage in the Senate.

Article. VI.

All Debts contracted and Engagements entered into, before the Adoption of this Constitution, shall be as valid against the United States under this Constitution, as under the Confederation.

This Constitution, and the Laws of the United States which shall be made in Pursuance thereof; and all Treaties made, or which shall be made, under the Authority of the United States, shall be the supreme Law of the Land; and the Judges in every State shall be bound thereby, any Thing in the Constitution or Laws of any State to the Contrary notwithstanding.

The Senators and Representatives before mentioned, and the Members of the several State Legislatures, and all executive and judicial Officers, both of the United States and of the several States, shall be bound by Oath or Affirmation, to support this Constitution; but no religious Test shall ever be required as a Qualification to any Office or public Trust under the United States.

Article. VII.

The Ratification of the Conventions of nine States, shall be sufficient for the Establishment of this Constitution between the States so ratifying the Same.

The Word, 'the', being interlined between the seventh and eighth Lines of the first Page, the Word 'Thirty' being partly written on an Erazure in the fifteenth Line of the first Page, The Words 'is tried' being interlined between the thirty second and thirty third Lines of the first Page and the Word 'the' being interlined between the forty third and forty fourth Lines of the second Page.

Attest William Jackson Secretary

Done in Convention by the Unanimous Consent of the States present the Seventeenth Day of September in the Year of our Lord one thousand seven hundred and Eighty seven and of the Independence of the United States of America the Twelfth In witness whereof We have hereunto subscribed our Names,

G°. Washington
Presidt and deputy from Virginia

Delaware
Geo: Read
Gunning Bedford jun
John Dickinson
Richard Bassett
Jaco: Broom

Maryland
James McHenry
Dan of St Thos. Jenifer
Danl. Carroll

Virginia
John Blair
James Madison Jr.

North Carolina
Wm. Blount
Richd. Dobbs Spaight
Hu Williamson

South Carolina
J. Rutledge
Charles Cotesworth
Pinckney
Charles Pinckney
Pierce Butler

Georgia
William Few
Abr Baldwin

New Hampshire
John Langdon
Nicholas Gilman

Massachusetts
Nathaniel Gorham
Rufus King

Connecticut
Wm. Saml. Johnson

Roger Sherman

New York
Alexander Hamilton

New Jersey
Wil: Livingston
David Brearley
Wm. Paterson
Jona: Dayton

Pennsylvania
B Franklin
Thomas Mifflin
Robt. Morris
Geo. Clymer
Thos. FitzSimons
Jared Ingersoll
James Wilson
Gouv Morris

The first ten amendments to the Constitution, known collectively as 'The Bill of Rights', were passed by Congress in 1789 and ratified 15 December 1791.

AMENDMENT I

Congress shall make no law respecting an establishment of religion, or prohibiting the free exercise thereof; or abridging the freedom of speech, or of the press; or the right of the people peaceably to assemble, and to petition the Government for a redress of grievances.

AMENDMENT II

A well regulated Militia, being necessary to the security of a free State, the right of the people to keep and bear Arms, shall not be infringed.

AMENDMENT III

No Soldier shall, in time of peace be quartered in any house, without the consent of the Owner, nor in time of war, but in a manner to be prescribed by law.

AMENDMENT IV

The right of the people to be secure in their persons, houses, papers, and effects, against unreasonable searches and seizures, shall not be violated, and no Warrants shall issue, but upon probable cause, supported by Oath or affirmation, and particularly describing the place to be searched, and the persons or things to be seized.

AMENDMENT V

No person shall be held to answer for a capital, or otherwise infamous crime, unless on a presentment or indictment of a Grand Jury, except in cases arising in the land or naval forces, or in the Militia, when in actual service in time of War or public danger; nor shall any person be subject for the same offence to be twice put in jeopardy of life or limb; nor shall be compelled in any criminal case to be a witness against himself, nor be deprived of life, liberty, or property, without due process of law; nor shall private property be taken for public use, without just compensation.

AMENDMENT VI

In all criminal prosecutions, the accused shall enjoy the right to a speedy and public trial, by an impartial jury of the State and district wherein the crime shall have been committed, which district shall have been previously ascertained by law, and to be informed of the nature and cause of the accusation; to be confronted with the witnesses against him; to have compulsory process for obtaining witnesses in his favor, and to have the Assistance of Counsel for his defence.

AMENDMENT VII

In Suits at common law, where the value in controversy shall exceed twenty dollars, the right of trial by jury shall be preserved, and no fact tried by a jury, shall be otherwise re-examined in any Court of the United States, than according to the rules of the common law.

AMENDMENT VIII

Excessive bail shall not be required, nor excessive fines imposed, nor cruel and unusual punishments inflicted.

AMENDMENT IX

The enumeration in the Constitution, of certain rights, shall not be construed to deny or disparage others retained by the people.

AMENDMENT X

The powers not delegated to the United States by the Constitution, nor prohibited by it to the States, are reserved to the States respectively, or to the people.

AMENDMENT XI

Passed by Congress 4 March 1794. Ratified 7 February 1795.

The Judicial power of the United States shall not be construed to extend to any suit in law or equity, commenced or prosecuted against one of the United States by Citizens of another State, or by Citizens or Subjects of any Foreign State.

AMENDMENT XII

Passed by Congress 9 December 1803. Ratified 15 June 1804.

The Electors shall meet in their respective states and vote by ballot for President and Vice-President, one of whom, at least, shall not be an inhabitant of the same state with themselves; they shall name in their ballots the person voted for as President, and in distinct ballots the person voted for as Vice-President, and they shall make distinct lists of all persons voted for as President, and of all persons voted for as Vice-President, and of the number of votes for each, which lists they shall sign and certify, and transmit sealed to the seat of the government of the United States, directed to the President of the Senate;—The President of the Senate shall, in the presence of the Senate and House of Representatives, open all the certificates and the votes shall then be counted;—The person having the greatest number of votes for President, shall be the President, if such number be a majority of the whole number of Electors appointed; and if no person have such majority, then from the persons having the highest numbers not exceeding three on the list of those voted for as President, the House of Representatives shall choose immediately, by ballot, the President. But in choosing the President, the votes shall be taken by states, the representation from each state having one vote; a quorum for this purpose shall consist of a member or members from two-thirds of the states, and a majority of all the states shall be necessary to a choice. [And if the House of Representatives shall not choose a President whenever the right of choice shall devolve upon them, before the fourth day of March next following, then the Vice-President shall act as President, as in case of the death or other constitutional disability of the President.—]* The person having the greatest number of votes as Vice-President, shall be the Vice-President, if such number be a majority of the whole number of Electors appointed, and if no person have a majority, then from the two highest numbers on the list, the Senate shall choose the Vice-President; a quorum for the purpose shall consist of two-thirds of the whole number of Senators, and a majority of the whole number shall be necessary to a choice. But no person constitutionally ineligible to the office of President shall be eligible to that of Vice-President of the United States.

*Superseded by section 3 of the 20th amendment.

AMENDMENT XIII

Passed by Congress 31 January 1865. Ratified 6 December 1865.

Section 1.

Neither slavery nor involuntary servitude, except as a punishment for crime whereof the party shall have been duly convicted, shall exist within the United States, or any place subject to their jurisdiction.

Section 2.

Congress shall have power to enforce this article by appropriate legislation.

AMENDMENT XIV

Passed by Congress 13 June 1866. Ratified 9 July 1868.

Section 1.

All persons born or naturalized in the United States, and subject to the jurisdiction thereof, are citizens of the United States and of the State wherein they reside. No State shall make or enforce any law which shall abridge the privileges or immunities of citizens of the United States; nor shall any State deprive any person of life, liberty, or property, without due process of law; nor deny to any person within its jurisdiction the equal protection of the laws.

Section 2.

Representatives shall be apportioned among the several States according to their respective numbers, counting the whole number of persons in each State, excluding Indians not taxed. But when the right to vote at any election for the choice of electors for President and Vice-President of the United States, Representatives in Congress, the Executive and Judicial officers of a State, or the members of the Legislature thereof, is denied to any of the male inhabitants of such State, being twenty-one years of age,* and citizens of the United States, or in any way abridged, except for participation in rebellion, or other crime, the basis of representation therein shall be reduced in the proportion which the number of such male citizens shall bear to the whole number of male citizens twenty-one years of age in such State.

Section 3.

No person shall be a Senator or Representative in Congress, or elector of President and Vice-President, or hold any office, civil or military, under the United States, or under any State, who, having previously taken an oath, as a member of Congress, or as an officer of the United States, or as a member of any State legislature, or as an executive or judicial officer of any State, to support the Constitution of the United States, shall have engaged in insurrection or rebellion against the same, or given aid or comfort to the enemies thereof. But Congress may by a vote of two-thirds of each House, remove such disability.

Section 4.

The validity of the public debt of the United States, authorized by law, including debts incurred for payment of pensions and bounties for services in suppressing insurrection or rebellion, shall not be questioned. But neither the United States nor any State shall assume or pay any debt or obligation incurred in aid of insurrection or rebellion against the United States, or any claim for the loss or emancipation of any slave; but all such debts, obligations and claims shall be held illegal and void.

Section 5.

The Congress shall have the power to enforce, by appropriate legislation, the provisions of this article.

 *Changed by section 1 of the 26th amendment.

AMENDMENT XV

Passed by Congress 26 February 1869. Ratified 3 February 1870.

Section 1.

The right of citizens of the United States to vote shall not be denied or abridged by the United States or by any State on account of race, color, or previous condition of servitude–

Section 2.

The Congress shall have the power to enforce this article by appropriate legislation.

AMENDMENT XVI

Passed by Congress 2 July 1909. Ratified 3 February 1913.

The Congress shall have power to lay and collect taxes on incomes, from whatever source derived, without apportionment among the several States, and without regard to any census or enumeration.

AMENDMENT XVII

Passed by Congress 13 May 1912. Ratified 8 April 1913.

The Senate of the United States shall be composed of two Senators from each State, elected by the people thereof, for six years; and each Senator shall have one vote. The electors in each State shall have the qualifications requisite for electors of the most numerous branch of the State legislatures.

When vacancies happen in the representation of any State in the Senate, the executive authority of such State shall issue writs of election to fill such vacancies: Provided, That the legislature of any State may empower the executive thereof to make temporary appointments until the people fill the vacancies by election as the legislature may direct.

This amendment shall not be so construed as to affect the election or term of any Senator chosen before it becomes valid as part of the Constitution.

AMENDMENT XVIII

Passed by Congress 18 December 1917. Ratified 16 January 1919. Repealed by amendment 21.

Section 1.

After one year from the ratification of this article the manufacture, sale, or transportation of intoxicating liquors within, the importation thereof into, or the exportation thereof from the United States and all territory subject to the jurisdiction thereof for beverage purposes is hereby prohibited.

Section 2.

The Congress and the several States shall have concurrent power to enforce this article by appropriate legislation.

Section 3.

This article shall be inoperative unless it shall have been ratified as an amendment to the Constitution by the legislatures of the several States, as provided in the Constitution, within seven years from the date of the submission hereof to the States by the Congress.

AMENDMENT XIX

Passed by Congress 4 June 1919. Ratified 18 August 1920.

The right of citizens of the United States to vote shall not be denied or abridged by the United States or by any State on account of sex.

Congress shall have power to enforce this article by appropriate legislation.

AMENDMENT XX

Passed by Congress 2 March 1932. Ratified 23 January 1933.

Section 1.

The terms of the President and the Vice President shall end at noon on the 20th day of January, and the terms of Senators and Representatives at noon on the 3d day of January, of the years in which such terms would have ended if this article had not been ratified; and the terms of their successors shall then begin.

Section 2.

The Congress shall assemble at least once in every year, and such meeting shall begin at noon on the 3d day of January, unless they shall by law appoint a different day.

Section 3.

If, at the time fixed for the beginning of the term of the President, the President elect shall have died, the Vice President elect shall become President. If a President shall not have been chosen before the time fixed for the beginning of his term, or if the President elect shall have failed to qualify, then the Vice President elect shall act as President until a President shall have qualified; and the Congress may by law provide for the case wherein neither a President elect nor a Vice President shall have qualified, declaring who shall then act as President, or the manner in which one who is to act shall be selected, and such person shall act accordingly until a President or Vice President shall have qualified.

Section 4.

The Congress may by law provide for the case of the death of any of the persons from whom the House of Representatives may choose a President whenever the right of choice shall have devolved upon them, and for the case of the death of any of the persons from whom the Senate may choose a Vice President whenever the right of choice shall have devolved upon them.

Section 5.

Sections 1 and 2 shall take effect on the 15th day of October following the ratification of this article.

Section 6.

This article shall be inoperative unless it shall have been ratified as an amendment to the Constitution by the legislatures of three-fourths of the several States within seven years from the date of its submission.

AMENDMENT XXI

Passed by Congress 20 February 1933. Ratified 5 December 1933.

Section 1.

The eighteenth article of amendment to the Constitution of the United States is hereby repealed.

Section 2.

The transportation or importation into any State, Territory, or Possession of the United States for delivery or use therein of intoxicating liquors, in violation of the laws thereof, is hereby prohibited.

Section 3.

This article shall be inoperative unless it shall have been ratified as an amendment to the Constitution by conventions in the several States, as provided in the Constitution, within seven years from the date of the submission hereof to the States by the Congress.

AMENDMENT XXII

Passed by Congress 21 March 1947. Ratified 27 February 1951.

Section 1.

No person shall be elected to the office of the President more than twice, and no person who has held the office of President, or acted as President, for more than two years of a term to which some other person was elected President shall be elected to the office of President more than once. But this Article shall not apply to any person holding the office of President when this Article was proposed by Congress, and shall not prevent any person who may be holding the office of President, or acting as President, during the term within which this Article becomes operative from holding the office of President or acting as President during the remainder of such term.

Section 2.

This article shall be inoperative unless it shall have been ratified as an amendment to the Constitution by the legislatures of three-fourths of the several States within seven years from the date of its submission to the States by the Congress.

AMENDMENT XXIII

Passed by Congress 16 June 1960. Ratified 29 March 1961.

Section 1.

The District constituting the seat of Government of the United States shall appoint in such manner as Congress may direct:

A number of electors of President and Vice President equal to the whole number of Senators and Representatives in Congress to which the District would be entitled if it were a State, but in no event more than the least populous State; they shall be in addition to those appointed by the States, but they shall be considered, for the purposes of the election of President and Vice President, to be electors appointed by a State; and they shall meet in the District and perform such duties as provided by the twelfth article of amendment.

Section 2.

The Congress shall have power to enforce this article by appropriate legislation.

AMENDMENT XXIV

Passed by Congress 27 August 1962. Ratified 23 January 1964.

Section 1.

The right of citizens of the United States to vote in any primary or other election for President or Vice President, for electors for President or Vice President, or for Senator or Representative in Congress, shall not be denied or abridged by the United States or any State by reason of failure to pay poll tax or other tax.

Section 2.

The Congress shall have power to enforce this article by appropriate legislation.

AMENDMENT XXV

Passed by Congress 6 July 1965. Ratified 10 February 1967.

Section 1.

In case of the removal of the President from office or of his death or resignation, the Vice President shall become President.

Section 2.

Whenever there is a vacancy in the office of the Vice President, the President shall nominate a Vice President who shall take office upon confirmation by a majority vote of both Houses of Congress.

Section 3.

Whenever the President transmits to the President pro tempore of the Senate and the Speaker of the House of Representatives his written declaration that he is unable to discharge the powers and duties of his office, and until he transmits to them a written declaration to the contrary, such powers and duties shall be discharged by the Vice President as Acting President.

Section 4.

Whenever the Vice President and a majority of either the principal officers of the executive departments or of such other body as Congress may by law provide, transmit to the President pro tempore of the Senate and the Speaker of the House of Representatives their written declaration that the President is unable to discharge the powers and duties of his office, the Vice President shall immediately assume the powers and duties of the office as Acting President.

Thereafter, when the President transmits to the President pro tempore of the Senate and the Speaker of the House of Representatives his written declaration that no inability exists, he shall resume the powers and duties of his office unless the Vice President and a majority of either the principal officers of the executive department or of such other body as Congress may by law provide, transmit within four days to the President pro tempore of the Senate and the Speaker of the House of Representatives their written declaration that the President is unable to discharge the powers and duties of his office. Thereupon Congress shall decide the issue, assembling within forty-eight hours for that purpose if not in session. If the Congress, within twenty-one days after receipt of the latter written declaration, or, if Congress is not in session, within twenty-one days after Congress is required to assemble, determines by two-thirds vote of both Houses that the President is unable to discharge the powers and duties of his office, the Vice President shall continue to discharge the same as Acting President; otherwise, the President shall resume the powers and duties of his office.

AMENDMENT XXVI

Passed by Congress 23 March 1971. Ratified 1 July 1971.

Section 1.

The right of citizens of the United States, who are eighteen years of age or older, to vote shall not be denied or abridged by the United States or by any State on account of age.

Section 2.

The Congress shall have power to enforce this article by appropriate legislation.

AMENDMENT XXVII

Originally proposed 25 September 1789. Ratified 7 May 1992.

No law, varying the compensation for the services of the Senators and Representatives, shall take effect, until an election of representatives shall have intervened.

....

NOTE

1 This is the original text as transcribed by the National Archives and Records Administration (www.archives.gov/national-archives-experience/charters/constitution.html). Items in italics have been superseded or amended.

REFERENCES

ALDRICH, J. H. (1995), *Why Parties? The Origin and Transformation of Political Parties in America* (Chicago: University of Chicago Press)

ALDRICH, J. H. and D. W. ROHDE (2001), 'The Logic of Conditional Party Government: Revisiting the Electoral Connection', in L. C. DODD and B. I. OPPENHEIMER (eds.), *Congress Reconsidered* (7th edn) (Washington, DC: Congressional Quarterly Press)

AMAR, A. R. (2005), *America's Constitution: a Biography* (New York: Random House)

BAUM, L. (2001), *American Courts: Process and Policy*, 5th edn (Boston, MA: Houghton Mifflin)

BRONARS, S. G. and J. R. LOTT, Jr. (1997), 'Do Campaign Donations Alter How a Politician Votes? Or, Do Donors Support Candidates Who Value the Same Things That They Do?', *Journal of Law and Economics* 40 (October), 317–50

CHAMBERS, W. N. and W. D. BURNHAM (eds.) (1975), *The American Party Systems: Stages of Political Development* (New York: Oxford University Press)

COLE, J. (2003), 'The United States and Shi'ite Religious Factions in Post-Ba'thist Iraq', *Middle East Journal* 57 (Fall), 543–66

Council of State Governments (2002), *Book of the States, 2002* (Lexington, KY: Council of State Governments)

Court Statistics Project (2005), *State Court Caseload Statistics, 2004* (Williamsburg, VA: National Center for State Courts)

DARCY, R., S. WELCH and J. CLARK (1987), *Women, Elections, and Representation* (New York: Longman)

DAVIDSON, R. H. and W. J. OLESZEK (2000), *Congress and Its Members* (Washington, DC: Congressional Quarterly Press)

DINKIN, R. J. (1977), *Voting in Provincial America: a Study of Elections in the Thirteen Colonies, 1689–1776* (Westport, CT: Greenwood Press)

ELAZAR, D. (1966), *American Federalism: a View from the States* (New York: Crowell)

FIORINA, M. P. (1977), *Congress: Keystone of the Washington Establishment* (New Haven, CT: Yale University Press)

GREEN, J. C. (2002), 'Still Functioning After All These Years: Parties in the United States, 1960–2000', in P. WEBB, D. M. FARRELL, and I. HOLLIDAY (eds.), *Political Parties in Advanced Industrial Democracies* (Oxford: Oxford University Press)

HERRNSON, P. S. (1988), *Party Campaigning in the 1980s* (Cambridge, MA: Harvard University Press)

HILLYGUS, D. S and T. G. SHIELDS (2005), 'Moral Issues and Voter Decision Making in the 2004 Presidential Election', *PS: Political Science and Society* 38 (April), 201–10

JUNZ, A. J. (1960), *The Student Guide to Parliament* (London: Hansard Society)

KAU, J. B. and P. H. RUBIN (1982), *Congressmen, Constituents, and Contributors: Determinants of Roll Call Voting in the House of Representatives* (Boston, MA: Martinus Nijhoff)

KETTL, D. F. (1998), 'Reinventing Government: a Fifth-Year Report Card', A Report of the Brookings Institution's Center for Public Management, September

LAKOFF, G. (2004), *Don't Think of an Elephant* (White River Junction, VT: Chelsea Green)

LASSWELL, H. D. (1950), *Politics: Who Gets What, When, How* (New York: P. Smith)

LEWIS, G. B. (2005), 'Same-sex Marriage and the 2004 Presidential Election', *PS: Political Science and Society* 38 (April), 195–200

LIGHT, P. C. (1995), *Thickening Government: Hierarchy and the Diffusion of Responsibility* (Washington, DC: Brookings Institution)

LIGHT, P. C. (2004), 'Fact Sheet on the Continued Thickening of Government', Brookings Institution, 23 July. Available at: http://www.brookings.edu/views/papers/light/20040723.htm

MADDISON, A. J. (1995), *Monitoring the World Economy, 1820–1992* (Paris: Development Centre of the Organisation for Economic Co-operation and Development)

MAYHEW, D. R. (1974), *Congress: the Electoral Connection* (New Haven, CT: Yale University Press)

MAZMANIAN, D. A. (1974), *Third Parties in Presidential Elections* (Washington, DC: Brookings Institution)

MCCONNELL, J. W. (1942), *The Evolution of Social Class* (Washington, DC: American Council on Public Affairs)

MCCORMICK, R. P. (1973), *The Second American Party System: Party Formation in the Jacksonian Era* (Chapel Hill, NC: University of North Carolina Press)

ORNSTEIN, N. J. (1975), *Congress in Change: Evolution and Reform* (New York: Praeger)

PEASLEE, A. J. (1965–70), *Constitutions of Nations* (The Hague: Martinus Nijhoff)

PETROCIK, J. (1998), 'Reformulating the Party Coalitions: the "Christian Democratic" Republicans', Paper presented at the annual meeting of the American Political Science Association, Boston

ROHDE, D. W. (1991), *Parties and Leaders in the Postreform House* (Chicago: University of Chicago Press)

ROM, M. C. (1999), 'Transforming State Health and Welfare Programs', in V. GRAY, R. L. HANSON, and H. JACOB (eds.), *Politics in the American States: a Comparative Analysis* (Washington, DC: Congressional Quarterly Press)

ROSENSTONE, S. J. (1996), *Third Parties in America: Citizen Response to Major Party Failure* (Princeton, NJ: Princeton University Press)

ROSSITER, C. (1953), *Seedtime of the Republic: the Origin of the American Tradition of Political Liberty* (New York: Harcourt, Brace)

ROTTMAN, D. B., C. R. FLANGO, M. T. CANTRELL, R. HANSEN, and N. LaFOUNTAIN, (1999), 'Judicial Selection and Service, *State Court Organization, 1998* (Williamsburg, VA: National Center for State Courts)

SCHATTSCHNEIDER, E. E. (1942), *Party Government* (New York: Farrar and Rinehart)

SCHLESINGER, J. A. (1965), 'The Politics of the Executive', in H. JACOB and K. N. VINES (eds.), *Politics in the American States* (Boston, MA: Little, Brown)

TOCQUEVILLE, ALEXIS DE (1956 [1834]), *Democracy in America*, ed. and abridged by R. D. HEFFNER, (New York: Penguin)

WOLFINGER, R. E. (1974), *The Politics of Progress* (Englewood Cliffs, NJ: Prentice-Hall)

INDEX